P9-CSF-682

Todd Lammle's
CCNA®/CCENT® IOS Commands
Survival Guide

Todd Lammle

A Wiley Brand

Senior Acquisitions Editor: Jeff Kellum
Development Editor: Pete Gaughan
Technical Editors: Troy McMillan and Dax Mickelson
Production Editor: Eric Charbonneau
Editorial Manager: Pete Gaughan
Vice President and Executive Group Publisher: Richard Swadley
Associate Publisher: Chris Webb
Compositor: Craig Woods, Happenstance Type-O-Rama
Proofreader: Rebecca Rider
Indexer: Ted Laux
Project Coordinator, Cover: Todd Klemme
Cover Designer: Ryan Sneed
Cover Image: © Wiley

Copyright © 2014 by John Wiley & Sons, Inc., Indianapolis, Indiana

Published simultaneously in Canada

ISBN: 978-1-118-82004-9

ISBN: 978-1-118-81978-4 (ebk.)

ISBN: 978-1-118-82007-0 (ebk.)

No part of this publication may be reproduced, stored in a retrieval system or transmitted in any form or by any means, electronic, mechanical, photocopying, recording, scanning or otherwise, except as permitted under Sections 107 or 108 of the 1976 United States Copyright Act, without either the prior written permission of the Publisher, or authorization through payment of the appropriate per-copy fee to the Copyright Clearance Center, 222 Rosewood Drive, Danvers, MA 01923, (978) 750-8400, fax (978) 646-8600. Requests to the Publisher for permission should be addressed to the Permissions Department, John Wiley & Sons, Inc., 111 River Street, Hoboken, NJ 07030, (201) 748-6011, fax (201) 748-6008, or online at www.wiley.com/go/permissions.

Limit of Liability/Disclaimer of Warranty: The publisher and the author make no representations or warranties with respect to the accuracy or completeness of the contents of this work and specifically disclaim all warranties, including without limitation warranties of fitness for a particular purpose. No warranty may be created or extended by sales or promotional materials. The advice and strategies contained herein may not be suitable for every situation. This work is sold with the understanding that the publisher is not engaged in rendering legal, accounting, or other professional services. If professional assistance is required, the services of a competent professional person should be sought. Neither the publisher nor the author shall be liable for damages arising herefrom. The fact that an organization or Web site is referred to in this work as a citation and/or a potential source of further information does not mean that the author or the publisher endorses the information the organization or Web site may provide or recommendations it may make. Further, readers should be aware that Internet Web sites listed in this work may have changed or disappeared between when this work was written and when it is read.

For general information on our other products and services or to obtain technical support, please contact our Customer Care Department within the U.S. at (877) 762-2974, outside the U.S. at (317) 572-3993 or fax (317) 572-4002.

Wiley publishes in a variety of print and electronic formats and by print-on-demand. Some material included with standard print versions of this book may not be included in e-books or in print-on-demand. If this book refers to media such as a CD or DVD that is not included in the version you purchased, you may download this material at http://booksupport.wiley.com. For more information about Wiley products, visit www.wiley.com.

Library of Congress Control Number: 2013954097

TRADEMARKS: Wiley, the Wiley logo, and the Sybex logo are trademarks or registered trademarks of John Wiley & Sons, Inc. and/or its affiliates, in the United States and other countries, and may not be used without written permission. CCNA and CCENT are registered trademarks of Cisco Technology, Inc. All other trademarks are the property of their respective owners. John Wiley & Sons, Inc. is not associated with any product or vendor mentioned in this book.

10 9 8 7 6 5 4 3 2 1

Dear Reader,

Thank you for choosing *Todd Lammle's CCNA/CCENT IOS Commands Survival Guide*. This book is part of a family of premium-quality Sybex books, all of which are written by outstanding authors who combine practical experience with a gift for teaching.

Sybex was founded in 1976. More than 30 years later, we're still committed to producing consistently exceptional books. With each of our titles, we're working hard to set a new standard for the industry. From the paper we print on to the authors we work with, our goal is to bring you the best books available.

I hope you see all that reflected in these pages. I'd be very interested to hear your comments and get your feedback on how we're doing. Feel free to let me know what you think about this or any other Sybex book by sending me an email at contactus@sybex.com. If you think you've found a technical error in this book, please visit http://sybex.custhelp.com. Customer feedback is critical to our efforts at Sybex.

Best regards,

Chris Webb
Associate Publisher
Sybex, an Imprint of Wiley

Acknowledgments

Kudos to Jeff Kellum for coming up with the original idea for this book. This is one of my favorite books that I have written, and I am glad that I had the opportunity to write this new second edition.

Thanks to my developmental editor Pete Gaughan for his patience and gentle but effective direction and also thanks to my production editor Eric Charbonneau for helping me organize and keep my thoughts going in one direction—which is no easy task! Also, thanks to Troy McMillan and Dax Mickelson for their technical expertise. Finally, thanks to proofreader Rebecca Rider and compositor Craig Woods. All of these people helped create this fantastic title.

About the Author

Todd Lammle is the authority on Cisco Certification and internetworking. He is a world-renowned author, speaker, trainer, and consultant. Todd has three decades of experience working with LANs, WANs, and large licensed and unlicensed wireless networks, and lately he has been implementing large Cisco data centers worldwide. His three decades of real world experience is prevalent in his writing; he is not just an author but an experienced networking engineer with very practical experience working on the largest networks in the world. Todd has published over 60 books, including the very popular *CCNA: Cisco Certified Network Associate Study Guide*, *CCNA Wireless Study Guide*, and *CCNA Data Center Study Guide*, all from Sybex. He runs an international training and consulting company based in Colorado, Texas, and San Francisco.

Contents at a Glance

Contents

Introduction

I know it's kind of wrong to say this type of stuff about your own stuff, but I'm just going to do it—this is a really good book! It might even be the most interesting book I've written so far. A big reason for this is that its scope allowed me to go above and beyond covering the usual CCNA study guide material and I got to really detail the commands I used in the guide, plus a lot of additional commands that just happen to be some of my personal favorites.

Do remember that, although very cool indeed, this volume isn't intended to be a one-stop shop for passing the CCNA exams. Think of it and use it as a supplement to other study material—like, well, my Sybex CCNA study guide! But seriously, I want you to know that this book will complement anything, no matter what you have stashed in your personal arsenal to pass the exams—it's that good, and yes, I said it myself. By the way, know that lots of other people (who I didn't pay) think so too!

How to Use This Book

If you want a solid foundation for the serious and I hope successful goal of effectively preparing for the Cisco Certified Network Associate (CCNA) suite of exams—including the ICND1, ICND2, and the CCNA composite 200-120—then this is your baby! I've spent hundreds of hours putting together this book with the sole objective of helping you to pass the whole group of CCNA exams while actually learning learn how to configure Cisco routers, switches, and tons of other things too.

So, yes, this book is loaded with lots of valuable information, and you will get the most out of all that and your studying time if you understand how I put the book together.

To maximize your benefit from this book, I recommend the following study method:

1. My recommendation is to read the full Sybex *CCNA Study Guide* and then just start reading this book from Chapter 1 and don't stop until you're all the way through Chapter 11. This study method will really help you concentrate on the commands needed to cover the many CCENT/CCNA objectives.

2. Study each chapter carefully, making sure you fully understand the command covered in each chapter. Pay extra-close attention to any chapter that includes material covered that you struggled with when reading the full study guide.

3. Check out www.lammle.com for more Cisco exam prep questions and updates to this book and other Cisco books I have written. The questions found at www.lammle.com will be updated at least monthly, if not weekly or even daily! Before you take your test, be sure to visit my website for questions, videos, audios, and other useful information.

To learn every bit of the material covered in this book, you'll have to apply yourself regularly and with discipline. Try to set aside the same time period every day to study, and select a comfortable and quiet place to do so. If you work hard, you will be surprised at how quickly you learn this material.

What Does This Book Cover?

This book covers everything you need to know in order to understand the CCNA exam objective commands. However, taking the time to study and practice with routers or a router simulator is the real key to success.

You will learn the following information in this book:

- Chapter 1 introduces you to the Cisco Internetwork Operating System (IOS) and command-line interface (CLI). In this chapter you will learn how to turn on a router and configure the basics of the IOS, including setting passwords, banners, and more.

- Chapter 2 provides you with the management skills needed to run a Cisco IOS network. Backing up and restoring the IOS, as well as router configuration, are covered, as are the troubleshooting command tools necessary to keep a network up and running.

- Chapter 3 teaches you about IP routing. This is an important chapter, because you will learn how to build a network, add IP addresses, and route data between routers. You will also learn about static, default, and dynamic routing using RIP.

- Chapter 4 dives into more complex dynamic routing with Enhanced IGRP and OSPF routing.

- Chapter 5 gives you a background on layer-2 switching and how switches perform address learning and make forwarding and filtering decisions. Network loops and how to avoid them with the Spanning Tree Protocol (STP) will be discussed, as well as the 802.1w STP version.

- Chapter 6 covers virtual LANs and how you can use them in your internetwork. This chapter also covers the nitty-gritty of VLANs and the different concepts and protocols used with VLANs, as well as troubleshooting.

- Chapter 7 covers security and access lists, which are created on routers to filter the network. IP standard, extended, and named access lists are covered in detail.

- Chapter 8 covers Network Address Translation (NAT). Information and all the configuration commands, troubleshooting, and verification commands needed to understand the NAT CCNA objectives are covered in this chapter.

- Chapter 9 covers IPv6. This is a very fun chapter and has some great information. IPv6 is not the big, bad, scary monster that most people think it is. IPv6 is an objective on this new exam, so study this chapter carefully. This chapter is more technology based then configuration based to cover the current CCNA objectives. Keep an eye out at www.lammle.com for up-to-the-minute updates.

- Chapter 10 concentrates on Cisco wide area network (WAN) protocols. This chapter covers HDLC, PPP, and Frame Relay in depth. You must be proficient in all these protocols to be successful on the CCNA exam.

- Chapter 11 covers Cisco IP Services, which are the newest exam objectives added to the latest CCNA exam.

For up-to-the-minute updates covering additions or modifications to the CCNA certification exams, as well as additional study tools and review questions, be sure to visit the Todd Lammle forum and website at www.lammle.com or www.lammle.com/forum.

Cisco's Network Certifications

It used to be that to secure the holy grail of Cisco certifications—the CCIE—you passed only one written test before being faced with a grueling, formidable hands-on lab. This intensely daunting, all-or-nothing approach made it nearly impossible to succeed and predictably didn't work out too well for most people. Cisco responded to this issue by creating a series of new certifications, which not only made it easier to eventually win the highly coveted CCIE prize, it gave employers a way to accurately rate and measure the skill levels of prospective and current employees. This exciting paradigm shift in Cisco's certification path truly opened doors that few were allowed through before!

Beginning in 1998, obtaining the Cisco Certified Network Associate (CCNA) certification was the first milestone in the Cisco certification climb as well as the unofficial prerequisite to each of the more advanced levels. But that changed when Cisco announced the Cisco Certified Entry Network Technician (CCENT) certification. And then in March 2013, Cisco once again proclaimed that all-new tests would be required beginning in October of the same year; now the Cisco certification process looks like Figure I.1.

FIGURE I.1   The Cisco Certification Path

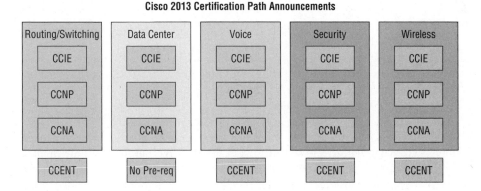

Cisco 2013 Certification Path Announcements

I have included only the most popular tracks in Figure I.1. In addition to the ones in this image, there are also tracks for Design, Service Provider, Service Provider Operations, and Video. Also note that the CCIE Voice certification has been retired as of February 2014.

The Cisco Routing and Switching (R/S) path is by far the most popular and could very well remain so, but soon you'll see the Data Center path become more and more of a focus as companies migrate to data center technologies. The Voice track also actually does provide a good job opportunity. Still, understanding the foundation of R/S before attempting any other certification track is something I highly recommend.

Even so, and as the figure shows, you only need your CCENT certification to get underway for most of the tracks. Also, note that there are a few other certification tracks you can go down that are not shown in the figure, although they're not as popular as the ones shown. You can find information on all Cisco certification tracks at www.cisco.com.

Cisco Certified Entry Network Technician (CCENT)

Don't be fooled by the oh-so-misleading name of this first certification because it absolutely isn't entry-level! Okay—maybe it's entry level for Cisco's certification path, but definitely not for someone without experience trying to break into the highly lucrative yet challenging IT job market! For the uninitiated, the CompTIA A+ and Network+ certifications aren't official prerequisites, but know that Cisco does expect you to have that type and level of experience before embarking on your Cisco certification journey.

All of this gets us to 2013, when the climb to Cisco supremacy just got much harder again. The innocuous-sounding siren's call of the CCENT can lure you to some serious trouble if you're not prepared, because it's actually much harder than the old CCNA ever was. This will rapidly become apparent once you start studying, but be encouraged! The fact that the certification process is getting harder really works better for you in the long run, because that which is harder to obtain only becomes that much more valuable when you finally do get it, right? Yes, indeed!

Another important factor to keep in mind is that the CCENT 100-101 exam, which is the exam this book was written for, costs $150 per attempt and it's anything but easy to pass! The good news is that this book will guide you step-by-step in building a strong foundation in routing and switching technologies. You really need to build on a strong technical foundation and stay away from exam cram type books, suspicious online material, and the like. They can help somewhat, but understand that you'll pass the Cisco certification exams only if you have a strong foundation and that you'll get that solid foundation only by reading as much as you can, performing the written labs and review questions in this book, and practicing lots and lots of hands-on labs. Additional practice exam questions, videos, and labs are offered on my website, and what seems like a million other sites offer additional material that can help you study.

However, there is one way to skip the CCENT exam and still meet the prerequisite required before moving on to any other certification track, and that path is through the

CCNA R/S composite exam. First, I'll discuss the Interconnecting Cisco Network Devices 2 (ICND2) exam, and then I'll tell you about the composite CCNA exam, which will provide you, when successful, with both the CCENT and the CCNA R/S certification.

Cisco Certified Network Associate Routing and Switching (CCNA R/S)

Once you have achieved your CCENT certification, you can take the ICND2 (200-101) exam in order to achieve your CCNA R/S certification. This is now the most popular certification Cisco has by far because it's the most sought-after certification of all employers.

As with the CCENT, this exam is also $150 per attempt—although thinking you can just skim a book and pass any of these exams would probably be a really expensive mistake! The CCENT/CCNA exams are extremely hard and cover a lot of material, so you have to really know your stuff. Taking a Cisco class or spending months with hands-on experience is definitely a requirement to succeed when faced with this monster!

And once you have your CCNA, you don't have to stop there—you can choose to continue and achieve an even higher certification, called the Cisco Certified Network Professional (CCNP). There are various ones as shown in Figure I.1. The CCNP R/S is still the most popular, with Voice certifications coming in at a close second. And I've got to tell you that the Data Center certification will be catching up fast. Also good to know is that anyone with a CCNP has all the skills and knowledge needed to attempt the notoriously dreaded but coveted CCIE lab. But just becoming a CCENT/CCNA can land you that job you've dreamed about and that's what this book is all about: helping you to get and keep a great job!

Still, why take two exams to get your CCNA if you don't have to? Cisco still has the composite exam called CCNA 200-120 that, if passed, will land you with your CCENT and your CCNA R/S via only one test priced accordingly at $300. Some people like the one test approach, some people like the two-test approach, but this book will help you with either path you choose.

Why Become a CCENT and CCNA R/S?

Cisco, like Microsoft and other vendors that provide certification, has created the certification process to give administrators a set of skills and to equip prospective employers with a way to measure those skills or match certain criteria. And as you probably know, becoming a CCNA R/S is certainly the initial, key step on a successful journey toward a new, highly rewarding, and sustainable networking career.

The CCNA program was created to provide a solid introduction not only to the Cisco Internetwork Operating System (IOS) and Cisco hardware but also to internetworking in general, making it helpful to you in areas that are not exclusively Cisco's. And regarding today's certification process, it's not unrealistic that network managers—even those without Cisco equipment—require Cisco certifications for their job applicants.

Rest assured that if you make it through the CCNA and are still interested in Cisco and internetworking, you're headed down a path to certain success!

What Skills Do You Need to Become a CCENT?

This exam tests a candidate for the knowledge and skills required to successfully install, operate, and troubleshoot a small branch office network.

The exam includes topics on the operation of IP data networks, LAN switching technologies, IPv6, IP routing technologies, IP services (DHCP, NAT, ACLs), network device security, and basic troubleshooting.

What Skills Do You Need to Become a CCNA R/S?

The ICND2 exam (exam 200-101) tests a candidate for the knowledge and skills required to successfully install, operate, and troubleshoot a small to medium-size enterprise branch network. The exam includes topics on LAN switching technologies, IP routing technologies, IP services (FHRP, syslog, SNMP v2 and v3), troubleshooting, and WAN technologies.

Another test you can take instead of taking both of the ICND1 and ICND2 is the composite CCNA v2.0 exam, number 200-120.

How Do You Become a CCNA R/S with Just One Test?

The way to become a CCNA R/S is to pass one little test (CCNA Composite exam 200-120) without having to take the CCENT exam. Then—poof!—you're a CCNA R/S. Oh, but don't you wish it were that easy? True, it's just one test, but it's a whopper, and to pass it you must possess enough knowledge to understand what the test writers are saying.

Good to know is that Cisco offers the two-step process I discussed earlier in this introduction that you can follow to become a CCNA. It's easier than taking that one ginormous exam, but don't think the two-test method is easy. It takes work! However, it can be done; you just need to stick with your studies.

The two-test method involves passing the following:

Exam 100-101: Interconnecting Cisco Networking Devices 1 (ICND1)

Exam 200-101: Introduction to Cisco Networking Devices 2 (ICND2)

I can't stress this point enough: It's critical that you have some hands-on experience with Cisco routers. If you can get ahold of some basic routers and switches, you're set; but if you can't, I've worked hard to provide hundreds of configuration examples throughout this book to help network administrators, or people who want to become network administrators, learn the skills they need to pass the CCENT and CCNA exams.

 For Cisco certification hands-on training with Todd Lammle, please see www.lammle.com. Each student will get hands-on experience by configuring at least three routers and two switches—no sharing of equipment!

Where Do You Take the Exams?

You may take the CCENT or any Cisco exam at any of the Pearson VUE authorized testing centers (www.vue.com) or call 877-404-EXAM (3926).

To register for a Cisco exam, follow these steps:

1. Determine the number of the exam you want to take.

2. Register with the nearest Pearson VUE testing center. At this point, you will be asked to pay in advance for the exam. At the time of this writing, the CCENT and ICND2 exams are $125 and must be taken within one year of payment. You can schedule exams up to six weeks in advance or as late as the day you want to take it—but if you fail a Cisco exam, you must wait six days before you will be allowed to retake it. If something comes up and you need to cancel or reschedule your exam appointment, contact Pearson VUE at least 24 hours in advance.

3. When you schedule the exam, you'll get instructions regarding all appointment and cancellation procedures, the ID requirements, and information about the testing-center location.

Tips for Taking Your CCNA Exams

The CCNA exams contains about 55 questions and must be completed in 75 to 90 minutes or less. This information can change per exam. You must get a score of about 80 to 85 percent to pass this exam, but again, each exam can be different.

Many questions on the exam have answer choices that at first glance look identical—especially the syntax questions! Remember to read through the choices carefully because close doesn't cut it. If you get commands in the wrong order or forget one measly character, you'll get the question wrong.

Also, never forget that the right answer is the Cisco answer. In many cases, more than one appropriate answer is presented, but the *correct* answer is the one that Cisco recommends. On the exam, you're always instructed to pick one, two, or three, never "choose all that apply." The latest CCNA exams may include the following test formats:

- Multiple-choice single answer
- Multiple-choice multiple answer
- Drag-and-drop
- Fill-in-the-blank
- Router simulations

In addition to multiple choice and fill-in response questions, Cisco Career Certifications exams may include performance simulation exam items. They do allow partial command responses. For example, show running-config, or sh run would be acceptable.

Here are some general tips for exam success:

- Arrive early at the exam center so you can relax and review your study materials.

- Read the questions *carefully*. Don't jump to conclusions. Make sure you're clear about *exactly* what each question asks.

- When answering multiple-choice questions that you're not sure about, use the process of elimination to get rid of the obviously incorrect answers first. Doing this greatly improves your odds if you need to make an educated guess.

- You can no longer move forward and backward through the Cisco exams, so double-check your answer before clicking Next since you can't change your mind.

After you complete an exam, you'll get immediate, online notification of your pass or fail status, a printed Examination Score Report that indicates your pass or fail status, and your exam results by section. (The test administrator will give you the printed score report.) Test scores are automatically forwarded to Cisco within five working days after you take the test, so you don't need to send your score to them. If you pass the exam, you'll receive confirmation from Cisco, typically within two to four weeks, sometimes longer.

This book covers everything CCNA related. For up-to-date information on Todd Lammle Cisco Authorized CCNA CCNP and CCIE boot camps, please see www.lammle.com.

How to Contact the Author

You can reach Todd Lammle through GlobalNet Training Solutions, Inc. (www.globalnettc.com), his training and systems integration company; or through his forum at www.lammle.com/forum.

Chapter

1

Basic IOS Commands

This book starts by introducing you to the Cisco Internetwork Operating System (IOS). The IOS is what runs Cisco routers as well as some Cisco switches, and it's what allows you to configure the devices. You use the command-line interface (CLI) to configure a router, and that is what I'll show you in this chapter.

The Cisco router IOS software is responsible for the following important tasks:

- Carrying network protocols and functions
- Connecting high-speed traffic between devices
- Adding security to control access and stop unauthorized network use
- Providing scalability for ease of network growth and redundancy
- Supplying network reliability for connecting to network resources

You can access the Cisco IOS through the console port of a router, from a modem into the auxiliary (or aux) port, or even through Telnet and Secure Shell (SSH). Access to the IOS command line is called an *exec session*.

Once you have attached your console cable (this is a rolled cable, sometimes referred to as a *rollover cable*) to the router and have started your terminal software, you will be ready to power on the router. Assuming that this is a new router, it will have no configuration and thus will need to have, well, everything set up. In this chapter, first I'll cover the power-on process of the router, and then I'll introduce the setup script.

For up-to-the minute updates for this chapter, please see www.lammle.com.

Booting the Router

The following messages appear when you first boot or reload a router:

```
System Bootstrap, Version 15.1(4)M6, RELEASE SOFTWARE (fc1)
Technical Support: http://www.cisco.com/techsupport
Copyright (c) 2006 by cisco Systems, Inc.
Initializing memory for ECC
c2811 platform with 262144 Kbytes of main memory
```

```
Main memory is configured to 64 bit mode with ECC enabled
Upgrade ROMMON initialized
program load complete, entry point: 0x8000f000, size: 0xcb80
program load complete, entry point: 0x8000f000, size: 0xcb80
program load complete, entry point: 0x8000f000, size: 0x14b45f8
Self decompressing the image :
    ###################################################################
    ########################################## [OK]
 [some output cut]

Cisco IOS Software, 2800 Software (C2800NM-ADVSECURITYK9-M), Version
    15.1(4)M6,RELEASE SOFTWARE (fc1)
Technical Support: http://www.cisco.com/techsupport
Copyright (c) 1986-2006 by Cisco Systems, Inc.
Compiled Fri 17-Nov-06 12:02 by prod_rel_team
Image text-base: 0x40093160, data-base: 0x41AA0000

[some output cut]

Cisco 2811 (revision 49.46) with 249856K/12288K bytes of memory.
Processor board ID FTX1049A1AB
2 FastEthernet interfaces
4 Serial(sync/async) interfaces
1 Virtual Private Network (VPN) Module
DRAM configuration is 64 bits wide with parity enabled.
239K bytes of non-volatile configuration memory.
62720K bytes of ATA CompactFlash (Read/Write)
```

Notice the following in the previous messages:

- The type of router (2811) and the amount of memory (262,144KB)
- The version of software the router is running (15.1(4)M6)
- The interfaces on the router (two Fast Ethernet and four serial)

Figure 1.1 shows a picture of an 1841 router, which is what is called an *integrated services router* (ISR), just like the 2811 router output shown earlier.

FIGURE 1.1　A Cisco 1841 router

An 1841 router holds most of the same interfaces as a 2800 router, but it's smaller and less expensive.

Setup Mode

If the router has no initial configuration, you will be prompted to use setup mode to establish an initial configuration. You can also enter setup mode at any time from the command line by typing the command **setup** from something called *privileged mode*. Setup mode covers only some global commands and is generally just not helpful. Here is an example:

```
Would you like to enter the initial configuration dialog? [yes/no]: y

At any point you may enter a question mark '?' for help.
Use ctrl-c to abort configuration dialog at any prompt.
Default settings are in square brackets '[]'.

Basic management setup configures only enough connectivity
for management of the system, extended setup will ask you
to configure each interface on the system

Would you like to enter basic management setup? [yes/no]: y
Configuring global parameters:

  Enter host name [Router]:Ctrl+C
Configuration aborted, no changes made.
```

 You can exit setup mode at any time by pressing Ctrl+C.

Router Configuration Modes

One key to navigating the CLI is to always be aware of which router configuration mode you are currently in (see Table 1.1). You can tell which configuration mode you are in by watching the CLI prompt.

TABLE 1.1   Router Configuration Modes

Mode	Definition	Example
User EXEC mode	Limited to basic monitoring commands	Router>

Mode	Definition	Example
Privileged EXEC mode	Provides access to all other router commands	`Router#`
Global configuration mode	Commands that affect the entire system	`Router(config)#`
Specific configuration modes	Commands that affect interfaces, subinterfaces, routing processes, or lines only	`Router(config-subif)#`

Once you understand the different modes, you will need to be able to move from one mode to another within the CLI. The commands in Table 1.2 allow you to navigate between the assorted CLI modes.

TABLE 1.2   Moving Between Modes

Command	Meaning
`Router>`**`enable`**	Changes from user EXEC to privileged EXEC mode
`Router#`**`disable`**	Changes to user EXEC from privileged EXEC mode
`Router#`**`config term`**	Changes to global configuration mode from privileged mode
`Router(config)#`**`exit`**	Exits from any configuration mode to privileged mode (Ctrl+Z is also commonly used)
`Router(config)#`**`interface <int>`**	Enters interface configuration mode from global configuration mode
`Router(config)#`**`interface <subint>`**	Enters subinterface configuration mode from global configuration mode
`Router(config)#`**`line <line>`**	Enters line configuration mode from global configuration mode
`Router(config)#`**`router eigrp 1`**	Enters router configuration mode from global configuration mode

Editing and Help Features

One difference between a good and a great CLI engineer is the ability to quickly edit the line being entered into the router. Great CLI engineers can quickly recall previously entered commands and modify them, which is often much quicker than reentering the entire command. Table 1.3 shows some of the editing commands most commonly used.

TABLE 1.3 CLI Editing Commands

Command	Meaning
Ctrl+P or Up arrow	Shows last command entered
Ctrl+N or Down arrow	Shows previous commands entered
show history	Shows last 10 commands entered by default
show terminal	Shows terminal configurations and history buffer size
terminal history size	Changes buffer size (the maximum is 256)
Ctrl+A	Moves your cursor to the beginning of the line
Ctrl+E	Moves your cursor to the end of the line
Esc+B	Moves back one word
Ctrl+B	Moves back one character
Ctrl+F	Moves forward one character
Esc+F	Moves forward one word
Ctrl+D	Deletes a single character
Backspace	Deletes a single character
Ctrl+R	Redisplays a line
Ctrl+U	Erases a line
Ctrl+W	Erases a word
Ctrl+Z	Ends configuration mode and returns to EXEC mode
Tab	Finishes typing a command for you

The CLI also provides extensive online help. Any great CLI engineer will have an excessively worn question-mark key on the keyboard! Table 1.4 shows some examples of using the online help.

TABLE 1.4 Online Help Commands

Command	Meaning
Router#**?**	Shows all available commands
Router#**c?**	Shows all available commands beginning with the letter *c*
Router#**clock ?**	Shows all available options for the clock command

Using the Question Mark

The only command is the question mark; however, it does make a difference where you use it. When entering complex IOS commands, it is common to use the question mark repeatedly while entering the command, as in the following example:

```
Router#clock ?
  read-calendar    Read the hardware calendar into the clock
  set              Set the time and date
  update-calendar  Update the hardware calendar from the clock
Router#clock set ?
  hh:mm:ss  Current Time
Router#clock set 11:15:11 ?
  <1-31>  Day of the month
  MONTH   Month of the year
Router#clock set 11:15:11 25 aug ?
  <1993-2035>  Year
Router#clock set 11:15:11 25 aug 2014 ?
  <cr>
Router#clock set 11:15:11 25 aug 2014
*Aug 25 11:15:11.000: %SYS-6-CLOCKUPDATE: System clock has been updated from
18:52:53 UTC Wed Feb 28 2014 to 11:15:11 UTC Sat Aug 25 2014, configured from
console by cisco on console.
```

Using the Pipe

The pipe (|) allows you to wade through all the configurations or other long outputs and get straight to your goods fast. Table 1.5 shows the pipe commands.

TABLE 1.5   Pipe Commands

Command	Meaning
Router#**sh running-config	?**	Shows the options for the pipe command. These include the ability to begin, include, exclude, and so on.
Router#**sh run	begin interface**	Shows the running configuration, beginning at the interface configurations.
Router#**sh ip route	include 192.168.3.32**	Shows all entries in the IP routing table that include the IP address 192.168.3.32.

Here's an example of using the pipe command to view just interface information on a router:

```
Router#sh run | ?
  append    Append redirected output to URL (URLs supporting append operation
            only)
  begin     Begin with the line that matches
  exclude   Exclude lines that match
  include   Include lines that match
  redirect  Redirect output to URL
  section   Filter a section of output
  tee       Copy output to URL
!
Router#sh run | begin interface
interface FastEthernet0/0
 description Sales VLAN
 ip address 10.10.10.1 255.255.255.248
 duplex auto
 speed auto
!
```

Configuring a Router

In the following sections, I'll introduce the commands used to do basic router configuration. You'll use these commands (or should use them) on every router you configure.

Hostnames

You can set the identity of the router with the `hostname` command. This is only locally significant, which means it has no bearing on how the router performs name lookups or how the router works on the internetwork. Table 1.6 shows the command for setting a router's hostname.

TABLE 1.6   Setting a Router Hostname

Command	Meaning
Router(config)#**hostname** *name*	Sets the hostname of this router

Here's an example of setting a hostname on a router:

```
Router#config t
Router(config)#hostname Todd
Todd(config)#
```

Banners

You can create a banner to give anyone who shows up on the router exactly the information you want them to have. Make sure you're familiar with these four available banner types: exec process creation banner, incoming terminal line banner, login banner, and message of the day banner (all illustrated in Table 1.7).

TABLE 1.7   Setting a Banner

Command	Meaning
Router(config)#**banner motd #**	Enters a banner MOTD message and ends the message with the # character
Router(config)#**banner exec #**	Enters a banner exec message and ends the message with the # character
Router(config)#**banner incoming #**	Enters a banner incoming message and ends the message with the # character
Router(config)#**banner login #**	Enters a banner login message and ends the message with the # character

The following describes the various banners:

MOTD banner   The MOTD banner will be displayed whenever anyone attaches to the router, regardless of how they access the router.

Exec banner   You can configure a line activation (exec) banner to be displayed when an EXEC process (such as a line activation or incoming connection to a VTY line) is created. By simply starting a user exec session through a console port, you'll activate the exec banner.

Incoming banner   You can configure a banner to be displayed on terminals connected to reverse Telnet lines. This banner is useful for providing instructions to users who use reverse Telnet.

Login banner   You can configure a login banner to be displayed on all connected terminals. This banner is displayed after the MOTD banner but before the login prompts. The login banner can't be disabled on a per-line basis, so to globally disable it, you have to delete it with the no banner login command.

Passwords

You can use five passwords to secure your Cisco routers: console, auxiliary, Telnet (VTY), enable password, and enable secret. However, other commands are necessary to complete the password configurations on a router or switch, as shown in Table 1.8.

TABLE 1.8   Setting Passwords

Command	Meaning
Todd(config)#**enable password todd**	Sets the enable password to Todd.
Todd(config)#**enable secret todd**	Sets the enable secret password to Todd. Supersedes the enable password.
Todd(config)#**line *line***	Changes to line mode to configure the console, aux, and VTY (Telnet).
Todd(config-line)#**password password**	The line password for aux, console, and VTY (Telnet) are all set in line configuration mode.
Todd(config-line)#**login**	When a line is configured to use a password, the login command must be set to prompt for login.
Todd(config)#**service password-encryption**	Encrypts the passwords in the clear-text configuration file (both running-config and startup-config).

Setting Passwords

Here's an example of setting all your passwords and then encrypting them in the clear text configuration file:

```
Todd#config t
Todd(config)#line aux ?
  <0-0>  First Line number
Todd(config)#line aux 0
Todd(config-line)#password aux
Todd(config-line)#login
Todd(config-line)#line con 0
Todd(config-line)#password console
Todd(config-line)#login
Todd(config-line)#exit
Todd(config)#line vty 0 ?
  <1-1180>  Last Line number
  <cr>
Todd(config)#line vty 0 1180
Todd(config-line)#password telnet
Todd(config-line)#login
Todd(config)#enable password todd
Todd(config)#enable secret globalnet
Todd(config)#service password-encryption
Todd(config)#do show run
Building configuration...
[outut cut]
!
enable secret 5 $1$S0a2$rLcwXpbme3zIrl2.TS1kX.
enable password 7 010709005F
!
[output cut]
!
line con 0
 exec-timeout 1 40
 password 7 050809013243420C
 logging synchronous
 login
line aux 0
 password 7 03054E13
 login
line vty 0 4
```

```
 password 7 105A0C150B1206
 login
line vty 5 1180
 password 7 0010160A0A5E1F
 login
!
 [output cut]
```
Todd(config)#no service password-encryption

Some other console helpful commands include the following. This sets the console time-out in second and minutes from 0-35791:

Todd(config-line)#**exec-timeout ?**

This redisplays interrupted console input:

Todd(config-line)#**logging synchronous**

Here's an example of setting the exec-timeout and logging synchronous commands:

```
Todd)#config t
Todd(config)#line con 0
Todd(config-line)#exec-timeout ?
  <0-35791>  Timeout in minutes
Todd(config-line)#exec-timeout 0 ?
  <0-2147483>  Timeout in seconds
  <cr>
Todd(config-line)#exec-timeout 0 100
Todd(config-line)#logging synchronous
```

Setting Up Secure Shell (SSH)

Instead of Telnet, you can use *Secure Shell*, which creates a more secure session than the Telnet application that uses an unencrypted data stream. SSH uses encrypted keys to send data so that your username and password are not sent in the clear. Table 1.9 lists the commands.

TABLE 1.9 SSH Commands

Command	Meaning
ip domain-name Lammle.com	Sets your domain name. You must set this.
crypto key generate rsa general-keys modulus	Sets the size of the key up to 2048.

Command	Meaning
`ip ssh time-out`	Sets the idle timeout up to 120 seconds.
`ip ssh authentication-retries`	Sets the max failed attempts up to 120.
`line vty` *first-line last_line*	Chooses your VTY lines to configure.
`transport input ssh telnet`	Tells the router to use SSH and then Telnet. You do not need the `telnet` command at the end of the line, but if you don't use it, only SSH will work on the router.

Here's an example of how you set up SSH on a router:

1. Set your hostname:

```
Router(config)#hostname Todd
```

2. Set the domain name—both the hostname and domain name are required for the encryption keys to be generated:

```
Todd(config)#ip domain-name Lammle.com
```

3. Set the username to allow SSH client access:

```
Todd(config)#username Todd password Lammle
```

4. Generate the encryption keys for securing the session:

```
Todd(config)#crypto key generate rsa
The name for the keys will be: Todd.Lammle.com
Choose the size of the key modulus in the range of 360 to
4096 for your General Purpose Keys. Choosing a key modulus
Greater than 512 may take a few minutes.

How many bits in the modulus [512]: 1024
% Generating 1024 bit RSA keys, keys will be non-exportable...
[OK] (elapsed time was 6 seconds)

Todd(config)#
1d14h: %SSH-5-ENABLED: SSH 1.99 has been enabled*June 24
19:25:30.035: %SSH-5-ENABLED: SSH 1.99 has been enabled
```

5. Enable SSH version 2 on the router—not mandatory, but strongly suggested:

```
Todd(config)#ip ssh version 2
```

6. Connect to the VTY lines of the switch:

```
Todd(config)#line vty 0 15
```

7. Configure your access protocols:

```
Todd(config-line)#transport input ?
  all     All protocols
  none    No protocols
  ssh     TCP/IP SSH protocol
  telnet  TCP/IP Telnet protocol
```

Beware of this next line, and make sure you never use it in production because it's a horrendous security risk:

```
Todd(config-line)#transport input all
```

I recommend using the next line to secure your VTY lines with SSH:

```
Todd(config-line)#transport input ssh ?
  telnet  TCP/IP Telnet protocol
  <cr>
```

I actually do use Telnet once in a while when a situation arises that specifically calls for it. It just doesn't happen very often. But if you want be able to use SSH or Telnet, here's how you do that:

```
Todd(config-line)#transport input ssh telnet
```

Know that if you don't use the keyword telnet at the end of the command string, then only SSH will work on the device. You can go with either, just so long as you understand that SSH is way more secure than Telnet.

Router Interfaces

Interface configuration is one of the most important router configurations, because without interfaces, a router is pretty much a completely useless object. Plus, interface configurations must be totally precise to enable communication with other devices. Network layer addresses, media type, bandwidth, and other administrator commands are all used to configure an interface. Table 1.10 shows the commands.

TABLE 1.10   Router Interface Commands

Command	Meaning
Todd(config)#**interface fastethernet** *slot/port*	Enters interface configuration mode from global configuration mode.
Todd(config)#**interface serial** *slot/port*	Same as the previous command, except for serial interface 0/0/0 rather than Fast Ethernet interface.
Todd(config-if)#**shutdown**	Shuts down an interface.
Todd(config-if)#**no shutdown**	Enables an interface that is shut down.
Todd(config-if)#**ip address** *address mask*	Configures an interface with an IP address and a subnet mask.
Todd(config-if)#**ip address** *address mask* **secondary**	Adds a secondary IP address to an interface.
Todd(config-if)#**description** *description*	Adds a description to an interface.
Todd(config-if)#**clock rate** *rate*	Sets the clock rate of a serial interface in bits per second.
Todd(config-if)#**bandwidth** *rate*	Sets the bandwidth of an interface in kilobits per second.
Todd#**show interface** *interface*	Displays the status and configuration of the Fast Ethernet interface.
Todd#**clear counters** *interface*	Clears the display counters on the serial interface.
Todd#**sh ip interface** *interface*	Displays the layer-3 properties of an interface.
Todd#**sh ip int brief**	Displays the IP interfaces in a summarized table. This is one of the most useful show commands!

Let's take a look at setting both an IP address and a secondary IP address on an interface, and then we'll verify the configuration:

```
Todd(config)#interface fastethernet 0/0
Todd(config)#interface serial 0/0/0
```

```
Todd(config-if)#shutdown
Jul 30 15:31:23.542: %LINK-5-CHANGED: Interface Serial0/0/0, changed state to
administratively down
Jul 30 15:31:24.542: %LINEPROTO-5-UPDOWN: Line protocol on Interface
Serial0/0/0, changed state to down
Todd(config-if)#no shutdown
Jul 30 15:31:27.566: %LINK-3-UPDOWN: Interface Serial0/0/0, changed state to up
Jul 30 15:31:28.566: %LINEPROTO-5-UPDOWN: Line protocol on Interface
Serial0/0/0, changed state to up
Todd(config-if)#ip address 172.16.10.1 255.255.255.0
Todd(config-if)#ip address 172.16.20.1 255.255.255.0 ?
  secondary  Make this IP address a secondary address
  <cr>
Todd(config-if)#ip address 172.16.20.1 255.255.255.0 secondary
Todd(config-if)#description Serial link to Miami
Todd(config-if)#clock rate 1000000
Todd(config-if)#bandwidth 1000
Todd(config-if)#exit
Todd(config)#exit
Todd#show interface s0/0/0
Serial0/0/0 is up, line protocol is up
  Hardware is GT96K Serial
  Description: Serial link to Miami
  Internet address is 172.16.10.1/24
  MTU 1500 bytes, BW 1000 Kbit, DLY 20000 usec,
     reliability 255/255, txload 1/255, rxload 1/255
  Encapsulation HDLC, loopback not set
  Keepalive set (10 sec)
  Last input 00:00:04, output 00:00:08, output hang never
  Last clearing of "show interface" counters 2d05h
  Input queue: 0/75/0/0 (size/max/drops/flushes); Total output drops: 0
  Queueing strategy: fifo
  Output queue: 0/40 (size/max)
  5 minute input rate 0 bits/sec, 0 packets/sec
  5 minute output rate 0 bits/sec, 0 packets/sec
     34632 packets input, 2479012 bytes, 0 no buffer
     Received 34031 broadcasts, 0 runts, 0 giants, 0 throttles
     0 input errors, 0 CRC, 0 frame, 0 overrun, 0 ignored, 0 abort
     34372 packets output, 2303104 bytes, 0 underruns
     0 output errors, 0 collisions, 5 interface resets
     0 output buffer failures, 0 output buffers swapped out
```

```
      112 carrier transitions
      DCD=up  DSR=up  DTR=up  RTS=up  CTS=up
```

Todd#**clear counters s0/0/0**
Clear "show interface" counters on this interface [confirm]**[enter]**
Jul 30 15:39:02.818: %CLEAR-5-COUNTERS: Clear counter on interface Serial0/0/0
by console
Todd#**sh ip interface s0/0/0**
Serial0/0/0 is up, line protocol is up
　　Internet address is 172.16.10.1/24
　　Broadcast address is 255.255.255.255
　　Address determined by setup command
　　MTU is 1500 bytes
　　Helper address is not set
　　Directed broadcast forwarding is disabled
　　Secondary address 172.16.20.1/24
　　Secondary address 172.16.30.1/24
　　Outgoing access list is not set
　　Inbound access list is not set
　　Proxy ARP is enabled
　　Local Proxy ARP is disabled
　　Security level is default
　　Split horizon is enabled
　　ICMP redirects are always sent
　　ICMP unreachables are always sent
　　ICMP mask replies are never sent
　　IP fast switching is enabled
　　IP fast switching on the same interface is enabled
　　IP Flow switching is disabled
　　IP CEF switching is enabled
　　IP CEF Fast switching turbo vector
　　[output cut]
Todd#**sh ip int brief**

```
Interface        IP-Address     OK? Method Status                Protocol
FastEthernet0/0  192.168.21.1   YES manual up                    up
FastEthernet0/1  unassigned     YES unset  administratively down down
Serial0/0/0      172.16.10.1    YES manual up                    up
Serial0/0/1      unassigned     YES unset  administratively down down
Todd#
```

Viewing, Saving, and Erasing Configurations

Once you have gone to all the work of creating a configuration, you will need to know how to save it, and maybe even delete it. Table 1.11 shows the commands used to manipulate configurations.

TABLE 1.11   Commands to Manipulate Configurations

Command	Meaning
Todd#**copy running-config startup-config**	Saves the running configuration to NVRAM
Todd#**show running-config**	Shows the running configuration on the terminal
Todd#**show startup-config**	Shows the start-up configuration (in NVRAM) on the terminal
Todd#**erase startup-config**	Erases the configuration stored in NVRAM

You can manually save the file from DRAM to NVRAM by using the copy running-config startup-config command (you can use the shortcut copy run start also):

```
Todd#copy running-config startup-config
Destination filename [startup-config]? [press enter]
Building configuration...
[OK]
Todd#
Building configuration...

Todd#show running-config
Building configuration...

Current configuration : 3343 bytes
!
version 15.0
[output cut]
```

The sh start command—one of the shortcuts for the show startup-config command—shows you the configuration that will be used the next time the router is reloaded. It also tells you how much NVRAM is being used to store the startup-config file. Here's an example:

```
Todd#show startup-config
Using 1978 out of 245752 bytes
!
```

```
version 15.0
[output cut]
```

```
Todd#erase startup-config
Erasing the nvram filesystem will remove all configuration files!
    Continue? [confirm][enter]
[OK]
Erase of nvram: complete
Todd#
*Feb 28 23:51:21.179: %SYS-7-NV_BLOCK_INIT: Initialized the geometry of nvram
Todd#sh startup-config
startup-config is not present
Todd#reload
Proceed with reload? [confirm]System configuration has been modified.
    Save? [yes/no]: n
```

Using the *show* Command

Obviously, show running-config would be the best way to verify your configuration, and show startup-config would be the best way to verify the configuration that will be used the next time the router is reloaded, right?

Table 1.12 shows some basic command you might use every day in a production environment.

TABLE 1.12   Everyday Commands

Command	Meaning
show running config	This shows the configuration that router is using.
show startup-config	This shows the configuration that the router will use when the router is reload.
show interface	This shows the status of all interfaces.
show ip interface	This shows the IP configuration on all interfaces.
show ip interface brief	This command provides a quick overview of the router's interfaces, including the logical address and status.

TABLE 1.12   Everyday Commands *(continued)*

Command	Meaning
show protocols	This shows the status of layers 1 and 2 of each interface as well as the IP addresses used.
show controllers	This shows whether an interface is a DCE or DTE interface.

The show running-config command is important and could very well be one of the most used commands on a Cisco router. The show running-config command shows the configuration that the router is running. The show startup-config shows the backup config, or the configuration that will be used the next time the router is booted. You can view the files by typing **show running-config** or **show startup-config** from privileged mode. The sh run command, which is a shortcut for show running-config, tells us that we're viewing the current configuration:

```
Todd#sh run
Building configuration...

Current configuration : 855 bytes
!
! Last configuration change at 23:20:06 UTC Mon Mar 1 1993
!
version 15.0
[output cut]
```

The sh start command—one of the shortcuts for the show startup-config command—shows us the configuration that will be used the next time the router is reloaded. It also tells us how much NVRAM is being used to store the startup-config file. Here's an example:

```
Todd#sh start
Using 855 out of 524288 bytes
!
! Last configuration change at 23:20:06 UTC Mon Mar 1 1993
!
version 15.0
[output cut]
```

But beware—if you try and view the configuration and see

```
Todd#sh start
startup-config is not present
```

you have not saved your running-config to NVRAM, or you've deleted the backup configuration! To do this, execute the copy run start command.

The show interface command is important, and that's what I'll discuss in this section. Here's what it looks like:

```
Router#sh int s0/0/0
Serial0/0 is up, line protocol is down
```

If you see that the line is up but the protocol is down, as shown earlier, you're experiencing a clocking (keepalive) or framing problem—possibly an encapsulation mismatch. Check the keepalives on both ends to make sure that they match, that the clock rate is set (if needed), and that the encapsulation type is the same on both ends. The previous output would be considered a Data Link layer problem.

If you discover that both the line interface and the protocol are down, it's a cable or interface problem. The following output would be considered a physical layer problem:

```
Router#sh int s0/0/0
Serial0/0 is down, line protocol is down
```

If one end is administratively shut down (as shown next), the remote end would present as down and down:

```
Router#sh int s0/0/0
Serial0/0 is administratively down, line protocol is down
```

To enable the interface, use the command no shutdown from interface configuration mode:

```
Router#config t
Router(config)#int s0/0/0
Router(config-if)#no shutdown
```

You can get a nice brief overview of the interfaces with the show interface brief command:

```
Router#show ip int brief
Interface        IP-Address      OK? Method Status     Protocol
FastEthernet0/0  unassigned      YES unset  up         up
FastEthernet0/1  unassigned      YES unset  up         up
Serial0/0/0      unassigned      YES unset  up         down
Serial0/0/1      unassigned      YES unset  up         up
Serial0/1/0      unassigned      YES unset  administratively down down
```

```
Todd#sh protocols
Global values:
  Internet Protocol routing is enabled
FastEthernet0/0 is up, line protocol is up
  Internet address is 192.168.21.1/24
FastEthernet0/1 is administratively down, line protocol is down
Serial0/0/0 is up, line protocol is up
  Internet address is 172.16.10.1/24
Serial0/0/1 is administratively down, line protocol is down
Todd#
```

The show controllers command displays information about the physical interface itself. It'll also give you the type of serial cable plugged into a serial port. Usually, this will be only a DTE cable that plugs into a type of data service unit (DSU).

```
Router#sh controllers serial 0/0
HD unit 0, idb = 0x1229E4, driver structure at 0x127E70
buffer size 1524 HD unit 0, V.35 DTE cable
cpb = 0xE2, eda = 0x4140, cda = 0x4000
```

```
Router#sh controllers serial 0/1
HD unit 1, idb = 0x12C174, driver structure at 0x131600
buffer size 1524 HD unit 1, V.35 DCE cable
cpb = 0xE3, eda = 0x2940, cda = 0x2800
```

Troubleshooting with the *show interfaces* Command

Let's take a look at the output of the show interfaces command one more time before I move onto the next chapter. There are some important statistics in this output that are important for the Cisco objectives.

```
275496 packets input, 35226811 bytes, 0 no buffer
  Received 69748 broadcasts (58822 multicasts)
  0 runts, 0 giants, 0 throttles
  0 input errors, 0 CRC, 0 frame, 0 overrun, 0 ignored
  0 watchdog, 58822 multicast, 0 pause input
  0 input packets with dribble condition detected
  2392529 packets output, 337933522 bytes, 0 underruns
  0 output errors, 0 collisions, 1 interface resets
  0 babbles, 0 late collision, 0 deferred
  0 lost carrier, 0 no carrier, 0 PAUSE output
  0 output buffer failures, 0 output buffers swapped out
```

Finding where to start when troubleshooting an interface can be the difficult part, but certainly we'll look for the number of input errors and CRCs right away. Typically we'd see those statistics increase with a duplex error, but it could be another Physical layer issue such as the cable might be receiving excessive interference or the network interface cards might have a failure. Typically you can tell if it is interference when the CRC and input errors output grow but the collision counters do not.

Let's take a look at some of the output:

No buffer   This isn't a number you want to see incrementing. This means you don't have any buffer room left for incoming packets. Any packets received once the buffers are full are discarded. You can see how many packets are dropped with the ignored output.

Ignored   If the packet buffers are full, packets will be dropped. You see this increment along with the no buffer output. Typically if the no buffer and ignored outputs are incrementing, you have some sort of broadcast storm on your LAN. This can be caused by a bad NIC or even a bad network design.

Runts   Frames that did not meet the minimum frame size requirement of 64 bytes. Typically caused by collisions.

Giants   Frames received that are larger than 1518 bytes.

Input Errors   This is the total of many counters: runts, giants, no buffer, CRC, frame, over-run, and ignored counts.

CRC   At the end of each frame is a Frame Check Sequence (FCS) field that holds the answer to a cyclic redundancy check (CRC). If the receiving host's answer to the CRC does not match the sending host's answer, then a CRC error will occur.

Frame   This output increments when frames received are of an illegal format, or not complete, which is typically incremented when a collision occurs.

Packets Output   Total number of packets (frames) forwarded out to the interface.

Output Errors   Total number of packets (frames) that the switch port tried to transmit but for which some problem occurred.

Collisions   When transmitting a frame in half-duplex, the NIC listens on the receiving pair of the cable for another signal. If a signal is transmitted from another host, a collision has occurred. This output should not increment if you are running full-duplex.

Late Collisions   If all Ethernet specifications are followed during the cable install, all collisions should occur by the 64th byte of the frame. If a collision occurs after 64 bytes, the late collisions counter increments. This counter will increment on a duplex mismatched interface or if cable length exceeds specifications.

Chapter 2

Managing a Cisco Internetwork

Here in Chapter 2, I'll show you the commands for managing Cisco routers on an internetwork. The Internetwork Operating System (IOS) and configuration files reside in different locations in a Cisco device, so it's really important to understand both where these files are located and how they work.

You'll be learning about the main components of a router, the router boot sequence, and the configuration register, including how to use the configuration register for password recovery. After that, you'll find out how to manage routers by using the copy command with a Trivial File Transfer Protocol (TFTP) host when using the Cisco IOS File System (IFS).

I'll wrap up the chapter by exploring the Cisco Discovery Protocol, showing how to resolve hostnames, and presenting some important Cisco IOS troubleshooting techniques.

 For up-to-the minute updates for this chapter, please see www.lammle.com.

Understanding the Internal Components of a Cisco Router

To configure and troubleshoot a Cisco internetwork, you need to know the major components of Cisco routers and understand what each one does. Table 2.1 describes the major Cisco router components.

TABLE 2.1 Cisco Router Components

Component	Description
Bootstrap	Stored in the microcode of the ROM, the bootstrap brings a router up during initialization. It will boot the router and then load the IOS.
Power-on self-test (POST)	Stored in the microcode of the ROM, the POST is used to check the basic functionality of the router hardware and determines which interfaces are present.

Component	Description
ROM monitor	Stored in the microcode of the ROM, the ROM monitor is used for manufacturing, testing, and troubleshooting.
Mini-IOS	Called the *RXBOOT* or *bootloader* by Cisco, the mini-IOS is a small IOS in ROM that can be used to open an interface and load a Cisco IOS into flash memory. The mini-IOS can also perform a few other maintenance operations.
Random-access memory (RAM)	Used to hold packet buffers, ARP cache, routing tables, and the software and data structures that allow the router to function. The running-config file is stored in RAM, and most routers expand the IOS from flash into RAM upon boot.
Read-only memory (ROM)	Used to start and maintain the router. Holds the POST and the bootstrap program, as well as the mini-IOS.
Flash memory	Used to store the Cisco IOS by default. Flash memory is not erased when the router is reloaded. It is electronically erasable programmable read-only memory (EEPROM) created by Intel.
Nonvolatile RAM (NVRAM)	Used to hold the router and switch configuration. NVRAM is not erased when the router or switch is reloaded. Does not store an IOS. The configuration-register file is stored in NVRAM.
Configuration register	Used to control how the router boots up. This value can be found as the last line of the **show version** command output, and by default it is set to 0x2102, which tells the router to load the IOS from flash memory as well as to load the configuration from NVRAM.

Managing the Configuration Register

All Cisco routers have a 16-bit software register that's written into NVRAM. By default, the *configuration register* is set to load the Cisco IOS from *flash memory* and to look for and load the startup-config file from NVRAM.

Checking the Current Configuration Register Value

You can see the current value of the configuration register by using the show version command (sh version or show ver for short), as demonstrated in Table 2.2.

TABLE 2.2   The *show version* Command

Command	Meaning
show version	Directs the router where to load the IOS and configuration files from

The only way to view the configuration register is through the show version command:

```
Router#sh version
Cisco IOS Software, 2800 Software (C2800NM-ADVSECURITYK9-M),Version 15.1(4)M6,
RELEASE SOFTWARE (fc1)
[output cut]
Configuration register is 0x2102
```

The last information given from this command is the value of the configuration register. In this example, the value is 0x2102, which is the default setting. The configuration register setting of 0x2102 tells the router to look in NVRAM for the boot sequence.

Changing the Configuration Register

You can change the configuration register value to modify how the router boots and runs. These are the main reasons you would want to change the configuration register:

- To force the system into the ROM monitor mode
- To select a boot source and default boot filename
- To enable or disable the Break function
- To control broadcast addresses
- To set the console terminal baud rate
- To load operating software from ROM
- To enable booting from a TFTP server

Table 2.3 shows the two commands we'll use to edit the configuration register:

TABLE 2.3   Configuration Register

Command	Meaning
config-register	Directs the router where to load the IOS and configuration files from
show flash	Displays a list of directories and files in flash memory

Here is an example of how to change the configuration register and then I'll show you how to verify:

```
Router(config)#config-register 0x2101
Router(config)#^Z
Router#sh ver
[output cut]
Configuration register is 0x2102 (will be 0x2101 at next
  reload)
```

Here is the router after setting the configuration register to 0x2101 and reloading:

```
Router(boot)#sh ver
Cisco IOS Software, 2800 Software (C2800NM-ADVSECURITYK9-M), Version 15.1(4)M6,
RELEASE SOFTWARE (fc1)
[output cut]

ROM: System Bootstrap, Version 15.1(4)M6, RELEASE SOFTWARE (fc1)

Router uptime is 3 minutes
System returned to ROM by power-on
System image file is "flash:c2800nm-advsecurityk9-mz.151-4.M6.bin"
[output cut]

Configuration register is 0x2101
```

At this point, if you typed **show flash**, you'd still see the IOS in flash memory ready to go. But in the previous code you told the router to load from ROM, which is why the hostname shows up with (boot) here:

```
Router#sh flash
-#- --length-- -----date/time------ path
1     45392400 Apr 14 2013 05:31:44 +00:00 c2800nm-advsecurityk9-mz.151-4.M6.bin
18620416 bytes available (45395968 bytes used)
```

If you want to set the configuration register back to the default, just type this:

```
Router(boot)#config t
Router(boot)(config)#config-register 0x2102
Router(boot)(config)#^Z
Router(boot)#reload
```

Recovering Passwords

If you're locked out of a router because you forgot the password, you can change the configuration register to help you get back on your feet.

To recover a password, you need to turn on bit 6. Doing this will tell the router to ignore the NVRAM contents. The configuration register value to turn on bit 6 is 0x2142.

Here are the main steps to password recovery:

1. Boot the router and interrupt the boot sequence by performing a break, which will take the router into ROM monitor mode.

2. Change the configuration register to turn on bit 6 (with the value 0x2142).

3. Reload the router.

4. Enter privileged mode.

5. Copy the startup-config file to running-config.

6. Change the password.

7. Reset the configuration register to the default value.

8. Save the router configuration.

9. Reload the router (optional).

Table 2.4 shows our password recovery commands:

TABLE 2.4   Configuration Register Commands

Command	Meaning
Ctrl+Break	Key combination used to interrupt router boot sequence
confreg	Rommon command for modifying the configuration register
config-register	Directs the router where to load the IOS and configuration files from
copy start run	Copies the startup-config file to RAM and names it running-config
config t	Takes you to global config
enable secret *password*	Sets the enable password
reload	Reboots the router

Interrupting the Router Boot Sequence

Your first step is to boot the router and perform a break. This is usually done by pressing the Ctrl+Break key combination when using HyperTerminal while the router first reboots.

After you've performed a break, you should see something like this for a 2600 series router (it is pretty much the same output for the ISR series):

```
System Bootstrap, Version 15.0(13r)T, RELEASE SOFTWARE (fc1)
Copyright (c) 1999 by cisco Systems, Inc.
TAC:Home:SW:IOS:Specials for info
PC = 0xfff0a530, Vector = 0x500, SP = 0x680127b0
C2600 platform with 32768 Kbytes of main memory
PC = 0xfff0a530, Vector = 0x500, SP = 0x80004374
monitor: command "boot" aborted due to user interrupt
rommon 1 >
```

Notice the line monitor: command "boot" aborted due to user interrupt. At this point, you will be at the rommon 1> prompt, which is called *ROM monitor mode*.

Reloading the Router and Entering Privileged Mode

At this point, you need to reset the router like this:

- From the ISR/2600 series router, type **I** (for initialize) or **reset**.
- From the 2500 series router, type **I**.

The router will reload and ask whether you want to use setup mode (because no startup-config is used). Type **no** to enter setup mode, press Enter to go into user mode, and then type **enable** to go into privileged mode.

Viewing and Changing the Configuration

Now you're past the point where you would need to enter the user-mode and privileged-mode passwords in a router. Copy the startup-config file to the running-config file:

```
copy startup-config running-config
```

or use the following shortcut:

```
copy start run
```

The configuration is now running in *random access memory (RAM)*, and you're in privileged mode, meaning you can now view and change the configuration. But you can't view the enable secret setting for the password since it is encrypted. To change the password, do this:

```
config t
enable secret todd
```

Cisco ISR/2600 Series Commands

To change the bit value on a Cisco ISR/2600 series router, you just enter the command at the rommon 1> prompt:

```
rommon 1 >confreg 0x2142
You must reset or power cycle for new config to take effect
rommon 2 >reset
```

Resetting the Configuration Register and Reloading the Router

After you're finished changing passwords, set the configuration register back to the default value with the config-register command:

config t
config-register 0x2102

Finally, save the new configuration by typing **copy running-config startup-config**, and reload the router. I will discuss in more detail the use of the copy command in a minute.

Using Boot System Commands

There are some boot commands you can play with that will help you manage the way your router boots the Cisco IOS, but let's remember, we're talking about the router's IOS here, *not* the router's configuration! To change the IOS the router loads, use the boot command in Table 2.5:

TABLE 2.5   The boot Command

Command	Meaning
boot	Allows the modification of where or what the system will boot. The configuration and IOS files can both be changed.

The boot command has a lot of options. Let's take a look at the most important ones:

```
Router>en
Router#config t
Enter configuration commands, one per line.  End with CNTL/Z.
```

```
Router(config)#boot ?
  bootstrap  Bootstrap image file
  config     Configuration file
  host       Router-specific config file
  network    Network-wide config file
  system     System image file
```

The boot system command will allow you to tell the router which file to boot from flash memory:

```
Router(config)#boot system ?
  WORD   TFTP filename or URL
  flash  Boot from flash memory
  ftp    Boot from a server via ftp
  mop    Boot from a Decnet MOP server
  rcp    Boot from a server via rcp
  rom    Boot from rom
  tftp   Boot from a tftp server
Router(config)#boot system flash c2800nm-advsecurityk9-mz.124-12.bin
```

Backing Up and Restoring the Cisco IOS

Before you upgrade or restore a Cisco IOS, you really should copy the existing file to a *TFTP host* as a backup just in case the new image crashes and burns.

But before you back up or restore an IOS image, you need to check these things:

- Make sure you can access the network server.
- Ensure that the network server has adequate space for the code image.
- Verify the file naming and path requirement.
- The copy flash tftp command must be supplied with the IP address of the workstation if you are copying from the router flash.
- And if you're copying "into" flash, you need to verify there's enough room in flash memory to accommodate the file to be copied.

Verifying Flash Memory

The ISR router discussed in Table 2.6 has 64MB of RAM, and roughly half of the memory is in use.

TABLE 2.6   Verifying Flash Commands

Command	Meaning
show flash	Used to find the amount of available memory
show version	Useful in determining the amount of memory

The show flash and show version are probably two of your most important commands. Let's go through the outputs of each:

```
Router#sh flash
-#- --length-- -----date/time------ path
1     45392400 Apr 14 2013 05:31:44 +00:00 c2800nm-advsecurityk9-mz.151-4.M6.bin
18620416 bytes available (45395968 bytes used)
```

The amount of flash is actually easier to tally using the show version command on the ISR routers:

```
Router#show version
[output cut]
Cisco 2811 (revision 49.46) with 249856K/12288K bytes of memory.
Processor board ID FTX1049A1AB
2 FastEthernet interfaces
4 Serial(sync/async) interfaces
1 Virtual Private Network (VPN) Module
DRAM configuration is 64 bits wide with parity enabled.
239K bytes of non-volatile configuration memory.
62720K bytes of ATA CompactFlash (Read/Write)
```

Backing Up the Cisco IOS

The copy command has become more powerful over the past few years. Let's use it to discuss backing up the IOS of a router. There are various places to back up an IOS, and a TFTP server is a common place.

The copy command shown in Table 2.7 allows us to manage our file systems.

TABLE 2.7 The copy Command

Command	Meaning
copy	Used to backup or restore a file to or from a device

There are many new options that are part of the copy command in the new ISR routers. The most important of these is the copy `flash tftp` and copy `tftp flash` commands. Let's take a look:

```
Router#copy ?
  /erase          Erase destination file system.
  /noverify       Don't verify image signature before reload.
  /verify         Verify image signature before reload.
  archive:        Copy from archive: file system
  cns:            Copy from cns: file system
  flash:          Copy from flash: file system
  ftp:            Copy from ftp: file system
  http:           Copy from http: file system
  https:          Copy from https: file system
  ips-sdf         Copy from current IPS signature configuration
  null:           Copy from null: file system
  nvram:          Copy from nvram: file system
  pram:           Copy from pram: file system
  rcp:            Copy from rcp: file system
  running-config  Copy from current system configuration
  scp:            Copy from scp: file system
  startup-config  Copy from startup configuration
  system:         Copy from system: file system
  tftp:           Copy from tftp: file system
  xmodem:         Copy from xmodem: file system
  ymodem:         Copy from ymodem: file system

Router#copy flash tftp
Source filename []?c2800nm-advsecurityk9-mz.151-4.M6.bin
Address or name of remote host []?1.1.1.2
Destination filename [c2800nm-advsecurityk9-mz.124-12.bin]?[enter]
!!!!!!!!!!!!!!!!!!!!!!!!!!!!!!!!!!!!!!!!!!!!!!!!!!!!!!!!!!!!!!!!!!!!!!!!!!!!!!!!!!!
!!!!!!!
21710744 bytes copied in 60.724 secs (357532 bytes/sec)
Router#
```

Restoring or Upgrading the Cisco Router IOS

What happens if you need to restore the Cisco IOS to flash memory to replace an original file that has been damaged or if you want to upgrade the IOS? You can download the file from a TFTP server to flash memory by using the copy tftp flash command:

```
Router#copy tftp flash
Address or name of remote host []?1.1.1.2
Source filename []?c2800nm-advsecurityk9-mz.151-4.M6.bin
Destination filename [c2800nm-advsecurityk9-mz.151-4.M6.bin]?[enter]
%Warning:There is a file already existing with this name
Do you want to over write? [confirm][enter]
Accessing tftp://1.1.1.2/c2800nm-advsecurityk9-mz.124-12.bin...
Loading c2800nm-advsecurityk9-mz.151-4.M6.bin from 1.1.1.2 (via
FastEthernet0/0): !!!!!!!!!!!!!!!!!!!!!!!!!!!!!!!!!!!!!!!!!!!!!!!!!!!!!!!!!!!!!!!!
!!!!!!!!!!!!!!!!!!!!!!!!!
[OK - 21710744 bytes]

21710744 bytes copied in 82.880 secs (261954 bytes/sec)
Router#
```

Using the Cisco IOS File System (Cisco IFS)

Cisco has created a file system called Cisco IFS that allows you to work with files and directories just like you would from a Windows DOS prompt.

You use Cisco IFS commands pretty much the same way you use the copy command described earlier:

- For backing up the IOS
- For upgrading the IOS
- For viewing text files

Table 2.8 is a list of the most used Cisco IFS commands:

TABLE 2.8   The Cisco IFS Commands

Command	Meaning
PWD	Shows the working directory
show file	Gives you information about a specified file or file system
dir	Lets you view files in a directory (the default directory is flash:/)

Command	Meaning
copy	Upgrades, restores, or backs up an IOS
more	Displays the contents of a file
delete	Deletes a file from a system or directory
erase/format	Erases or formats a file system
CD	Changes directories
MKDIR/RMDIR	Creates and deletes directories

These Cisco IFS commands can get confusing. Let's work through a few of them:

```
Router#pwd
flash:
Router#dir
Directory of flash:/
    1  -rw-    13937472   Dec 20 2006 19:58:18 +00:00   c1841-ipbase-mz.124-1c.bin
    2  -rw-        1821   Dec 20 2006 20:11:24 +00:00   sdmconfig-18xx.cfg
    3  -rw-     4734464   Dec 20 2006 20:12:00 +00:00   sdm.tar
    4  -rw-      833024   Dec 20 2006 20:12:24 +00:00   es.tar
    5  -rw-     1052160   Dec 20 2006 20:12:50 +00:00   common.tar
    6  -rw-        1038   Dec 20 2006 20:13:10 +00:00   home.shtml
    7  -rw-      102400   Dec 20 2006 20:13:30 +00:00   home.tar
    8  -rw-      491213   Dec 20 2006 20:13:56 +00:00   128MB.sdf
    9  -rw-     1684577   Dec 20 2006 20:14:34 +00:00   securedesktop-ios-
3.1.1.27-k9.pkg
   10  -rw-      398305   Dec 20 2006 20:15:04 +00:00   sslclient-win-1.1.0.154.pkg

32071680 bytes total (8818688 bytes free)
Router#show file info flash:c1841-ipbase-mz.124-1c.bin
flash:c1841-ipbase-mz.124-1c.bin:
  type is image (elf) []
  file size is 13937472 bytes, run size is 14103140 bytes
  Runnable image, entry point 0x8000F000, run from ram
Router#delete flash:c1841-ipbase-mz.124-1c.bin
Delete filename [c1841-ipbase-mz.124-1c.bin]?[enter]
Delete flash:c1841-ipbase-mz.124-1c.bin? [confirm][enter]
Router#sh flash
```

```
-#- --length-- -----date/time------ path
1          1821 Dec 20 2006 20:11:24 +00:00 sdmconfig-18xx.cfg
2       4734464 Dec 20 2006 20:12:00 +00:00 sdm.tar
3        833024 Dec 20 2006 20:12:24 +00:00 es.tar
4       1052160 Dec 20 2006 20:12:50 +00:00 common.tar
5          1038 Dec 20 2006 20:13:10 +00:00 home.shtml
6        102400 Dec 20 2006 20:13:30 +00:00 home.tar
7        491213 Dec 20 2006 20:13:56 +00:00 128MB.sdf
8       1684577 Dec 20 2006 20:14:34 +00:00 securedesktop-ios-3.1.1.27-k9.pkg
9        398305 Dec 20 2006 20:15:04 +00:00 sslclient-win-1.1.0.154.pkg
22757376 bytes available (9314304 bytes used)
R1#sh file info flash:c1841-ipbase-mz.124-1c.bin
%Error opening flash:c1841-ipbase-mz.124-1c.bin (File not found)
Router#
Router#copy tftp://1.1.1.2//c1841-advipservicesk9-mz.124-12.bin/ flash:/ c1841-
advipservicesk9-mz.124-12.bin
Source filename [/c1841-advipservicesk9-mz.124-12.bin/]?[enter]
Destination filename [c1841-advipservicesk9-mz.124-12.bin]?[enter]
Loading /c1841-advipservicesk9-mz.124-12.bin/ from 1.1.1.2 (via
FastEthernet0/0): !!!!!!!!!!!!!!!!!!!!!!!!!!!!!!!!!!!!!!!!
[output cut]
!!!!!!!!!!!!!!!!!!!!!!!!!!!!!!!!!!!!!!!!!!!!!!!!!!!!!
[OK - 22103052 bytes]
22103052 bytes copied in 72.008 secs (306953 bytes/sec)
Router#sh flash
-#- --length-- -----date/time------ path
1          1821 Dec 20 2006 20:11:24 +00:00 sdmconfig-18xx.cfg
2       4734464 Dec 20 2006 20:12:00 +00:00 sdm.tar
3        833024 Dec 20 2006 20:12:24 +00:00 es.tar
4       1052160 Dec 20 2006 20:12:50 +00:00 common.tar
5          1038 Dec 20 2006 20:13:10 +00:00 home.shtml
6        102400 Dec 20 2006 20:13:30 +00:00 home.tar
7        491213 Dec 20 2006 20:13:56 +00:00 128MB.sdf
8       1684577 Dec 20 2006 20:14:34 +00:00 securedesktop-ios-3.1.1.27-k9.pkg
9        398305 Dec 20 2006 20:15:04 +00:00 sslclient-win-1.1.0.154.pkg
10     22103052 Mar 10 2007 19:40:50 +00:00 c1841-advipservicesk9-mz.124-12.bin
651264 bytes available (31420416 bytes used)
Router#
Router#sh file information flash:c1841-advipservicesk9-mz.124-12.bin
```

```
flash:c1841-advipservicesk9-mz.124-12.bin:
  type is image (elf) []
  file size is 22103052 bytes, run size is 22268736 bytes
  Runnable image, entry point 0x8000F000, run from ram
```

Backing Up and Restoring the Cisco Configuration

Any changes you make to the router configuration are stored in the running-config file. And if you don't enter a copy run start command after you make a change to running-config, that change will go "poof!" if the router reboots or gets powered down. So, you probably want to make another backup of the configuration information just in case the router or switch completely dies on you. Even if your machine is healthy and happy, the backup is good to have for reference and documentation reasons.

In the following sections, I'll describe how to copy the configuration of a router to a TFTP server and how to restore that configuration.

Backing Up the Cisco Router Configuration

The file commands you'll need are listed in Table 2.9:

TABLE 2.9 Verifying and Backing Up Your Configuraiton

Command	Meaning
show running-config	Displays the running configuration file from RAM
show startup-config	Displays the start-up configuration file from NVRAM
copy	Copies configuration and image files
erase	Deletes configuration and image files

Verifying the Current Configuration

To verify the configuration in DRAM, use the show running-config command (sh run for short), like this:

```
Router#show running-config
Building configuration...
```

```
Current configuration : 776 bytes
!
version 15.1
```

Verifying the Stored Configuration

Next, you should check the configuration stored in NVRAM. To see this, use the show startup-config command (sh start for short), like this:

```
Router#show startup-config
Using 776 out of 245752 bytes
!
version 15.1
```

Copying the Current Configuration to NVRAM

You'll then need to copy the current configuration to NVRAM:

```
Router#copy running-config startup-config
Destination filename [startup-config]?[enter]
Building configuration...
[OK]
Router#


Router#copy running-config ?
  archive:       Copy to archive: file system
  flash:         Copy to flash: file system
  ftp:           Copy to ftp: file system
  http:          Copy to http: file system
  https:         Copy to https: file system
  ips-sdf        Update (merge with) IPS signature configuration
  null:          Copy to null: file system
  nvram:         Copy to nvram: file system
  rcp:           Copy to rcp: file system
  running-config Update (merge with) current system configuration
  scp:           Copy to scp: file system
  startup-config Copy to startup configuration
  syslog:        Copy to syslog: file system
  system:        Copy to system: file system
  tftp:          Copy to tftp: file system
  xmodem:        Copy to xmodem: file system
  ymodem:        Copy to ymodem: file system
```

Copying the Configuration to a TFTP Server

Once the file is copied to NVRAM, you can make a second backup to a TFTP server by using the copy running-config tftp command (copy run tftp for short), like this:

```
Router#copy running-config tftp
Address or name of remote host []?1.1.1.2
Destination filename [router-confg]?todd-confg
!!
776 bytes copied in 0.800 secs (970 bytes/sec)
Router#
```

Restoring the Cisco Router Configuration

If you did copy the router's configuration to a TFTP server as a second backup, you can restore the configuration using the copy tftp running-config command (copy tftp run for short) or the copy tftp startup-config command (copy tftp start for short), as shown here (the old command that provides this function is config net):

```
Router#copy tftp running-config
Address or name of remote host []?1.1.1.2
Source filename []?todd-confg
Destination filename[running-config]?[enter]
Accessing tftp://1.1.1.2/todd-confg...
Loading todd-confg from 1.1.1.2 (via FastEthernet0/0): !
[OK - 776 bytes]
776 bytes copied in 9.212 secs (84 bytes/sec)
Router#
*Mar  7 17:53:34.071: %SYS-5-CONFIG_I: Configured from tftp://1.1.1.2/todd-confg
by console
Router#
```

Erasing the Configuration

To delete the startup-config file on a Cisco router, use the command erase startup-config, like this:

```
Router#erase startup-config
Erasing the nvram filesystem will remove all configuration files! Continue?
[confirm][enter]
[OK]
Erase of nvram: complete
```

```
*Mar  7 17:56:20.407: %SYS-7-NV_BLOCK_INIT: Initialized the geometry of nvram
Router#reload
System configuration has been modified. Save? [yes/no]:n
Proceed with reload? [confirm][enter]
 *Mar  7 17:56:31.059: %SYS-5-RELOAD: Reload requested by console. Reload
Reason: Reload Command.
```

This command deletes the contents of NVRAM on the router. By typing **reload** at privileged mode and typing **no** to saving the changes, the router will reload and come up into setup mode.

Using the Cisco IOS File System to Manage Your Router's Configuration (Cisco IFS)

Using the old, faithful copy command is still useful, and I recommend it. However, you still need to know about the Cisco IFS. I'll first show how to use the show file command to see the contents of NVRAM and RAM:

```
Router#show file information nvram:startup-config
nvram:startup-config:
  type is config
Router#cd nvram:
Router#pwd
nvram:/
Router#dir
Directory of nvram:/

  190  -rw-          830                 <no date>  startup-config
  191  ----            5                 <no date>  private-config
  192  -rw-          830                 <no date>  underlying-config
    1  -rw-            0                 <no date>  ifIndex-table
196600 bytes total (194689 bytes free)
Router#cd system:
Router#pwd
system:/
Router#dir ?
  /all            List all files
  /recursive      List files recursively
  all-filesystems List files on all filesystems
  archive:        Directory or file name
  cns:            Directory or file name
```

```
    flash:          Directory or file name
    null:           Directory or file name
    nvram:          Directory or file name
    system:         Directory or file name
    xmodem:         Directory or file name
    ymodem:         Directory or file name
    <cr>
Router#dir
Directory of system:/

    3   dr-x          0              <no date>  lib
   33   dr-x          0              <no date>  memory
    1   -rw-        750              <no date>  running-config
    2   dr-x          0              <no date>  vfiles
Router#config net
Host or network configuration file [host]?[enter]
This command has been replaced by the command:
        'copy <url> system:/running-config'
Address or name of remote host [255.255.255.255]?
Router#copy tftp://1.1.1.2/todd-confg system://running-config
Destination filename [running-config]?[enter]
Accessing tftp://1.1.1.2/todd-confg...Loading todd-confg from 1.1.1.2 (via
FastEthernet0/0): !
[OK - 776 bytes]
[OK]
776 bytes copied in 13.816 secs (56 bytes/sec)
Router#
*Mar 10 22:12:59.819: %SYS-5-CONFIG_I: Configured from tftp://1.1.1.2/todd-confg
by console
```

Using Cisco Discovery Protocol (CDP)

Cisco Discovery Protocol (CDP) is a proprietary protocol designed by Cisco to help administrators collect information about both locally attached and remote devices. By using CDP, you can gather hardware and protocol information about neighbor devices, which is useful information for troubleshooting and documenting the network!

In the following sections, I'll discuss the CDP timer and CDP commands used to verify your network.

Getting CDP Timers and Holdtime Information

I'll start with the basic commands that describe how CDP works, and then I'll show how to use CDP to gather more advanced information. Table 2.10 shows a list of the CDP commands. You must know these!

TABLE 2.10   Cisco Discovery Protocol

Command	Meaning
show cdp	Displays cdp timer and holdtime values
cdp holdtime	Configures the cdp holdtimer
cdp timer	Configures the cdp timer
cdp enable	Globally enables cdp; to disable, use the no form of the command
show cdp neighbor	Displays information about directly connected neighbors
show cdp neighbor detail	Displays detailed information about neighbors including IOS and layer-3 information
show cdp entry * protocol	Displays just the layer-3 information, such as the IP address
show cdp entry * version	Displays the version information of directly connected neighbors
show cdp traffic	Displays interface cdp traffic statistics
show cdp interface	Displays interface status information

The cdp timer and holdtime is typically never changed, but you can and here is how you would do that:

- The *CDP timer* is how often CDP packets are transmitted to all active interfaces.
- The *CDP holdtime* is the amount of time that the device will hold packets received from neighbor devices.

```
Router#sh cdp
Global CDP information:
        Sending CDP packets every 60 seconds
        Sending a holdtime value of 180 seconds
        Sending CDPv2 advertisements is enabled
```

```
Router(config)#cdp ?
  advertise-v2      CDP sends version-2 advertisements
  holdtime          Specify the holdtime (in sec) to be sent in packets
  log               Log messages generated by CDP
  run               Enable CDP
  source-interface  Insert the interface's IP in all CDP packets
  timer             Specify rate (in sec) at which CDP packets are sent  run
Router (config)#cdp holdtime ?
  <10-255> Length  of time  (in sec) that receiver must keep this packet
Router (config)#cdp timer ?
  <5-254>  Rate at which CDP packets are sent (in sec)
```

Gathering Neighbor Information

I can't stress to you enough how important CDP is. Let's go through the CDP commands and please study the output.

The following output shows the show cdp neighbor command used on my ISR router:

```
Router#sh cdp neighbors
Capability Codes: R - Router, T - Trans Bridge, B - Source Route Bridge
                  S - Switch, H - Host, I - IGMP, r - Repeater
Device ID    Local Intrfce   Holdtme   Capability   Platform  Port ID
ap           Fas 0/1         165          T I       AIR-AP124 Fas 0
R2           Ser 0/1/0       140         R S I      2801      Ser 0/2/0
R3           Ser 0/0/1       157         R S I      1841      Ser 0/0/1
R1           Ser 0/2/0       154         R S I      1841      Ser 0/0/1
R1           Ser 0/0/0       154         R S I      1841      Ser 0/0/0
Router#
```

Another command that will deliver the goods on neighbor information is the show cdp neighbor detail command (show cdp nei de for short). This command can be run on both routers and switches, and it displays detailed information about each device connected to the device on which you're running the command. Check out this router output for an example:

```
Router#sh cdp neighbors detail
-------------------------
Device ID: R2
Entry address(es):
  IP address: 10.4.4.2
Platform: Cisco 2801,  Capabilities: Router Switch IGMP
Interface: Serial0/1/0,  Port ID (outgoing port): Serial0/2/0
Holdtime : 135 sec
```

```
Version :
Cisco IOS Software, 2801 Software (C2801-ADVENTERPRISEK9-M), Experimental
Version 15.0(20050525:193634) [jezhao-ani 145]
Copyright (c) 1986-2005 by Cisco Systems, Inc.
Compiled Fri 27-May-05 23:53 by jezhao

advertisement version: 2
VTP Management Domain: ''

Corp#
Corp#show cdp entry * protocol
Protocol information for ap :
  IP address: 10.1.1.2
Protocol information for R2 :
  IP address: 10.4.4.2
Protocol information for R3 :
  IP address: 10.5.5.1
Protocol information for R1 :
  IP address: 10.3.3.2
Protocol information for R1 :
  IP address: 10.2.2.2
Corp#show cdp entry * version
Version information for ap :
  Cisco IOS Software, C1240 Software (C1240-K9W7-M), Version 12.3(8)JEA, RELEASE
SOFTWARE (fc2)
Technical Support: http://www.cisco.com/techsupport
Copyright (c) 1986-2006 by Cisco Systems, Inc.
Compiled Wed 23-Aug-06 16:45 by kellythw

Version information for R2 :
  Cisco IOS Software, 2801 Software (C2801-ADVENTERPRISEK9-M), Experimental
Version 15.0(20050525:193634) [jezhao-ani 145]
Copyright (c) 1986-2005 by Cisco Systems, Inc.
Compiled Fri 27-May-05 23:53 by jezhao

Version information for R3 :
  Cisco IOS Software, 1841 Software (C1841-IPBASE-M), Version 15.0(1c), RELEASE
SOFTWARE (fc1)
Technical Support: http://www.cisco.com/techsupport
Copyright (c) 1986-2005 by Cisco Systems, Inc.
Compiled Tue 25-Oct-05 17:10 by evmiller
```

```
  --More--
[output cut]
```

Gathering Interface Traffic Information

The show cdp traffic command displays information about interface traffic, including the number of CDP packets sent and received and the errors with CDP.

The following output shows the show cdp traffic command used on the Corp router:

```
Router#sh cdp traffic
CDP counters :
        Total packets output: 911, Input: 524
        Hdr syntax: 0, Chksum error: 0, Encaps failed: 2
        No memory: 0, Invalid packet: 0, Fragmented: 0
        CDP version 1 advertisements output: 0, Input: 0
        CDP version 2 advertisements output: 911, Input: 524
Router#
```

Gathering Port and Interface Information

The show cdp interface command gives you the CDP status on router interfaces or switch ports:

```
Router#sh cdp interface
FastEthernet0/0 is administratively down, line protocol is down
  Encapsulation ARPA
  Sending CDP packets every 60 seconds
  Holdtime is 180 seconds
FastEthernet0/1 is up, line protocol is up
  Encapsulation ARPA
  Sending CDP packets every 60 seconds
  Holdtime is 180 seconds
Serial0/0/0 is up, line protocol is up
  Encapsulation HDLC
  Sending CDP packets every 60 seconds
  Holdtime is 180 seconds
Serial0/0/1 is up, line protocol is up
  Encapsulation HDLC
  Sending CDP packets every 60 seconds
  Holdtime is 180 seconds
```

```
Serial0/1/0 is up, line protocol is up
   Encapsulation HDLC
   Sending CDP packets every 60 seconds
   Holdtime is 180 seconds
Serial0/2/0 is up, line protocol is up
   Encapsulation HDLC
   Sending CDP packets every 60 seconds
   Holdtime is 180 seconds
```

Using Telnet

Telnet, part of the TCP/IP protocol suite, is a powerful program that allows your computer to act like a dumb terminal and run programs on another computer. Table 2.11 shows the commands you need to know:

TABLE 2.11   Telnet Commands

Command	Meaning
telnet	Makes your terminal a dumb terminal. You can only run programs on another computer, not copy files.
show sessions	Shows the routers into which you are telnetted.
show users	Shows the routers that are telnetted into your router.
exit	Closes a Telnet session.
disconnect	Closes a remote Telnet session.
clear line line-number	Clears a session connected to your router.

Telnet is a virtual terminal protocol that allows you to connect to remote devices, gather information, and run programs.

You can issue the telnet command from any router prompt, like this:

```
Router#telnet 10.2.2.2
Trying 10.2.2.2 ... Open
```

```
Password required, but none set

[Connection to 10.2.2.2 closed by foreign host]
Router#
```

As you can see, I didn't set my passwords—how embarrassing! Remember that the VTY ports on a router are configured as login, meaning you have to either set the VTY passwords or use the no login command.

On a Cisco router, you don't need to use the telnet command; you can just type in an IP address from a command prompt, and the router will assume you want to telnet to the device. Here's how that looks by using just the IP address:

```
Router#10.2.2.2
Trying 10.2.2.2 ... Open

Password required, but none set

[Connection to 10.2.2.2 closed by foreign host]
Router#
```

Telnetting into Multiple Devices Simultaneously

If you telnet to a router or switch, you can end the connection by using exit at any time. But what if you want to keep your connection to a remote device but still come back to your original router console? To do that, you can press the Ctrl+Shift+6 key combination, release it, and then press X.

Here's an example of connecting to multiple devices from my console:

```
Router#10.2.2.2
Trying 10.2.2.2 ... Open

User Access Verification

Password:
R1>
Router#
```

In this example, I telnetted to the R1 router and then typed the password to enter user mode. I next pressed Ctrl+Shift+6 and then X (but you can't see that because it doesn't show on the screen output). Notice that my command prompt is now back at the Router# prompt.

Checking Telnet Connections

To see the connections made from your router to a remote device, use the show sessions command, like so:

```
Corp#sh sessions
Conn Host                 Address            Byte  Idle Conn Name
   1 10.2.2.2             10.2.2.2             0     0 10.2.2.2
*  2 10.1.1.2             10.1.1.2             0     0 10.1.1.2
Corp#
```

See that asterisk (*) next to connection 2? It means that session 2 was your last session. You can return to your last session by pressing Enter twice. You can also return to any session by typing the number of the connection and pressing Enter.

Checking Telnet Users

You can list all active consoles and VTY ports in use on your router with the show users command:

```
Corp#sh users
   Line        User       Host(s)           Idle         Location
*  0 con 0                10.1.1.2          00:00:01
                          10.2.2.2          00:01:06
```

In the command's output, con represents the local console. In this example, the console is connected to two remote IP addresses or, in other words, two devices. In the next example, I typed **sh users** on the ap device that the Corp router had telnetted into and that is connected via line 1:

```
Corp#sh sessions
Conn Host                 Address            Byte  Idle Conn Name
   1 10.1.1.2             10.1.1.2             0     0 10.1.1.2
*  2 10.2.2.2             10.2.2.2             0     0 10.2.2.2
Corp#1
[Resuming connection 1 to 10.1.1.2 ... ]
ap>sh users
   Line        User       Host(s)           Idle         Location
*  1 vty 0                idle              00:00:00 10.1.1.1
ap>
```

This output shows that the console is active and that VTY port 1 is being used. The asterisk represents the current terminal session from which the show user command was entered.

Closing Telnet Sessions

You can end Telnet sessions a few different ways—using exit or disconnect is probably the easiest and quickest:

```
ap>exit
```

```
[Connection to 10.1.1.2 closed by foreign host]
Corp#
```

Since the ap device was my last session, I just pressed Enter twice to return to that session. To end a session from a local device, use the disconnect command:

```
Corp#sh session
Conn Host                Address              Byte  Idle Conn Name
   2 10.2.2.2            10.2.2.2                0     0 10.2.2.2
Corp#disconnect ?
  <0-0>  The number of an active network connection
  qdm    Disconnect QDM web-based clients
  ssh    Disconnect an active SSH connection
Corp#disconnect 2
Closing connection to 10.2.2.2 [confirm][enter]
Corp#
```

If you want to end a session of a device attached to your local device through Telnet, you should first check to see whether any devices are telnetted into your router. To get that information, use the show users command like this:

```
R1#sh users
    Line       User        Host(s)              Idle       Location
*  0 con 0                 idle              00:00:00
   vty 194                 idle              00:00:21 10.2.2.1
```

This output shows that VTY has IP address 10.2.2.1 connected. That's the Corp router. Also notice that the Corp router connected to line 194—remember, you cannot choose which line you connect to! This is why I set the same password on all lines.

To clear the connection, use the clear line # command:

```
R1#clear line 194
[confirm][enter]
 [OK]
R1#sh users
    Line       User        Host(s)              Idle       Location
*  0 con 0                 idle              00:00:00
```

This output confirms that the line has been cleared.

Resolving Hostnames

To use a hostname rather than an IP address to connect to a remote device, the device that you are using to make the connection must be able to translate the hostname to an IP address.

You can resolve hostnames to IP addresses in two ways: building a host table on each router or building a Domain Name System (DNS) server, which is similar to a dynamic host table. Table 2.12 is a list of important commands that can be used to help you resolve hostnames on a router:

TABLE 2.12   Hosts Table Commands

Command	Meaning
ip host	Creates a static host table on your router
show hosts	Displays the host table on your router
ip domain-lookup	Enables the DNS service
ip name-server	Configures your device with the IP address of a DNS server
ip domain-name	Configures domain suffix for fully qualified domain name

Building a Host Table

A *host table* provides name resolution only on the router that it was built upon. The command to build a host table on a router is as follows:

ip host *host_name tcp_port_number ip_address*

The default is TCP port number 23, but you can create a session using Telnet with a different TCP port number if you want. You can also assign up to eight IP addresses to a hostname.

Here's an example of configuring a host table on the Corp router with two entries to resolve the names for the R1 router and the ap device:

```
Corp#config t
Enter configuration commands, one per line.  End with CNTL/Z.
Corp(config)#ip host R1 ?
  <0-65535>   Default telnet port number
  A.B.C.D     Host IP address
```

```
 additional  Append addresses
 mx          Configure a MX record
 ns          Configure an NS record
 srv         Configure a SRV record
Corp(config)#ip host R1 10.2.2.2 ?
 A.B.C.D  Host IP address
 <cr>
Corp(config)#ip host R1 10.2.2.2
Corp(config)#ip host ap 10.1.1.2
```

Notice in the previous router configuration that I can just keep adding IP addresses to reference a host, one after another, up to eight IP address. And to see the newly built host table, just use the show hosts command:

```
Corp(config)#do show hosts
Default domain is not set
Name/address lookup uses domain service
Name servers are 255.255.255.255

Codes: UN - unknown, EX - expired, OK - OK, ?? - revalidate
       temp - temporary, perm - permanent
       NA - Not Applicable None - Not defined
Host                    Port Flags      Age Type   Address(es)
ap                      None (perm, OK)  0   IP     10.1.1.2
R1                      None (perm, OK)  0   IP     10.2.2.2
Corp(config)#^Z
Corp#
```

You can see the two hostnames plus their associated IP addresses in the preceding router output. The perm in the Flags column means the entry is manually configured. If it said temp, it would be an entry that was resolved by DNS. Here is an example of a router resolving a hostname and then telnetting to the resolved IP address:

```
Corp#r1
Trying R1 (10.2.2.2)... Open

User Access Verification

Password:
R1>Ctrl+Shift+6
Corp#ap
Trying ap (10.1.1.2)... Open
```

```
User Access Verification

Password:
ap>Ctrl+Shift+6
Corp#
Corp#sh sessions
Conn Host              Address           Byte  Idle Conn Name
   1 r1                10.2.2.2             0     1 r1
*  2 ap                10.1.1.2             0     0 ap
Corp#
```

If you want to remove a hostname from the table, just use the no ip host command, like this:

```
RouterA(config)#no ip host R1
```

The problem with the host table method is that you would need to create a host table on each router to be able to resolve names. And if you have a whole bunch of routers and want to resolve names, using DNS is a much better choice!

Using DNS to Resolve Names

If you have a lot of devices and don't want to create a host table in each device, you can use a DNS server to resolve hostnames.

Anytime a Cisco device receives a command it doesn't understand, it will try to resolve it through DNS by default. Watch what happens when I type the special command **todd** at a Cisco router prompt:

```
Corp#todd
Translating "todd"...domain server (255.255.255.255)
Translating "todd"...domain server (255.255.255.255)
Translating "todd"...domain server (255.255.255.255)
% Unknown command or computer name, or unable to find
  computer address
Corp#
```

You can get around this and prevent a time-consuming DNS lookup by using the no ip domain-lookup command on your router from global configuration mode.

If you have a DNS server on your network, you need to add a few commands to make DNS name resolution work:

```
Corp#config t
Corp(config)#ip domain-lookup
Corp(config)#ip name-server ?
  A.B.C.D  Domain server IP address (maximum of 6)
```

```
Corp(config)#ip name-server 192.168.0.70
Corp(config)#ip domain-name lammle.com
Corp(config)#^Z
Corp#
```

After the DNS configurations are set, you can test the DNS server by using a hostname to ping or telnet a device like this:

```
Corp#ping R1
Translating "R1"...domain server (192.168.0.70) [OK]
Type escape sequence to abort.
Sending 5, 100-byte ICMP Echos to 10.2.2.2, timeout is
  2 seconds:
!!!!!
Success rate is 100 percent (5/5), round-trip min/avg/max
  = 28/31/32 ms
```

Checking Network Connectivity and Troubleshooting

You can use the ping and traceroute commands to test connectivity to remote devices, and you can use both of them with many protocols, not just IP.

The debug command and the show processes command you need to troubleshoot a router are listed in Table 2.13:

TABLE 2.13   Troubleshooting Commands

Command	Meaning
ping	Tells you whether a host on an internetwork is alive and has an IP stack enabled, and is used for deeper diagnostics as well.
traceroute	Tells you the path a packet takes to find a remote host
debug	Enables packet-level debugging used for troubleshooting a router or network
undebug	The undebug command will disable debugging output on the router
show processes	Show the processes used on a router and CPU cycles

Using the *ping* Command

So far, you've seen many examples of pinging devices to test IP connectivity and name resolution using the DNS server. To see all the different protocols that you can use with the ping program, type **ping ?**, like so:

```
Corp#ping ?
  WORD  Ping destination address or hostname
  clns  CLNS echo
  ip    IP echo
  srb   srb echo
  tag   Tag encapsulated IP echo
  <cr>
```

The ping output displays the minimum, average, and maximum times it takes for a ping packet to find a specified system and return. Here's an example:

```
Corp#ping R1
Translating "R1"...domain server (192.168.0.70)[OK]
Type escape sequence to abort.
Sending 5, 100-byte ICMP Echos to 10.2.2.2, timeout
  is 2 seconds:
!!!!!
Success rate is 100 percent (5/5), round-trip min/avg/max
  = 1/2/4 ms
Corp#
```

Using the *traceroute* Command

The traceroute command (or trace for short) shows the path a packet takes to get to a remote device. It uses time to live (TTL) timeouts and ICMP error messages to outline the path a packet takes through an internetwork to arrive at a remote host. Let's take a look at the traceroute command being used on a router:

```
Corp#traceroute ?
  WORD       Trace route to destination address or hostname
  appletalk  AppleTalk Trace
  clns       ISO CLNS Trace
  ip         IP Trace
  ipv6       IPv6 Trace
  ipx        IPX Trace
  <cr>
```

The trace command shows the hops that a packet traverses on its way to a remote device. Here's an example:

```
Corp#traceroute r1

Type escape sequence to abort.
Tracing the route to R1 (10.2.2.2)

  1 R1 (10.2.2.2) 4 msec *  0 msec
Corp#
```

Debugging

The debug command is a troubleshooting command that's available from privileged exec mode (of Cisco IOS). It's used to display information about various router operations and the related traffic generated or received by the router, plus any error messages.

```
Corp>debug ?
% Unrecognized command
Corp>en
Corp#debug ?
  aaa                     AAA Authentication, Authorization and Accounting
  access-expression       Boolean access expression
  adjacency               adjacency
  all                     Enable all debugging
[output cut]
```

If you have the freedom to pretty much take out a router and you really want to have some fun with debugging, use the debug all command:

```
Corp#debug all

This may severely impact network performance. Continue? (yes/[no]):yes

All possible debugging has been turned on

2d20h: SNMP: HC Timer 824AE5CC fired
2d20h: SNMP: HC Timer 824AE5CC rearmed, delay = 20000
2d20h: Serial0/0: HDLC myseq 4, mineseen 0, yourseen 0, line down
2d20h:
2d20h: Rudpv1 Sent: Pkts 0,  Data Bytes 0,  Data Pkts 0
2d20h: Rudpv1 Rcvd: Pkts 0,  Data Bytes 0,  Data Pkts 0
```

```
2d20h: Rudpv1 Discarded: 0,  Retransmitted 0
2d20h:
2d20h: RIP-TIMER: periodic timer expired
2d20h: Serial0/0: HDLC myseq 5, mineseen 0, yourseen 0, line down
2d20h: Serial0/0: attempting to restart
2d20h: PowerQUICC(0/0): DCD is up.
2d20h: is_up: 0 state: 4 sub state: 1 line: 0
2d20h:
2d20h: Rudpv1 Sent: Pkts 0,  Data Bytes 0,  Data Pkts 0
2d20h: Rudpv1 Rcvd: Pkts 0,  Data Bytes 0,  Data Pkts 0
2d20h: Rudpv1 Discarded: 0,  Retransmitted 0
2d20h: un all
All possible debugging has been turned off
Corp#
```

To disable debugging on a router, just use the command no in front of the debug command:

```
Corp#no debug all
```

I typically just use the undebug all command since it is so easy when using the shortcut:

```
Corp#un all
```

Remember that instead of using the debug all command, it's almost always better to use specific commands—and only for short periods of time. Here's an example of deploying debug ip rip that will show you rip updates being sent and received on a router:

```
Corp#debug ip rip
RIP protocol debugging is on
Corp#
1w4d: RIP: sending v2 update to 224.0.0.9 via Serial0/0 (192.168.12.1)
1w4d: RIP: build update entries
1w4d:    10.10.10.0/24 via 0.0.0.0, metric 2, tag 0
1w4d:    171.16.125.0/24 via 0.0.0.0, metric 3, tag 0
1w4d:    172.16.12.0/24 via 0.0.0.0, metric 1, tag 0
1w4d:    172.16.125.0/24 via 0.0.0.0, metric 3, tag 0
1w4d: RIP: sending v2 update to 224.0.0.9 via Serial0/2 (172.16.12.1)
1w4d: RIP: build update entries
1w4d:    192.168.12.0/24 via 0.0.0.0, metric 1, tag 0
1w4d:    192.168.22.0/24 via 0.0.0.0, metric 2, tag 0
1w4d: RIP: received v2 update from 192.168.12.2 on Serial0/0
1w4d:    192.168.22.0/24 via 0.0.0.0 in 1 hops
Corp#un all
```

Using the *sh processes* Command

You really have to be careful when using the debug command on your devices. If your router's CPU utilization is consistently at 50 percent or more, it's probably not a good idea to type in the debug all command unless you want to see what a router looks like when it crashes!

```
Corp#sh processes
CPU utilization for five seconds: 2%/0%; one minute: 0%; five minutes: 0%
 PID QTy       PC Runtime (ms)    Invoked   uSecs    Stacks TTY Process
   1 Cwe 8034470C           0          1       0 5804/6000   0 Chunk Manager
   2 Csp 80369A88           4       1856       2 2616/3000   0 Load Meter
   3 M*          0         112         14 800010656/12000   0 Exec
   5 Lst 8034FD9C      268246      52101    5148 5768/6000   0 Check heaps
   6 Cwe 80355E5C          20          3    6666 5704/6000   0 Pool Manager
   7 Mst 802AC3C4           0          2       0 5580/6000   0 Timers
[output cut]
```

So basically, the output from the show processes command shows that the router is happily able to process debugging commands without being overloaded.

Chapter

3

IP Routing

In this chapter, I'll discuss the commands that configure the IP routing process. This is an important subject to understand since it pertains to all routers and configurations that use IP. *IP routing* is the process of moving packets from one network to another network using routers. And as before, by *routers* I mean Cisco routers, of course!

Once all routers know about all networks, a *routed protocol* can be used to send user data (packets) through the established enterprise. Routed protocols are assigned to an interface and determine the method of packet delivery. Examples of routed protocols are IP and IPv6.

For up-to-the minute updates for this chapter, please see www.lammle.com.

Routing Basics

Once you create an internetwork by connecting your WANs and LANs to a router, you'll need to configure logical network addresses, such as IP addresses, to all hosts on the internetwork so that they can communicate across that internetwork.

If your network has no routers, then it should be apparent that you are not routing. Routers route traffic to all the networks in your internetwork. To be able to route packets, a router must know, at a minimum, the following:

- The destination address
- The neighbor routers from which it can learn about remote networks
- Possible routes to all remote networks
- The best route to each remote network
- How to maintain and verify routing information

The router learns about remote networks from neighbor routers or from an administrator. The router then builds a *routing table* (a map of the internetwork) that describes how to find the remote networks. If a network is directly connected, then the router already knows how to get to it.

If a network isn't directly connected to the router, the router must learn how to get to the remote network in one of two ways: by using *static routing*, meaning someone must type all network locations into the routing table, or by using something called *dynamic routing*.

Figure 3.1 shows a simple two-router network. Lab_A has one serial interface and three LAN interfaces.

FIGURE 3.1   A simple routing example

By using the command show ip route in Table 3.1, you can see the routing table (map of the internetwork) that Lab_A uses to make forwarding decisions:

TABLE 3.1   The show ip route Command and Meaning

Command	Meaning
show ip route	Displays a routers table of known or learned destination networks

And here is the output of the routing table:

```
Lab_A#sh ip route
[output cut]
Gateway of last resort is not set
10.0.0.0/8 is variably subnetted, 8 subnets, 2 masks
C       10.10.10.0/24 is directly connected, FastEthernet0/0
L       10.10.10.1/32 is directly connected, FastEthernet0/0
C       10.10.20.0/24 is directly connected, FastEthernet0/1
L       10.10.20.1/32 is directly connected, FastEthernet0/1
C       10.10.30.0/24 is directly connected, FastEthernet0/2
```

```
L       10.10.30.1/32 is directly connected, FastEthernet0/2
C       10.10.40.0/24 is directly connected, Serial0/0
L       10.10.40.1/32 is directly connected, Serial0/0
```

Let's take a look at the information you get from the routing table. All the way to the left in each of the listings is a C. Now, if you look at a routing table on a real router, you will see a legend right above the table. The C tells you that each of these networks is directly connected to this router. I will be talking about many more of the codes in the legend as we go along. The next bit of information from the listings is the actual network that the router knows about. The table then tells you that each of the entries is directly connected and finally the interface you have to send packets out of to reach the given network. But wait—what about that L in the routing table—that's new, isn't it? Yes it is, because in the new Cisco IOS 15 code, Cisco defines a different route, called a local route. Each has a /32 prefix defining a route just for the one address. So in this example, the router has relied upon these routes that list their own local IP addresses to more efficiently forward packets to the router itself.

For another example, look at the output of a corporate router's routing table, and it will say you have now turned on RIP:

```
Corp#sh ip route
[output cut]
R     192.168.215.0 [120/2] via 192.168.20.2, 00:00:23, Serial0/0
R     192.168.115.0 [120/1] via 192.168.20.2, 00:00:23, Serial0/0
R     192.168.30.0 [120/1] via 192.168.20.2, 00:00:23, Serial0/0
C     192.168.20.0/24 is directly connected, Serial0/0
L     192.168.20.2/32 is directly connected, Serial0/0
C     192.168.214.0/24 is directly connected, FastEthernet0/0
L     192.168.214.1/32 is directly connected, FastEthernet0/0
```

You can now see there is a little bit more information the routing table is displaying to you. Again, from the far left there is an R. The R tells you that this entry or route was learned by the router through the RIP routing protocol. The entry displays the network for you again, but now you can see some new pieces. The two numbers in the brackets are important. The first number tells the administrative distance of the route. The second number gives you the metric of the route. Here is the output of the entire top portion of the routing table so you can see all the routing codes:

```
Corp#sh ip route
Codes: L - local, C - connected, S - static, R - RIP, M - mobile, B - BGP
       D - EIGRP, EX - EIGRP external, O - OSPF, IA - OSPF inter area
       N1 - OSPF NSSA external type 1, N2 - OSPF NSSA external type 2
       E1 - OSPF external type 1, E2 - OSPF external type 2
       i - IS-IS, su - IS-IS summary, L1 - IS-IS level-1, L2 - IS-IS level-2
```

```
ia - IS-IS inter area, * - candidate default, U - per-user static route
o - ODR, P - periodic downloaded static route, H - NHRP, l - LISP
+ - replicated route, % - next hop override
```

Static Routing

Now that you can get basic information from the router out of the routing table, you can start putting some information into the routing table. Static routing is a pretty simple way to put in information, and it is where we will start.

Static routing occurs when you manually add routes in each router's routing table. Static routing has pros and cons, but that's true for all routing processes.

Static routing has the following benefits:

- There is no overhead on the router CPU, which means you could buy a cheaper router than you would use if you were using dynamic routing.

- There is no bandwidth usage between routers, which means you could save money on WAN links.

- It adds security, because the administrator can choose to allow routing access to certain networks only.

Static routing has the following disadvantages:

- The administrator must really understand the internetwork and how each router is connected in order to configure routes correctly.

- If a network is added to the internetwork, the administrator has to add a route to it on all routers—by hand.

- It's not feasible in large networks because maintaining it would be a full-time job in itself.

That said, Table 3.2 lists the command syntax you use to add a static route to a routing table:

TABLE 3.2 The ip route Command

Command	Meaning
ip route	Configures static route information for a router to possibly use in its routing table

Here are the options:

ip route [*destination_network*] [*mask*] [*next-hop_address* or
  exitinterface] [*administrative_distance*] [permanent]

Table 3.3 describes the command and each option in the string.

TABLE 3.3   Static Routing Commands and Options

Option	Meaning
destination_network	The network you're placing in the routing table.
mask	The subnet mask being used on the network.
next-hop_address	The address of the next-hop router that will receive the packet and forward it to the remote network. This is a router interface that's on a directly connected network.
exitinterface	Used in place of the next-hop address if you want and shows up as a directly connected route.
administrative_distance	By default, static routes have an administrative distance of 1 (or even 0 if you use an exit interface instead of a next-hop address).
permanent	If the interface is shut down or the router can't communicate to the next-hop router, the route will automatically be discarded from the routing table. Choosing the permanent option keeps the entry in the routing table no matter what happens.

Here is a sample static route, complete with the network to be added, its mask, and the next-hop address to which the data will be sent:

```
Router(config)#ip route 172.16.3.0 255.255.255.0 192.168.2.4
```

However, suppose the static route looked like this:

```
Router(config)#ip route 172.16.3.0 255.255.255.0 192.168.2.4 150
```

The 150, at the end of the command, changes the default administrative distance (AD) of 1 to 150. Remember that the AD is the trustworthiness of a route, where 0 is best and 255 is worst.

Here's one more example:

```
Router(config)#ip route 172.16.3.0 255.255.255.0 s0/0/0
```

Instead of using a next-hop address, you can use an exit interface that will make the route show up as a directly connected network. Functionally, the next-hop and exit interfaces work the same way.

Default Routing

You can use *default routing* to send packets with a remote destination network not in the routing table to the next-hop router. You should use default routing only on stub networks—those with only one exit path out of the network.

To configure a default route, you use wildcards in the network address and mask locations of a static route. In fact, you can just think of a default route as a static route that uses wildcards instead of network and mask information.

By using a default route, you can create just one static route entry instead. This sure is easier than typing in all those routes! Here is an example using my router with a WLAN interface installed:

```
Router(config)#ip route 0.0.0.0 0.0.0.0 10.1.11.1
Router (config)#ip classless
Router (config)#do show ip route
  Gateway of last resort is 10.1.11.1 to network 0.0.0.0
  10.0.0.0/24 is subnetted, 2 subnets
C    10.1.11.0 is directly connected, Vlan1
L    10.1.11.1/32 is directly connected, Vlan1
C    10.1.12.0 is directly connected, Dot11Radio0
L    10.1.12.1/32 is directly connected, Dot11Radio0
S*   0.0.0.0/0 [1/0] via 10.1.11.1
Router (config)#
```

If you look at the routing table, you'll see only the two directly connected networks plus an S*, which indicates this entry is a candidate for a default route. I could have completed the default route command another way:

```
Router (config)#ip route 0.0.0.0 0.0.0.0 Fa0/0
```

What this is telling you is that if you don't have an entry for a network in the routing table, just forward it out FastEthernet0/0. Table 3.4 defines the ip classless command:

TABLE 3.4 Default Routing

Command	Meaning
ip classless	Enables classless features, allowing different subnet sizes

All Cisco routers are classful routers, meaning they expect a default subnet mask on each interface of the router. When a router receives a packet for a destination subnet that's not in the routing table, it will drop the packet by default. If you're using default routing, you must use the `ip classless` command because it is possible that no remote subnets will be in the routing table. Here is example:

```
Router(config)#ip classless
```

Table 3.5 defines the `ip default-network` command used with RIP:

TABLE 3.5   Advanced Static Route Commands

Command	Meaning
ip default-network	Configures a gateway of last resort and allows it to be advertised

There's another command you can use to configure a gateway of last resort—the `ip default-network` command. Figure 3.2 shows a network that needs to have a gateway of last resort statement configured.

FIGURE 3.2   Configuring a gateway of last resort

Here are three commands (all providing the same solution) for adding a gateway of last resort on the gateway router to the ISP:

```
Gateway(config)#ip route 0.0.0.0 0.0.0.0 217.124.6.1

Gateway(config)#ip route 0.0.0.0 0.0.0.0 s0/0

Gateway(config)#ip default-network 217.124.6.0
```

As I said before, all three of these commands would accomplish the goal of setting the gateway of last resort, but there are some small differences between them. First, the exit interface solution would be used over the other two solutions because it has an AD of 0. Also, the `ip default-network` command would advertise the default network when you configure an IGP (like RIP) on the router. This is so other routers in your internetwork will receive this route as a default route automatically.

I'll discuss one last topic before moving on to dynamic routing. If you have the routing table output as shown here, what happens if the router receives a packet from 10.1.6.100 destined for host 10.1.8.5?

```
Corp#sh ip route
[output cut]
Gateway of last resort is 10.1.5.5 to network 0.0.0.0

R     10.1.3.0 [120/1] via 101.2.2, 00:00:00, Serial 0/0
C     10.1.2.0  is directly connected, Serial0/0
C     10.1.5.0  is directly connected, Serial0/1
C     10.1.6.0  is directly connected, Fastethernet0/0
R*    0.0.0.0/0 [120/0] via 10.1.5.5, 00:00:00 Serial 0/1
```

This is a tad different from what I've shown you up until now because the default route is listed as R*, which means it's a RIP-injected route. This is because someone configured the `ip default-network` command on a remote router as well as configuring RIP, causing RIP to advertise this route through the internetwork as a default route. Since the destination address is 10.1.8.5 and there is no route to network 10.1.8.0, the router would use the default route and send the packet out serial 0/1.

Routing Protocol Basics

You should know some important facts about routing protocols before getting deeper into RIP. Specifically, you need to understand administrative distances, the three kinds of routing protocols, and routing loops. I'll cover each of these in more detail in the following sections.

Administrative Distances (ADs)

The *AD* is used to rate the trustworthiness of routing information received on a router from a neighbor router. An AD is an integer from 0 to 255, where 0 is the most trusted and 255 means no traffic will be passed via this route.

Table 3.6 shows the default administrative distances that a Cisco router uses to decide which route to take to a remote network.

TABLE 3.6   Default Administrative Distances

Route Source	Default AD
Connected interface	0
Static route	1
EIGRP	90
IGRP	100
OSPF	110
RIP	120
External EIGRP	170
Unknown	255 (this route will never be used)

Table 3.7 defines the commands to change the AD of RIP on your router:

TABLE 3.7   Router Rip Commands

Command	Meaning
router rip	Enables RIP routing
distance	Changes the default administrative distance

Each routing protocol has a default AD; you can, however, change the AD for specific routes or for a routing protocol. Earlier when I added 150 to the end of the static route entry, I changed the AD for that specific route. If I want to change the AD for a routing protocol, I must use the distance command.

```
Router(config)#router rip
Router(config-router)#distance 150
```

Routing Information Protocol (RIP)

Routing Information Protocol (RIP) is a true distance-vector routing protocol. RIP sends the complete routing table to all active interfaces every 30 seconds. RIP uses the hop count only to determine the best way to a remote network, but it has a maximum allowable hop count of 15 by default, meaning that 16 is deemed unreachable. RIP works well in small networks, but it's inefficient on large networks with slow WAN links or on networks with a large number of routers installed.

RIP Timers

RIP uses four kinds of timers to regulate its performance; Table 3.8 describes them.

TABLE 3.8   RIP Timers

Timer	Meaning
route update timer	Sets the interval (typically 30 seconds) between periodic routing updates, in which the router sends a complete copy of its routing table to all neighbors.
route invalid timer	Determines the length of time that must elapse (180 seconds) before a router determines that a route has become invalid. It will come to this conclusion if it hasn't heard any updates about a particular route for that period. When that happens, the router will send out updates to all its neighbors letting them know that the route is invalid.
holddown timer	This sets the amount of time during which routing information is suppressed. Routes will enter into the holddown state when an update packet is received that indicates the route is unreachable. This continues either until an update packet is received with a better metric or until the holddown timer expires. The default is 180 seconds.
route flush timer	Sets the time between a route becoming invalid and its removal from the routing table (240 seconds). Before it's removed from the table, the router notifies its neighbors of that route's impending demise. The value of the route invalid timer must be less than that of the route flush timer. This gives the router enough time to tell its neighbors about the invalid route before the local routing table is updated.

Table 3.9 lists the commands to change the timers.

TABLE 3.9 RIP Timer Commands

Command	Meaning
router rip	Enables rip routing
timers	Changes the default RIP timers

The command to configure the RIP timers is timers under the RIP configuration mode. Here is an example of setting the timers to their defaults:

```
Router(config-router)#timers basic 30 180 180 240
```

Enabling RIP

To configure RIP routing, just turn on the protocol with the router rip command and tell the RIP routing protocol which networks to advertise. Table 3.10 shows the basic configuration of enabling RIP:

TABLE 3.10 RIP Commands

Command	Meaning
router rip	Starts and enable a RIP routing process
network	Configures a network to advertise and enable interfaces into the routing process

Here's an example:

```
Router#config t
Router(config)#router rip
Router(config-router)#network 10.0.0.0
```

That's it. Two or three commands, and you're done—that sure makes your job a lot easier than when using static routes, doesn't it? However, keep in mind the extra router CPU process and bandwidth you're consuming.

Notice I didn't type subnets, only the classful network address (all subnet bits and host bits off!). It is the job of the routing protocol to find the subnets and populate the routing tables. Since you have no router buddies running RIP, you won't see any RIP routes in the routing table yet.

Remember that RIP uses the classful address when configuring the network address. Because of this, all subnet masks must be the same on all devices in the network (this is called *classful routing*).

To clarify this, let's say you're using a Class B network address of 172.16.0.0/24 with subnets 172.16.10.0, 172.16.20.0, and 172.16.30.0. You would type only the classful network address of 172.16.0.0 and let RIP find the subnets and place them in the routing table.

Holding Down RIP Propagations

You probably don't want your RIP network advertised everywhere on your LAN and WAN. There's not a whole lot to be gained by advertising your RIP network to the Internet, now, is there?

To stop route updates from being sent out an interface, use the command in Table 3.11:

TABLE 3.11   Holding Down Rip Propagations

Command	Meaning
passive-interface	Prevents an interface from fully participating in a routing process

Here's an example of how to configure a passive interface on a router using the CLI:

```
Lab_A#config t
Lab_A(config)#router rip
Lab_A(config-router)#network 192.168.10.0
Lab_A(config-router)#passive-interface serial 0/0
```

This command will stop RIP updates from being propagated out serial interface 0/0, but serial interface 0/0 can still receive RIP updates.

RIP Version 2 (RIPv2)

I'll now spend a few paragraphs discussing RIPv2 before moving into the distance-vector, Cisco-proprietary routing protocol EIGRP.

RIP version 2 (RIPv2) is mostly the same as RIP version 1 (RIPv1). Both RIPv1 and RIPv2 are *distance-vector protocols*, which means each router running RIP sends its complete routing tables out all active interfaces at periodic time intervals. Also, the timers and loop-avoidance schemes are the same in both RIP versions—that is, holddown timers and split horizon rule. Both RIPv1 and RIPv2 are configured as classful addressing (but RIPv2 is considered classless because subnet information is sent with each route update), and both have the same administrative distance (120). Table 3.12 describes the difference between the two protocols.

TABLE 3.12 RIPv1 vs. RIPv2

RIPv1	RIPv2
Distance vector	Distance vector
Maximum hop count of 15	Maximum hop count of 15
Classful	Classless
Broadcast based	Uses Multicast 224.0.0.9
No support for VLSM	Supports VLSM networks
No authentication	Allows for MD5 authentication
No support for discontiguous networks	Supports discontiguous networks

Table 3.13 lists the commands for basic configuration of RIPv2 and for using authentication with RIPv2.

TABLE 3.13 RIPv2 Authentication Commands

Command	Meaning
`version`	Configures the version of RIP which is running.
`key` **key**	Specifies a specific key on the kay chain.
`key chain` **name**	This just creates a key chain name. Multiple keys can be on the key chain.
`Key-string` **string**	This is the authentication string that is sent and received in the packets by the routing protocol being authenticated.
`ip rip authentication key-chain` **chain_name**	Enables authentication on the interface and configures the key chain that will be used.
`ip rip authentication mode md5`	Optional, but highly recommended. If you do not add the md5 authentication, then the key-chain is sent in clear text.

Configuring RIPv2 is pretty straightforward. Here's an example:

```
Lab_C(config)#router rip
Lab_C(config-router)#network 192.168.40.0
Lab_C(config-router)#network 192.168.50.0
Lab_C(config-router)#version 2
```

That's it--just add the command version 2 at the (config-router)# prompt, and you are now running RIPv2. Now, let's add authentication to the RIP route updates.

```
Lab_C#config t
Lab_C(config)#key chain todd
Lab_C(config)#key 1
Lab_C(config)#key-string 12345
Lab_C(config)#interface serial 0/0
Lab_C(config-if)#ip rip authentication key-chain todd
Lab_C(config-if)#ip rip authentication mode md5
```

OK, let's verify RIP routing.

Verifying RIP

The following commands in Table 3.14 are used for the verification of RIP routing.

TABLE 3.14 Verifying RIP

Command	Meaning
show ip route	Displays the routers routing table
show ip protocols	Displays the routing protocols and interfaces used with all routing protocols configured on your router
debug ip rip	Show rip updates being sent and received on your router

The *show ip protocols* Command

The show ip protocols command shows you the routing protocols that are configured on your router. Looking at the following output, you can see that RIP is running on the router and the timers that RIP uses:

```
R3#sh ip protocols
Routing Protocol is "rip"
```

```
Outgoing update filter list for all interfaces is not set
Incoming update filter list for all interfaces is not set
Sending updates every 30 seconds, next due in 24 seconds
Invalid after 180 seconds, hold down 180, flushed after 240
Redistributing: rip
Default version control: send version 1, receive version 1
  Interface          Send  Recv  Triggered RIP  Key-chain
  FastEthernet0/1     1     1
  Serial0/0/1         1     1
Automatic network summarization is not in effect
Maximum path: 4
Routing for Networks:
  10.0.0.0
Passive Interface(s):
  FastEthernet0/0
  Serial0/0/0
Routing Information Sources:
  Gateway         Distance      Last Update
  10.1.11.2         120         00:00:10
  10.1.5.1          120         00:00:22
Distance: (default is 120)
```

Let's discuss what the above output provides to us:

RIP is sending updates every 30 seconds, which is the default.

The timers used in distance vector are also shown.

Notice further down that RIP is routing for directly connected interfaces Fa0/1, and s0/0/0. To the right of the interfaces are the version listed—RIPv1.

F0/0 and s0/0/0 are listed as passive interfaces (they will not send RIP information out).

The neighbors it found are 10.1.11.2 and 10.1.5.1. The last entry is the default AD for RIP (120).

The *debug ip rip* Command

The debug ip rip command shows routing updates as they are sent and received on the router to the console session. If you are telnetted into the router, you'll need to use the terminal monitor command to be able to receive the output from the debug commands.

You can see in this output that RIP is both sending and receiving (the metric is the hop count):

```
R3#debug ip rip
RIP protocol debugging is on
R3#terminal monitor
*Mar 17 19:08:34.371: RIP: sending v1 update to 255.255.255.255 via Serial0/0/1
(10.1.5.2)
```

```
*Mar 17 19:08:34.371: RIP: build update entries
*Mar 17 19:08:34.371:    subnet 10.1.10.0 metric 1
*Mar 17 19:08:34.371:    subnet 10.1.11.0 metric 1
*Mar 17 19:08:34.371:    subnet 10.1.12.0 metric 2
```
*Mar 17 19:08:40.107: RIP: received v1 update from 10.1.5.1 on Serial0/0/1
```
*Mar 17 19:08:40.107:       10.1.1.0 in 1 hops
*Mar 17 19:08:40.107:       10.1.2.0 in 1 hops
*Mar 17 19:08:40.107:       10.1.3.0 in 1 hops
*Mar 17 19:08:40.107:       10.1.4.0 in 1 hops
*Mar 17 19:08:40.107:       10.1.6.0 in 2 hops
*Mar 17 19:08:40.107:       10.1.7.0 in 2 hops
*Mar 17 19:08:40.107:       10.1.8.0 in 2 hops
*Mar 17 19:08:40.107:       10.1.9.0 in 2 hops
```
*Mar 17 19:08:47.535: RIP: sending v1 update to 255.255.255.255 via
FastEthernet0/1 (10.1.11.1)
```
*Mar 17 19:08:47.535: RIP: build update entries
*Mar 17 19:08:47.535:    subnet 10.1.1.0 metric 2
*Mar 17 19:08:47.535:    subnet 10.1.2.0 metric 2
*Mar 17 19:08:47.535:    subnet 10.1.3.0 metric 2
*Mar 17 19:08:47.535:    subnet 10.1.4.0 metric 2
*Mar 17 19:08:47.535:    subnet 10.1.5.0 metric 1
*Mar 17 19:08:47.535:    subnet 10.1.6.0 metric 3
*Mar 17 19:08:47.535:    subnet 10.1.7.0 metric 3
*Mar 17 19:08:47.535:    subnet 10.1.8.0 metric 3
*Mar 17 19:08:47.535:    subnet 10.1.9.0 metric 3
*Mar 17 19:08:47.535:    subnet 10.1.10.0 metric 1
```
*Mar 17 19:08:49.331: RIP: received v1 update from 10.1.11.2 on FastEthernet0/1
```
*Mar 17 19:08:49.331:       10.1.12.0 in 1 hops
R3#undeug all
```

Let's talk about the parts I highlighted in bold. First, RIP is sending v1 packet to 255.255.255.255—an "all-hands" broadcast, out interface Serial0/0/1, via 10.1.5.2. This is where RIPv2 will come in handy. Why? Well, RIPv2 doesn't send broadcasts; it used the multicast 224.0.0.9. So even though the RIP packets could be transmitted onto a network with no routers, all hosts would just ignore them, making RIPv2 a bit of an improvement over RIPv1. On this R3, I'm using the passive interface so I'm not sending broadcasts out to a LAN with any routers connected. Continuing with the debug ip rip command, let's take a quick look at a route update when using RIPv2 with MD5 authentication.

```
R3#debug ip rip
 RIP protocol debugging is on
*May  3 20:48:37.046: RIP: received packet with MD5 authentication
*May  3 20:48:37.046: RIP: received v2 update from 192.168.10.1 on Serial0/0
*May  3 20:48:37.050:    10.0.0.0/8 via 0.0.0.0 in 1 hops
```

Chapter 4

Enhanced IGRP (EIGRP) and Open Shortest Path First (OSPF)

Enhanced Interior Gateway Routing Protocol (EIGRP) is a proprietary Cisco protocol that runs on Cisco routers. It is important for you to understand EIGRP because it is probably one of the two most popular routing protocols in use today. In this chapter, I'll show you the many features of EIGRP and describe how it works, with particular focus on the unique way it discovers, selects, and advertises routes.

I'll also introduce you to the Open Shortest Path First (OSPF) routing protocol, which is the other popular routing protocol in use today. I'll explain commands to use in order to implement single-area OSPF in specific networking environments and demonstrate how to verify that everything is running smoothly.

For up-to-the minute updates for this chapter, please see www.lammle.com.

Understanding EIGRP Basics

A number of powerful features make EIGRP a real standout from RIP and other protocols. The main ones are listed here:

- Support for IP and IPv6 (and some other useless routed protocols) via protocol-dependent modules
- Considered classless (same as RIPv2 and OSPF)
- Support for VLSM/CIDR
- Support for summaries and discontiguous networks
- Efficient neighbor discovery
- Communication via Reliable Transport Protocol (RTP)
- Best path selection via Diffusing Update Algorithm (DUAL)

Configuring EIGRP

Although EIGRP can be configured for IP, IPv6, IPX, and AppleTalk, as a future Cisco Certified Network Associate, you really need to focus only on configuring IP for now.

You can enter EIGRP commands from two modes: router configuration mode and interface configuration mode. *Router configuration mode* enables the protocol, determines which networks will run EIGRP, and sets global characteristics. *Interface configuration mode* allows the customization of summaries, metrics, timers, and bandwidth.

To start an EIGRP session on a router, use the `router eigrp` command followed by the autonomous system number of your network. You then enter the network numbers connected to the router using the `network` command followed by the network number. Table 4.1 defines the minimum commands to enable EIGRP on your router:

TABLE 4.1   Basic EIGRP Commands

Command	Meaning
router eigrp	Starts an EIGRP routing process for a given autonomous system
network	Configures a network to be advertised in the routing protocol and the interface to enable and include in the process

Here's an example of enabling EIGRP for autonomous system 20 on a router connected to two networks, with the network numbers being 10.3.1.0/24 and 172.16.10.0/24:

```
Router#config t
Router(config)#router eigrp 20
Router(config-router)#network 172.16.0.0
Router(config-router)#network 10.0.0.0
```

Remember—as with RIP, you use the classful network address, which means all host bits are turned off.

Holding Down EIGRP Propagations

Say you need to stop EIGRP from working on a specific interface, such as a BRI interface or a serial connection to the Internet. To do that, you would flag the interface as passive using the `passive-interface` *interface* command, as discussed in Chapter 3 with RIP. The following command (Table 4.2) shows you how to make interface serial 0/1 a passive interface: The passive-interface command is configured under the routing protocol, not the interface.

TABLE 4.2   Holding Down EIGRP Propagations

Command	Meaning
passive-interface	Configuring in EIGRP prevents the interface from participating in the routing process by preventing the sending and receiving of hello packets.

Here are the commands used in context:

```
Router(config)#router eigrp 20
Router(config-router)#passive-interface serial 0/1
```

Doing this will prohibit the interface from sending or receiving hello packets and, as a result, stop it from forming adjacencies. This means it won't send or receive route information on this interface.

Setting Maximum Paths and Hop Count

By default, EIGRP can provide equal-cost load balancing of up to four links (actually, all routing protocols do this). However, you can have EIGRP actually load balance across up to 32 links (equal or unequal) by using the following command: Typically you would not need to configure these commands, but here (Table 4.3) is how you see the maximum paths and hop count:

TABLE 4.3   Advanced EIGRP Commands

Command	Meaning
maximum-paths	Displays a routers table of known or learned destination networks
metric maximum-hops	Changes the hop count for EIGRP up to a maximum of 255

Here are the commands used in context:

```
Pod1R1(config)#router eigrp 10
Pod1R1(config-router)#maximum-paths ?
  <1-32>  Number of paths
```

In addition, EIGRP has a maximum hop count of 100 but can be set up to 255. Chances are you wouldn't want to ever change this, but if you did, here is how you would do it:

```
Pod1R1(config)#router eigrp 10
Pod1R1(config-router)#metric maximum-hops ?
  <1-255>  Hop count
```

As you can see from this router output, EIGRP can be set to a maximum of 255 hops, and even though it doesn't use hop count in the path metric calculation, it still uses the maximum hop count to limit the scope of the Autonomous System.

Using Redistribution Commands

From a router named R3, you just need to add the redistribution commands under EIGRP and RIP. Listed in Table 4.4 are the commands:

TABLE 4.4 Routing Protocol Redistribution Commands

Command	Meaning
redistribution	Displays a routers table of known or learned destination networks
metric	Sets the parameters for redistribution
bandwidth	Configures the bandwidth used for routing calculations
delay	Sets the delay of the link used for routing calculations
reliability	Not used by default with EIGRP, but sets the reliability of the link used with routing calculations if administratively set
load	Not used by default with EIGRP, but sets the load of the link used with routing calculations if administratively set
MTU	Not used by default with EIGRP, but sets the maximum transmission unit of the link used with routing calculations if administratively set

The commands seem a little convoluted, but once you work through them a few times, you'll start to feel more comfortable with redistribution. Take a look:

```
R3#config t
R3(config)#router eigrp 10
R3(config-router)#redistribute rip ?
  metric     Metric for redistributed routes
  route-map  Route map reference
  <cr>
R3(config-router)#redistribute rip metric ?
  <1-4294967295>  Bandwidth metric in Kbits per second
R3(config-router)#redistribute rip metric 10000000 ?
  <0-4294967295>  EIGRP delay metric, in 10 microsecond units
```

```
R3(config-router)#redistribute rip metric 10000000 20000 ?
  <0-255>  EIGRP reliability metric where 255 is 100% reliable
R3(config-router)#redistribute rip metric 10000000 20000 255 ?
  <1-255>  EIGRP Effective bandwidth metric (Loading) where 255 is 100% loaded
R3(config-router)#redistribute rip metric 10000000 20000 255 1 ?
  <1-65535>  EIGRP MTU of the path
R3(config-router)#redistribute rip metric 10000000 20000 255 1 1500
R3(config-router)#do show run | begin router eigrp 10
router eigrp 10
 redistribute rip metric 10000000 20000 255 1 1500
 passive-interface FastEthernet0/0
 passive-interface Serial0/0/0
 network 10.0.0.0
 no auto-summary
!
```

As you can see, I needed to change RIP's metric of hop count to match EIGRP's band-width metric, delay, reliability, load, and MTU. Even though EIGRP may use only bandwidth and delay of the line by default, when you configure redistribution, you have to configure all metric values.

The following output shows I'm redistributing EIGRP into RIP and changing the metric to hop count:

```
R3(config)#router rip
R3(config-router)#redistribute eigrp 10 ?
  metric     Metric for redistributed routes
  route-map  Route map reference
  <cr>
R3(config-router)#redistribute eigrp 10 metric ?
  <0-16>       Default metric
  transparent  Transparently redistribute metric

R3(config-router)#redistribute eigrp 10 metric 1
```

Configuring Discontiguous Networks

1. You need to be aware of one more configuration, as listed in Table 4.5, that has to do with autosummarization.

TABLE 4.5   Solving Discontiguous Networks

Command	Meaning
no auto-summary	Configures manual summarization and the propagation of all subnet entries in the routing table

Without the option of the no auto-summary command for both RIPv2 and EIGRP, discontiguous networks will never work.

```
Lab_A#config t
Lab_A(config)#router eigrp 100
Lab_A(config-router)#network 172.16.0.0
Lab_A(config-router)#network 10.0.0.0
Lab_A(config-router)#no auto-summary

Lab_B#config t
Lab_B(config)#router eigrp 100
Lab_B(config-router)#network 172.16.0.0
Lab_B(config-router)#network 10.0.0.0
Lab_B(config-router)#no auto-summary
```

By using the no auto-summary command, EIGRP will advertise all the subnets between the two routers. If the networks were larger, you could then provide manual summarization on these same boundaries.

By default auto-summarization is disabled on routers running 15 code; however, you need to be aware that the exam has both 12.4 and 15 IOS code routers in use and you need to disable auto-summarization on routers running the 12.4 IOS code.

Load Balancing with EIGRP

1. You might know that by default EIGRP can load balance up to four equal-cost links. But did you know that you can configure EIGRP to load balance across up to thirty-two equal/unequal-cost links to a remote network? Well, you can, so let's take a some EIGRP commands (Table 4.6) and do some load balancing as well.

TABLE 4.6   Load Balancing

Command	Meaning
show ip route	Displays the router's routing table
show ip eigrp topology	Shows the topology table used with EIGRP
variance	Sets a variance used for unequal-cost load balancing

Take a look at a routing table with EIGRP routing configured on the network:

```
R1#sh ip route
      10.0.0.0/24 is subnetted, 12 subnets
D        10.1.11.0 [90/2684416] via 10.1.3.1, 00:50:37, Serial0/0/1
                   [90/2684416] via 10.1.2.1, 00:50:37, Serial0/0/0
D        10.1.10.0 [90/2707456] via 10.1.3.1, 01:04:40, Serial0/0/1
                   [90/2707456] via 10.1.2.1, 01:04:40, Serial0/0/0
D        10.1.9.0 [90/2707456] via 10.1.3.1, 01:24:09, Serial0/0/1
                   [90/2707456] via 10.1.2.1, 01:24:09, Serial0/0/0
D        10.1.8.0 [90/2707456] via 10.1.3.1, 01:24:09, Serial0/0/1
                   [90/2707456] via 10.1.2.1, 01:24:09, Serial0/0/0
D        10.1.12.0 [90/2684416] via 10.1.3.1, 00:10:10, Serial0/0/1
                   [90/2684416] via 10.1.2.1, 00:10:10, Serial0/0/0
C        10.1.3.0 is directly connected, Serial0/0/1
C        10.1.2.0 is directly connected, Serial0/0/0
D        10.1.1.0 [90/2172416] via 10.1.3.1, 01:24:11, Serial0/0/1
                   [90/2172416] via 10.1.2.1, 01:24:11, Serial0/0/0
C        10.1.7.0 is directly connected, FastEthernet0/1
C        10.1.6.0 is directly connected, FastEthernet0/0
D        10.1.5.0 [90/2681856] via 10.1.3.1, 01:24:11, Serial0/0/1
                   [90/2681856] via 10.1.2.1, 01:24:11, Serial0/0/0
D        10.1.4.0 [90/2681856] via 10.1.3.1, 01:24:11, Serial0/0/1
                   [90/2681856] via 10.1.2.1, 01:24:11, Serial0/0/0
```

You can see that here you have two links to every route in the internetwork, and again, EIGRP will load balance across the s0/0/0 and s0/0/1 links by default because they're the same metric.

But how about bundling links? Well, EIGRP can allow you to do this too—with just a slightly different configuration! I'll show you how this works by configuring the links between the Corp and R1 router with the same subnet, meaning both links will have all interfaces within the same subnet. Check out my configuration:

```
Corp#config t
Corp(config)#int s0/0/1
Corp(config-if)#ip address 10.1.2.4 255.255.255.0

R1#config t
R1(config)#int s0/0/1
R1(config-if)#ip address 10.1.2.3 255.255.255.0
R1(config-if)#do show run | begin interface
interface Serial0/0/0
 description 1st Connection to Corp Router
 ip address 10.1.2.2 255.255.255.0
!
interface Serial0/0/1
 description 2nd connection to Corp Router
 ip address 10.1.2.3 255.255.255.0
```

Now both links have all four interfaces in the same subnet:

```
R1(config-if)#do show ip route
     10.0.0.0/24 is subnetted, 12 subnets
D       10.1.11.0 [90/2684416] via 10.1.2.4, 00:04:44, Serial0/0/1
                  [90/2684416] via 10.1.2.1, 00:04:44, Serial0/0/0
D       10.1.10.0 [90/2707456] via 10.1.2.4, 00:04:44, Serial0/0/1
                  [90/2707456] via 10.1.2.1, 00:04:44, Serial0/0/0
D       10.1.9.0 [90/2707456] via 10.1.2.4, 00:04:44, Serial0/0/1
                 [90/2707456] via 10.1.2.1, 00:04:44, Serial0/0/0
D       10.1.8.0 [90/2707456] via 10.1.2.4, 00:04:44, Serial0/0/1
                 [90/2707456] via 10.1.2.1, 00:04:44, Serial0/0/0
D       10.1.12.0 [90/2684416] via 10.1.2.4, 00:04:44, Serial0/0/1
                  [90/2684416] via 10.1.2.1, 00:04:44, Serial0/0/0
D       10.1.3.0 [90/3193856] via 10.1.2.4, 00:04:44, Serial0/0/1
                 [90/3193856] via 10.1.2.1, 00:04:44, Serial0/0/0
C       10.1.2.0 is directly connected, Serial0/0/0
                 is directly connected, Serial0/0/1
D       10.1.1.0 [90/2172416] via 10.1.2.4, 00:03:56, Serial0/0/1
                 [90/2172416] via 10.1.2.1, 00:03:56, Serial0/0/0
C       10.1.7.0 is directly connected, FastEthernet0/1
C       10.1.6.0 is directly connected, FastEthernet0/0
```

```
D       10.1.5.0 [90/2681856] via 10.1.2.4, 00:04:46, Serial0/0/1
                 [90/2681856] via 10.1.2.1, 00:04:46, Serial0/0/0
D       10.1.4.0 [90/2681856] via 10.1.2.4, 00:04:46, Serial0/0/1
                 [90/2681856] via 10.1.2.1, 00:04:46, Serial0/0/0
```

Now I'll show what's in the Corp topology table by using the show ip eigrp topology command. I'll cover this command more specifically in the "Verifying EIGRP" section.

```
Corp# sh ip eigrp topology
IP-EIGRP Topology Table for AS(10)/ID(10.1.5.1)
Codes: P - Passive, A - Active, U - Update, Q - Query, R - Reply,
       r - reply Status, s - sia Status
P 10.1.11.0/24, 1 successors, FD is 2172416
        via 10.1.5.2 (2172416/28160), Serial0/2/0
P 10.1.10.0/24, 1 successors, FD is 2172416
        via 10.1.5.2 (2195456/281600), Serial0/2/0
P 10.1.9.0/24, 1 successors, FD is 2195456
        via 10.1.4.2 (2195456/281600), Serial0/1/0
P 10.1.8.0/24, 1 successors, FD is 2195456
        via 10.1.4.2 (2195456/72960), Serial0/1/0
P 10.1.12.0/24, 1 successors, FD is 2172416
        via 10.1.5.2 (2172416/28160), Serial0/2/0
P 10.1.3.0/24, 1 successors, FD is 76839936
        via Connected, Serial0/0/1
        via 10.1.2.2 (9849856/7719936), Serial0/0/0, serno 89
P 10.1.2.0/24, 1 successors, FD is 2169856
        via Connected, Serial0/0/0
        via 10.1.2.2 (2681856/551936), Serial0/0/0
P 10.1.1.0/24, 1 successors, FD is 28160
        via Connected, FastEthernet0/1
P 10.1.7.0/24, 1 successors, FD is 793600
        via 10.1.2.2 (2195456/281600), Serial0/0/0
        via 10.1.3.2 (77081600/281600), Serial0/0/1
P 10.1.6.0/24, 1 successors, FD is 793600
        via 10.1.2.2 (2195456/281600), Serial0/0/0
        via 10.1.3.2 (77081600/281600), Serial0/0/1
P 10.1.5.0/24, 1 successors, FD is 2169856
        via Connected, Serial0/2/0
P 10.1.4.0/24, 1 successors, FD is 2169856
        via Connected, Serial0/1/0
```

Each entry also indicates the *feasible distance (FD)* to each remote network plus the next-hop neighbor through which packets will travel to their destinations. Plus, each entry also has two numbers in parentheses. The first indicates the feasible distance, and the second one indicates the advertised distance to a remote network.

Now here's where things get interesting—notice that under the 10.1.7.0 and 10.1.6.0 outputs there are two links to each network and the feasible distance and advertised distance are different. What this means is that you have one successor to the networks and one feasible successor—a backup route!

> For the route to be a feasible successor, its advertised distance must be less than the feasible distance of the successor route. That's so very cool! You need to remember that even though both routes to network 10.1.6.0 and 10.1.7.0 are in the topology table, only the successor route (the one with the lowest metrics) will be copied and placed into the routing table.

EIGRP will load balance across both links automatically when they are of equal variance (equal cost), but EIGRP can also load balance across unequal cost links if you use the `variance` command. Changing a variance value enables EIGRP to install multiple, loop-free routes with unequal cost in a local routing table.

For example, if the variance is set to 2, an unequal cost path with a metric less than two times the successor metric will be installed in the local routing table. Remember, an unequal cost path will be used only if it is a feasible successor.

Using Route Authentication with EIGRP

To enable authentication of EIGRP packets, use the following commands in Table 4.7 beginning in interface configuration mode:

TABLE 4.7   EIGRP Route Authentication

Command	Meaning
`interface` *interface*	Configure an interface type and enter interface configuration mode.
`ip authentication mode eigrp` *AS* `md5`	Enable MD5 authentication in EIGRP route update packets.
`ip authentication key-chain eigrp as` *key-chain*	Enable authentication of EIGRP packets.
`key chain` *name*	Identify the key chain.

TABLE 4.7   EIGRP Route Authentication *(continued)*

Command	Meaning
key *number*	In key chain configuration mode, identify the key number
key-string *text*	In key chain key configure mode, identify the key string
accept-lifetime *start-time*	(optional) specify the time period during which the key can be received
send-lifetime *start-time*	(optional) specify the time period during which the key can be sent

Let's take a look at these commands as used on a Cisco router:

```
Corp#config t
Corp(config)#int s0/0/1
Corp(config-if)#ip authentication mode eigrp 10 md5
Corp(config-if)#ip authentication key-chain eigrp 10 todd
Corp(config-if)#exit
Corp(config)#key chain todd
Corp(config-keychain)#key 1
Corp(config-keychain-key)#key-string 1234567890
Corp(config-keychain-key)#accept-lifetime 04:00:00 Jan  14 2008 infinite
Corp(config)#send-lifetime 04:00:00 Jan 14 2008 04:50:00 Jan 14 2008
```

Now, let's verify EIGRP.

Verifying EIGRP

You can use several commands, as defined in Table 4.8, on a router to help you trouble-shoot and verify the EIGRP configuration:

TABLE 4.8   Verifying EIGRP

Command	Meaning
show ip route eigrp	Shows only EIGRP entries in the routing table
show ip eigrp neighbors	Shows all EIGRP neighbors

Command	Meaning
show ip eigrp topology	Shows entries in the EIGRP topology table
debug eigrp packet	Shows hello packets sent/received between adjacent routers
debug ip eigrp notification	Shows EIGRP changes and updates as they occur on your network

Now return to the Corp router and see what it shows in the neighbor table:

```
Corp#sh ip eigrp neighbors
IP-EIGRP neighbors for process 10
H   Address      Interface    Hold Uptime    SRTT  RTO Q  Seq
                              (sec)          (ms)     Cnt Num
1   10.1.3.2     Se0/0/1      14 00:35:10     1    200 0  81
3   10.1.5.2     Se0/2/0      10 02:51:22     1    200 0  31
2   10.1.4.2     Se0/1/0      13 03:17:20     1    200 0  20
0   10.1.2.2     Se0/0/0      10 03:19:37     1    200 0  80
```

You can read the information in this output like this:

- The H field indicates the order in which the neighbor was discovered.

- The hold time is how long this router will wait for a hello packet to arrive from a specific neighbor.

- The uptime indicates how long the "neighborship" has been established.

- The SRTT field is the smooth round-trip timer—an indication of the time it takes for a round-trip from this router to its neighbor and back. This value is used to determine how long to wait after a multicast for a reply from this neighbor. If a reply isn't received in time, the router will switch to using unicasts in an attempt to complete the communication. The time between multicast attempts is specified by the Retransmission Time Out (RTO) field, described next.

- RTO is the amount of time EIGRP waits before retransmitting a packet from the retransmission queue to a neighbor.

- The Q value indicates whether there are any outstanding messages in the queue— consistently large values would indicate a problem.

- The Seq field indicates the sequence number of the last update from that neighbor— something that's used to maintain synchronization and avoid duplicate or out-of-sequence processing of messages.

Now let's see what's in the Corp topology table by using the show ip eigrp topology command. This should be interesting!

```
Corp#sh ip eigrp topology
IP-EIGRP Topology Table for AS(10)/ID(10.1.5.1)
Codes: P - Passive, A - Active, U - Update, Q - Query, R - Reply,
       r - reply Status, s - sia Status
P 10.1.11.0/24, 1 successors, FD is 2172416
        via 10.1.5.2 (2172416/28160), Serial0/2/0
P 10.1.10.0/24, 1 successors, FD is 2172416
        via 10.1.5.2 (2195456/281600), Serial0/2/0
P 10.1.9.0/24, 1 successors, FD is 2195456
        via 10.1.4.2 (2195456/281600), Serial0/1/0
P 10.1.8.0/24, 1 successors, FD is 2195456
        via 10.1.4.2 (2195456/72960), Serial0/1/0
P 10.1.12.0/24, 1 successors, FD is 2172416
        via 10.1.5.2 (2172416/28160), Serial0/2/0
P 10.1.3.0/24, 1 successors, FD is 76839936
        via Connected, Serial0/0/1
        via 10.1.2.2 (9849856/7719936), Serial0/0/0, serno 89
P 10.1.2.0/24, 1 successors, FD is 2169856
        via Connected, Serial0/0/0
        via 10.1.2.2 (2681856/551936), Serial0/0/0
```

- Notice that every route is preceded by a P. This means the route is in the *passive state*, which is good because routes in the *active state (A)* indicate that the router has lost its path to this network and is searching for a replacement. Each entry also indicates the FD to each remote network plus the next-hop neighbor through which packets will travel to their destinations. In addition, each entry also has two numbers in parentheses. The first indicates the feasible distance, and the second indicates the advertised distance to a remote network.

```
Corp#debug eigrp packet
EIGRP Packets debugging is on
    (UPDATE, REQUEST, QUERY, REPLY, HELLO, IPXSAP, PROBE, ACK, STUB, SIAQUERY,
SIAREPLY)
Corp#
*Mar 21 23:17:35.050: EIGRP: Sending HELLO on FastEthernet0/1
*Mar 21 23:17:35.050:   AS 10, Flags 0x0, Seq 0/0 idbQ 0/0 iidbQ un/rely 0/0
*Mar 21 23:17:35.270: EIGRP: Received HELLO on Serial0/1/0 nbr 10.1.4.2
*Mar 21 23:17:35.270:   AS 10, Flags 0x0, Seq 0/0 idbQ 0/0 iidbQ un/rely 0/0
peerQ un/rely 0/0
*Mar 21 23:17:35.294: EIGRP: Received HELLO on Serial0/0/0 nbr 10.1.2.2
```

```
*Mar 21 23:17:35.294:    AS 10, Flags 0x0, Seq 0/0 idbQ 0/0 iidbQ un/rely 0/0
peerQ un/rely 0/0
 *Mar 21 23:17:38.014: EIGRP: Received HELLO on Serial0/2/0 nbr 10.1.5.2
*Mar 21 23:17:38.014:    AS 10, Flags 0x0, Seq 0/0 idbQ 0/0 iidbQ un/rely 0/0
peerQ un/rely 0/0
```

- Since my Corp router is connected to three EIGRP neighbors and because the 224.0.0.10 multicast is sent out every five seconds, I didn't have any problem seeing the updates. The hello packets are sent out every active interface, as well as all the interfaces to which I have neighbors connected. Did you notice the AS number is provided in the update? This is because if a neighbor doesn't have the same AS number, the hello update would just be discarded.

I'll now show you one more important debugging command—the debug ip eigrp notification command (called debug ip eigrp events on pre-12.4 routers), plus the resulting output. The only time you'll see output from this command is if there's a problem on your network or you you've added or deleted a network from a router in your internetwork, which I demonstrate here by shutting down an interface on thr Corp router.

```
Corp(config)#int f0/1
Corp(config-if)#shut
*Mar 21 23:25:43.506: IP-EIGRP(Default-IP-Routing-Table:10): Callback: route_
adjust FastEthernet0/1
*Mar 21 23:25:43.506: IP-EIGRP: Callback: ignored connected AS 0 10.1.1.0/24
*Mar 21 23:25:43.506:              into: eigrp AS 10
*Mar 21 23:25:43.506: IP-EIGRP(Default-IP-Routing-Table:10): Callback:
callbackup_routes 10.1.1.0/24
Corp(config-if)#n
*Mar 21 23:25:45.506: %LINK-5-CHANGED: Interface FastEthernet0/1, changed state
to administratively down
*Mar 21 23:25:46.506: %LINEPROTO-5-UPDOWN: Line protocol on Interface
FastEthernet0/1, changed state to down
Corp(config-if)#no shut
Corp(config-if)#^Z
*Mar 21 23:25:49.570: %LINK-3-UPDOWN: Interface FastEthernet0/1, changed state
to up
*Mar 21 23:25:49.570: IP-EIGRP(Default-IP-Routing-Table:10): Callback: lostroute
10.1.1.0/24
*Mar 21 23:25:49.570: IP-EIGRP(Default-IP-Routing-Table:0): Callback: redist
connected (config change) FastEthernet0/1
*Mar 21 23:25:49.570: IP-EIGRP(Default-IP-Routing-Table:0): Callback: redist
connected (config change) Serial0/0/0
*Mar 21 23:25:49.570: IP-EIGRP(Default-IP-Routing-Table:0): Callback: redist
connected (config change) Serial0/0/1
*Mar 21 23:25:49.570: IP-EIGRP(Default-IP-Routing-Table:0): Callback: redist
connected (config change) Serial0/1/0
```

```
*Mar 21 23:25:49.570: IP-EIGRP(Default-IP-Routing-Table:0): Callback: redist
connected (config change) Serial0/2/0
*Mar 21 23:25:49.570: IP-EIGRP(Default-IP-Routing-Table:10): Callback: route_
adjust FastEthernet0/1
*Mar 21 23:25:50.570: %LINEPROTO-5-UPDOWN: Line protocol on Interface
FastEthernet0/1, changed state to up
```

Understanding Open Shortest Path First (OSPF) Basics

Open Shortest Path First (OSPF) is an open standards routing protocol that has been implemented by a wide variety of network vendors, including Cisco.

This works by using the Dijkstra algorithm. First a shortest path tree is constructed, and then the routing table is populated with the resulting best paths. OSPF converges quickly, although perhaps not as quickly as EIGRP, and it supports multiple, equal-cost routes to the same destination. Like EIGRP, it does support both IP and IPv6 routed protocols.

OSPF provides the following features:

- Consists of areas and autonomous systems
- Minimizes routing update traffic
- Allows scalability
- Supports VLSM/CIDR
- Has unlimited hop count
- Allows multivendor deployment (open standard)

Table 4.9 describes the characteristics of the RIP and OSPF protocols discussed thus far.

TABLE 4.9   Protocol Characteristics

Characteristic	OSPF	RIPv2	RIPv1
Type of protocol	Link-state	Distance Vector	Distance-vector
Classless support	Yes	Yes	No
VLSM support	Yes	Yes	No
Auto summarization	No	Yes	Yes
Manual summarization	Yes	No	No

Characteristic	OSPF	RIPv2	RIPv1
Discontiguous support	Yes	Yes	No
Route propagation	Multicast on change	Periodic multicast	Periodic broadcast
Path metric	Bandwidth	Hops	Hops
Hop count limit	None	15	15
Convergence	Fast	Slow	Slow
Peer authentication	Yes	Yes	No
Hierarchical network	Yes (using areas)	No (flat only)	No (flat only)
Updates	Event triggered	Route table updates	Route table updates
Route computation	Dijkstra	Bellman-Ford	Bellman-Ford

OSPF is supposed to be designed in a hierarchical fashion, which basically means you can separate the larger internetwork into smaller internetworks called *areas*. This is the best design for OSPF.

The reasons for creating OSPF in a hierarchical design include the following:

- To decrease routing overhead
- To speed up convergence
- To confine network instability to single areas of the network

Configuring OSPF

Configuring basic OSPF isn't as simple as RIP, and EIGRP, and it can get really complex once you factor in the many options that are allowed within OSPF.

These two elements are the basic elements of OSPF configuration:

- Enabling OSPF
- Configuring OSPF areas

Enabling OSPF

The easiest and also least scalable way to configure OSPF is to use just a single area. Doing this requires a minimum of two commands.

The command you use to activate the OSPF routing process is as follows:

```
Lab_A(config)#router ospf ?
<1-65535>
```

A value in the range 1–65,535 identifies the OSPF process ID. It's a unique number on this router that groups a series of OSPF configuration commands under a specific running process. Different OSPF routers don't have to use the same process ID in order to communicate. It's purely a local value that essentially has little meaning, but it cannot start at 0. It has to start at a minimum of 1.

Configuring OSPF Areas

After identifying the OSPF process, you need to identify the interfaces that you want to activate OSPF communications on, as well as the area in which each resides. This will also configure the networks you're going to advertise to others. OSPF uses wildcards in the configuration.

Here's an OSPF basic configuration example for you:

```
Lab_A#config t
Lab_A(config)#router ospf 1
Lab_A(config-router)#network 10.0.0.0 0.255.255.255
 area ?
  <0-4294967295>  OSPF area ID as a decimal value
  A.B.C.D         OSPF area ID in IP address format
Lab_A(config-router)#network 10.0.0.0 0.255.255.255
 area 0
```

> EIGRP can also be configured with wildcards as I demonstrated with OSPF, however, this is not common in a small to medium sized network.

Verifying OSPF Configuration

There are several ways to verify proper OSPF configuration and operation, and in the following sections I'll show you the OSPF show commands you need to know in order to do this. I'll start by showing the routing table of the Corp router. Here in Table 4.10 are the commands we'll use to verify OSPF.

TABLE 4.10   Verifying OSPF

Command	Meaning
show ip route	Displays the router's routing table
show ip ospf	Displays OSPF information for one or all OSPF processes running on the router
show ip ospf database	Shows the topological database used in OSPF
show ip ospf interface	Displays all interface-related OSPF information
show ip ospf neighbor	Summarizes the pertinent OSPF information regarding neighbors and the adjacency state
show ip ospf protocols	Shows routing protocol information

So, let's issue a show ip route command on the Corp router:

```
   10.0.0.0/24 is subnetted, 12 subnets
O       10.1.11.0 [110/65] via 10.1.5.2, 00:01:31, Serial0/2/0
O       10.1.10.0 [110/65] via 10.1.5.2, 00:01:31, Serial0/2/0
O       10.1.9.0 [110/74] via 10.1.4.2, 00:01:31, Serial0/1/0
O       10.1.8.0 [110/65] via 10.1.4.2, 00:01:31, Serial0/1/0
O       10.1.12.0 [110/66] via 10.1.5.2, 00:01:31, Serial0/2/0
C       10.1.3.0 is directly connected, Serial0/0/1
C       10.1.2.0 is directly connected, Serial0/0/0
C       10.1.1.0 is directly connected, FastEthernet0/1
O       10.1.7.0 [110/74] via 10.1.3.2, 00:01:32, Serial0/0/1
                 [110/74] via 10.1.2.2, 00:01:32, Serial0/0/0
O       10.1.6.0 [110/74] via 10.1.3.2, 00:01:32, Serial0/0/1
                 [110/74] via 10.1.2.2, 00:01:32, Serial0/0/0
C       10.1.5.0 is directly connected, Serial0/2/0
C       10.1.4.0 is directly connected, Serial0/1/0
```

The Corp router shows the found routes for all 12 networks, with the O representing OSPF internal routes (the Cs are obviously the directly connected networks). It also found the dual routes to networks 10.1.6.0 and 10.1.7.0. OSPF uses bandwidth only to determine the best path to a network.

Using the *show ip ospf* Command

You can use the show ip ospf command to display OSPF information for one or all OSPF processes running on the router. Information contained therein includes the router ID, area information, SPF statistics, and LSA timer information. Here's the output from the Corp router:

```
Corp#sh ip ospf
 Routing Process "ospf 132" with ID 10.1.5.1
 Start time: 04:32:04.116, Time elapsed: 01:27:10.156
 Supports only single TOS(TOS0) routes
 Supports opaque LSA
 Supports Link-local Signaling (LLS)
 Supports area transit capability
 Router is not originating router-LSAs with maximum metric
 Initial SPF schedule delay 5000 msecs
 Minimum hold time between two consecutive SPFs 10000 msecs
 Maximum wait time between two consecutive SPFs 10000 msecs
 Incremental-SPF disabled
 Minimum LSA interval 5 secs
 Minimum LSA arrival 1000 msecs
 LSA group pacing timer 240 secs
 Interface flood pacing timer 33 msecs
 Retransmission pacing timer 66 msecs
 Number of external LSA 0. Checksum Sum 0x000000
 Number of opaque AS LSA 0. Checksum Sum 0x000000
 Number of DCbitless external and opaque AS LSA 0
 Number of DoNotAge external and opaque AS LSA 0
 Number of areas in this router is 1. 1 normal 0 stub 0 nssa
 Number of areas transit capable is 0
 External flood list length 0
    Area BACKBONE(0)
        Number of interfaces in this area is 5
        Area has no authentication
        SPF algorithm last executed 00:14:52.220 ago
        SPF algorithm executed 14 times
        Area ranges are
        Number of LSA 6. Checksum Sum 0x03C06F
        Number of opaque link LSA 0. Checksum Sum 0x000000
        Number of DCbitless LSA 0
        Number of indication LSA 0
```

```
        Number of DoNotAge LSA 0
        Flood list length 0
```

Notice the router ID (RID) of 10.1.5.1, which is the highest IP address configured on the router.

Using the *show ip ospf database* Command

Using the show ip ospf database command will give you information about the number of routers in the internetwork (AS) plus the neighboring router's ID, and it is the topology database I mentioned earlier. Unlike the show ip eigrp topogogy command, this command shows the OSPF routers, not each and every link in the AS like EIGRP does.

The output is broken down by area. Here's some sample output, again from Corp:

```
Corp#sh ip ospf database

            OSPF Router with ID (10.1.5.1) (Process ID 132)

            Router Link States (Area 0)

Link ID         ADV Router      Age       Seq#       Checksum Link count
10.1.5.1        10.1.5.1        72        0x80000002 0x00F2CA 9
10.1.7.1        10.1.7.1        83        0x80000004 0x009197 6
10.1.9.1        10.1.9.1        73        0x80000001 0x00DA1C 4
10.1.11.1       10.1.11.1       67        0x80000005 0x00666A 4
10.1.12.1       10.1.12.1       67        0x80000004 0x007631 2

            Net Link States (Area 0)

Link ID         ADV Router      Age       Seq#       Checksum
10.1.11.2       10.1.12.1       68        0x80000001 0x00A337
```

You can see all five routers and the RID of each router (the highest IP address on each router). The router output shows the link ID—remember that an interface is also a link—and the RID of the router on that link under the ADV router (or *advertising* router).

Using the *show ip ospf interface* Command

The show ip ospf interface command displays all interface-related OSPF information. Data is displayed about OSPF information for all interfaces or for specified interfaces:

```
Corp#sh ip ospf interface f0/1
FastEthernet0/1 is up, line protocol is up
```

```
Internet Address 10.1.1.1/24, Area 0
Process ID 132, Router ID 10.1.5.1, Network Type BROADCAST, Cost: 1
Transmit Delay is 1 sec, State DR, Priority 1
Designated Router (ID) 10.1.5.1, Interface address 10.1.1.1
No backup designated router on this network
Timer intervals configured, Hello 10, Dead 40, Wait 40, Retransmit 5
  oob-resync timeout 40
  Hello due in 00:00:01
Supports Link-local Signaling (LLS)
Index 1/1, flood queue length 0
Next 0x0(0)/0x0(0)
Last flood scan length is 0, maximum is 0
Last flood scan time is 0 msec, maximum is 0 msec
Neighbor Count is 0, Adjacent neighbor count is 0
Suppress hello for 0 neighbor(s)
```

The information displayed by this command includes the following:

- Interface IP address
- Area assignment
- Process ID
- Router ID
- Network type
- Cost
- Priority
- DR/BDR election information (if applicable)
- Hello and dead timer intervals
- Adjacent neighbor information

The reason I used the show ip ospf interface f0/1 command is because I knew that there would be a designated router elected on the FastEthernet broadcast multiaccess network.

Using the *show ip ospf neighbor* Command

The show ip ospf neighbor command is really useful because it summarizes the pertinent OSPF information regarding neighbors and the adjacency state. If a DR or BDR exists, that information will also be displayed. Here's a sample:

```
Corp#sh ip ospf neighbor
Neighbor ID  Pri  State   Dead Time    Address     Interface
10.1.11.1     0   FULL/ - 00:00:37     10.1.5.2    Serial0/2/0
```

```
10.1.9.1      0   FULL/  - 00:00:34   10.1.4.2    Serial0/1/0
10.1.7.1      0   FULL/  - 00:00:38   10.1.3.2    Serial0/0/1
10.1.7.1      0   FULL/  - 00:00:34   10.1.2.2    Serial0/0/0
```

This is an important command to understand because it's extremely useful in production networks! Here are the R3 and 871W routers' outputs:

```
R3#sh ip ospf neighbor
Neighbor ID Pri  State   Dead Time    Address      Interface
10.1.5.1      0   FULL/  - 00:00:39   10.1.5.1    Serial0/0/1
10.1.11.2     1   FULL/BDR 00:00:31   10.1.11.2   FastEthernet0/1
871W#sh ip ospf nei
Neighbor ID  Pri  State   Dead Time    Address      Interface
10.1.11.1     1   FULL/DR  00:00:30   10.1.11.1    Vlan1
```

Since there's an Ethernet link (broadcast multiaccess) on the Corp router, there's going to be an election to determine which router will be the designated router and which router will be the nondesignated router. You can see that the 871W became the designate router, and it won because it had the highest IP address on the network. You can change this, but that's the default.

The reason that the Corp connections to R1, R2, and R3 don't have a DR or BDR listed in the output is that by default elections don't happen on point-to-point links. But you can see that the Corp router is fully adjacent to all three routers (and on both connections to R1) from its output.

Using the *show ip protocols* Command

The show ip protocols command is also useful whether you're running OSPF, EIGRP, IGRP, RIP, BGP, IS-IS, or any other routing protocol that can be configured on your router. It provides an excellent overview of the actual operation of all currently running protocols.

Check out the output from the Corp router:

```
Corp#sh ip protocols
Routing Protocol is "ospf 132"
  Outgoing update filter list for all interfaces is not set
  Incoming update filter list for all interfaces is not set
  Router ID 10.1.5.1
  Number of areas in this router is 1. 1 normal 0 stub 0 nssa
  Maximum path: 4
  Routing for Networks:
    10.1.1.1 0.0.0.0 area 0
    10.1.2.1 0.0.0.0 area 0
    10.1.3.1 0.0.0.0 area 0
```

```
    10.1.4.1 0.0.0.0 area 0
    10.1.5.1 0.0.0.0 area 0
Reference bandwidth unit is 100 mbps
 Routing Information Sources:
    Gateway          Distance        Last Update
    10.1.11.1             110        00:28:53
    10.1.11.2             110        00:28:53
    10.1.9.1              110        00:28:53
    10.1.7.1              110        00:28:53
 Distance: (default is 110)
```

Checking out this output, you can determine the OSPF process ID, OSPF router ID, type of OSPF area, networks and areas configured for OSPF, and the OSPF router IDs of neighbors—that's a lot. Read, that's efficient! And hold on a second. Did you notice the absence of timers like the ones you saw earlier in the RIP outputs from this command? That's because Link State routing protocols don't use timers to keep the network stable like Distance Vector routing algorithms do.

Debugging OSPF

Debugging is a great tool for any protocol, so let's take a look at Table 4.11 and a few debugging commands for troubleshooting OSPF:

TABLE 4.11 Debugging OSPF

Command	Meaning
debug ip ospf packet	Shows hello packets being sent and received on your router.
debug ip ospf hello	Shows hello packets being sent and received on your router. Shows more detail than the debug ip ospf packet output.
debug ip ospf adj	Shows DR and DBR elections on a broadcast and non-broadcast multiaccess network.

I'll start by showing you the output from the Corp router I got using the debug ip ospf packet command:

```
Corp#debug ip ospf packet
OSPF packet debugging is on
*Mar 23 01:20:42.199: OSPF: rcv. v:2 t:1 l:48 rid:172.16.10.3
    aid:0.0.0.0 chk:8075 aut:0 auk: from Serial0/1/0
```

```
Corp#
*Mar 23 01:20:45.507: OSPF: rcv. v:2 t:1 l:48 rid:172.16.10.2
     aid:0.0.0.0 chk:8076 aut:0 auk: from Serial0/0/0
*Mar 23 01:20:45.531: OSPF: rcv. v:2 t:1 l:48 rid:172.16.10.2
     aid:0.0.0.0 chk:8076 aut:0 auk: from Serial0/0/1
*Mar 23 01:20:45.531: OSPF: rcv. v:2 t:1 l:48 rid:172.16.10.4
     aid:0.0.0.0 chk:8074 aut:0 auk: from Serial0/2/0
*Mar 23 01:20:52.199: OSPF: rcv. v:2 t:1 l:48 rid:172.16.10.3
     aid:0.0.0.0 chk:8075 aut:0 auk: from Serial0/1/0
*Mar 23 01:20:55.507: OSPF: rcv. v:2 t:1 l:48 rid:172.16.10.2
     aid:0.0.0.0 chk:8076 aut:0 auk: from Serial0/0/0
*Mar 23 01:20:55.527: OSPF: rcv. v:2 t:1 l:48 rid:172.16.10.2
     aid:0.0.0.0 chk:8076 aut:0 auk: from Serial0/0/1
*Mar 23 01:20:55.531: OSPF: rcv. v:2 t:1 l:48 rid:172.16.10.4
     aid:0.0.0.0 chk:8074 aut:0 auk: from Serial0/2/0
```

In the previous output, you can see that the router is both sending and receiving hello packets every 10 seconds from neighbor (adjacent) routers. The next command will provide you with the same information but with more detail. For example, you can see the multicast address used (224.0.0.5) and the area:

```
Corp#debug ip ospf hello
*Mar 23 01:18:41.103: OSPF: Send hello to 224.0.0.5 area 0 on Serial0/1/0 from
10.1.4.1
*Mar 23 01:18:41.607: OSPF: Send hello to 224.0.0.5 area 0 on FastEthernet0/1
from 10.1.1.1
*Mar 23 01:18:41.607: OSPF: Send hello to 224.0.0.5 area 0 on Serial0/0/0 from
10.1.2.1
*Mar 23 01:18:41.611: OSPF: Send hello to 224.0.0.5 area 0 on Serial0/2/0 from
10.1.5.1
*Mar 23 01:18:41.611: OSPF: Send hello to 224.0.0.5 area 0 on Serial0/0/1 from
10.1.3.1
*Mar 23 01:18:42.199: OSPF: Rcv hello from 172.16.10.3 area 0 from Serial0/1/0
10.1.4.2
*Mar 23 01:18:42.199: OSPF: End of hello processing
*Mar 23 01:18:45.519: OSPF: Rcv hello from 172.16.10.2 area 0 from Serial0/0/0
10.1.2.2
*Mar 23 01:18:45.519: OSPF: End of hello processing
*Mar 23 01:18:45.543: OSPF: Rcv hello from 172.16.10.2 area 0 from Serial0/0/1
10.1.3.2
*Mar 23 01:18:45.543: OSPF: End of hello processing
*Mar 23 01:18:45.543: OSPF: Rcv hello from 172.16.10.4 area 0 from Serial0/2/0
10.1.5.2
*Mar 23 01:18:45.543: OSPF: End of hello processing
```

The last debug command I'll show you is the debug ip ospf adj command, which will show you elections as they occur on broadcast and nonbroadcast multiaccess networks:

```
Corp#debug ip ospf adj
OSPF adjacency events debugging is on
*Mar 23 01:24:34.823: OSPF: Interface FastEthernet0/1 going Down
*Mar 23 01:24:34.823: OSPF: 172.16.10.1 address 10.1.1.1 on FastEthernet0/1 is
dead, state DOWN
*Mar 23 01:24:34.823: OSPF: Neighbor change Event on interface FastEthernet0/1
*Mar 23 01:24:34.823: OSPF: DR/BDR election on FastEthernet0/1
*Mar 23 01:24:34.823: OSPF: Elect BDR 0.0.0.0
*Mar 23 01:24:34.823: OSPF: Elect DR 0.0.0.0
*Mar 23 01:24:34.823: OSPF: Elect BDR 0.0.0.0
*Mar 23 01:24:34.823: OSPF: Elect DR 0.0.0.0
*Mar 23 01:24:34.823:         DR: none    BDR: none
*Mar 23 01:24:34.823: OSPF: Flush network LSA immediately
*Mar 23 01:24:34.823: OSPF: Remember old DR 172.16.10.1 (id)
*Mar 23 01:24:35.323: OSPF: We are not DR to build Net Lsa for interface
FastEthernet0/1
*Mar 23 01:24:35.323: OSPF: Build router LSA for area 0, router ID 172.16.10.1,
seq 0x80000006
*Mar 23 01:24:35.347: OSPF: Rcv LS UPD from 172.16.10.2 on Serial0/0/1 length
148 LSA count 1
*Mar 23 01:24:40.703: OSPF: Interface FastEthernet0/1 going Up
*Mar 23 01:24:41.203: OSPF: Build router LSA for area 0, router ID 172.16.10.1,
seq 0x80000007
*Mar 23 01:24:41.231: OSPF: Rcv LS UPD from 172.16.10.2 on Serial0/0/1 length
160 LSA count 1
```

Chapter 5

Layer-2 Switching and Spanning-Tree Protocol (STP)

When Cisco discusses switching, it's talking about layer-2 switching unless otherwise mentioned. *Layer-2 switching* is the process of using the hardware address of devices on a LAN to segment a network. In this chapter I'll focus on the particulars of layer-2 switching so you can understand how it works.

OK, you know that switching breaks up large collision domains into smaller ones and that a collision domain is a network segment with two or more devices sharing the same bandwidth. A hub network is a typical example of this type of technology. But since each port on a switch is actually its own collision domain, you can make a much better Ethernet LAN network just by replacing your hubs with switches!

Routing protocols have processes for stopping network loops from occurring at the Network layer. However, if you have redundant physical links between your switches, routing protocols won't do a thing to stop loops from occurring at the Data Link layer. That's exactly the reason Spanning-Tree Protocol was developed—to put a stop to loops in a layer-2 switched network.

For up-to-the minute updates for this chapter, please see www.lammle.com.

Switching Services

Unlike bridges, which use software to create and manage filter tables, switches use application-specific integrated circuits (ASICs) to build and maintain their filter tables. But it's still OK to think of a layer-2 switch as a multiport bridge because their basic purpose is the same: to break up collision domains.

Layer-2 switches and bridges are faster than routers because they don't take up time looking at the Network layer header information. Instead, they look at the frame's hardware addresses before deciding to either forward the frame or flood it.

Switches create private dedicated collision domains and provide independent bandwidth on each port, unlike hubs.

Layer 2 switching provides the following:

- Hardware-based bridging (ASIC)
- Wire speed
- Low latency
- Low cost

Three Switch Functions at Layer 2

Table 5.1 describes the three distinct functions of layer-2 switching (you need to remember these!).

TABLE 5.1   Functions of Layer-2 Switching

Function	Meaning
Address learning	Layer-2 switches and bridges remember the source hardware address of each frame received on an interface, and they enter this information into a MAC database called a *forward/filter table*.
Forward/filter decisions	When a frame is received on an interface, the switch looks at the destination hardware address and finds the exit interface in the MAC database. The frame is forwarded out the specified destination port only.
Loop avoidance	If multiple connections between switches are created for redundancy purposes, network loops can occur. Spanning-Tree Protocol is used to stop network loops while still permitting redundancy.

Now I'll show the output of a show mac address-table command. The MAC table, as it is often called, will display the hardware addresses that the switch has learned. From this table the forwarding decisions are also made.

The following command in Table 5.2 is used to display the forward/filter table on a switch:

TABLE 5.2   Command and Meaning

Command	Meaning
show mac address-table	Displays the cache table of learned hardware addresses

Here is the output for the sh mac address-table command:

```
Switch#sh mac address-table
Vlan    Mac Address      Type        Ports
----    -----------      --------    -----
   1    0005.dccb.d74b   DYNAMIC     Fa0/1
   1    000a.f467.9e80   DYNAMIC     Fa0/3
   1    000a.f467.9e8b   DYNAMIC     Fa0/4
   1    000a.f467.9e8c   DYNAMIC     Fa0/3
   1    0010.7b7f.c2b0   DYNAMIC     Fa0/3
   1    0030.80dc.460b   DYNAMIC     Fa0/3
   1    0030.9492.a5dd   DYNAMIC     Fa0/1
   1    00d0.58ad.05f4   DYNAMIC     Fa0/1
```

Basic Switch Configurations

Slightly different from configuring an interface on a router is configuring a switch to talk on the network. Remember, a switch operates at layer 2, and therefore its layer-2 ports do not get IP addresses. The only layer-3 function a switch has is a VLAN, so that is where you'll configure its IP address. For the switch to communicate with a device that is not on the same subnet, it will also have to know where to find a router. You configure the switch with a default gateway (much like a host) for this reason. Here in Table 5.3 are the commands you need:

TABLE 5.3   Command and Meaning

Command	Meaning
enable	Takes you to privileged mode
config t	Takes you to global configuration mode
interface vlan	Enters VLAN configuration mode to configure parameters such as the IP address and mask
ip default-gateway	Configures a default gateway on a switch

Remember, you do not need an IP address on a switch, but here is an example of setting an IP address, mask and default-gateway on a switch:

```
Core>enable
Core#config t
Core(config)#int vlan 1
Core(config-if)#ip address 192.168.10.19 255.255.255.240
```

```
Core(config-if)#no shut

Core#config t
Core(config)#ip default-gateway 192.168.10.30
Core(config)#exit
Core#
```

Switch Security

So, just how do you stop someone from simply plugging a host into one of your switch ports—or worse, adding a hub, switch, or access point into the Ethernet jack in their office? By default, MAC addresses will just dynamically appear in your MAC forward/filter database. You can stop them in their tracks by using port security by using the following command from Table 5.4:

TABLE 5.4   Command and Meaning

Command	Meaning
switchport port-security	Configures access control of a switch port

To enable port security on a switch port, use the following:

```
Switch#config t
Switch(config)#int f0/1
Switch(config-if)#switchport port-security
```

Table 5.5 lists your options for the switchport port-security command.

TABLE 5.5   Options for *switchport port-security*

Options	Meaning
aging	Configures a timer for dynamically learned addresses to decay out of the cache.
mac-address	Configures a statically assigned secure hardware address for a given ports table.
maximum	Configures a max number of secure addresses for a given port.
violation	Configures an action should a violation on the port occur. There are three violation modes: protect, restrict, and shutdown.

Here is an example of setting port security on a switch port:

```
Switch#config t
Switch(config)#int f0/1
Switch(config-if)#switchport port-security ?
        aging           Port-security aging commands
        mac-address     Secure mac address
        maximum         Max secure addresses
        violation       Security violation mode
        <cr>
```

If you want to set up a switch port to allow only one host per port and shut down the port if this rule is violated, use the following commands:

```
Switch#config t
Switch(config)#int f0/1
Switch(config-if)#switchport port-security maximum 1
Switch(config-if)#switchport port-security violation shutdown
```

These commands are probably the most popular because they prevent users from connecting to a switch or access point into their office. A maximum of 1 means only one MAC address can be used on that port, and if the user tries to add another host on that segment, the switch port will then shut down. If that happens, you'd have to manually go into the switch and enable the port with a no shutdown command.

Probably one of my favorite commands is the sticky command. Not only does it perform a cool function, but it has a cool name! You can find this command under the mac-address command:

```
Switch(config-if)#switchport port-security mac-address sticky
Switch(config-if)#switchport port-security maximum 2
Switch(config-if)#switchport port-security violation shutdown
```

Basically, this provides static MAC address security without having to type in everyone's MAC address on the network!

Assigning Static MAC Addresses

If you use static mac-address assignments on every switch port, I hope you like to type a lot. If you do, Table 5.6 shows you how to do it.

TABLE 5.6   Command and Meaning

Command	Meaning
mac-address-table static *mac_ address* vlan *vlan-id* {drop | interface {*type slot/port*} | port- channel *number*} [auto-learn]	Sets a static MAC address on a switch inter- face. If you enable the auto-learn option, the switch will update the entry if the same MAC address is seen on a different port.

You can set a static MAC address in the MAC address table, but like setting static MAC port security, it's a ton of work. But in case you want to do it, here's how it's done:

```
S1#config t
S1(config)#mac-address-table static aaaa.bbbb.cccc vlan 1 int fa0/5
S1(config)#do show mac address-table
          Mac Address Table
-------------------------------------------

Vlan    Mac Address      Type       Ports
----    -----------      --------   -----
 All    0100.0ccc.cccc   STATIC     CPU
[output cut]
  1     0002.1762.b235   DYNAMIC    Po1
  1     0009.b79f.c080   DYNAMIC    Po1
  1     000d.29bd.4b87   DYNAMIC    Po1
  1     000d.29bd.4b88   DYNAMIC    Po1
  1     0016.4662.52b4   DYNAMIC    Fa0/4
  1     0016.4677.5eab   DYNAMIC    Po1
  1     001a.2f52.49d8   DYNAMIC    Po1
  1     001a.2fe7.4170   DYNAMIC    Fa0/8
  1     001a.e2ce.ff40   DYNAMIC    Po1
  1     0050.0f02.642a   DYNAMIC    Fa0/3
  1     aaaa.bbbb.cccc   STATIC     Fa0/5
Total Mac Addresses for this criterion: 31
S1(config)#
```

Here you can see that a static MAC address is now assigned permanently to interface fa0/5 and that it's also assigned to VLAN 1 only.

Spanning-Tree Operations

Spanning-Tree Protocol (STP) allows a switch to perform its third function, loop avoidance. Its job is to find all links in the network and shut down any redundant ones, thereby preventing network loops from occurring.

Let's look at changing the priority to force a switch to become the root of your STP network. Use the following command in Table 5.7 to change the bridge priority on a Catalyst switch:

TABLE 5.7   Command and Meaning

Command	Meaning
spanning-tree	Configures Spanning-Tree Protocol options

Table 5.8 shows the options for the spanning-tree command.

TABLE 5.8   Options for *spanning-tree*

Option	Meaning
spanning-tree vlan *vlan-id* [forward-time seconds | hello-time *seconds* | max-age seconds | priority *priority* | protocol *protocol* | [root {primary | secondary}	Configures a switch VLAN to have a specific STP priority
show spanning-tree	Shows the spanning-tree configuration for each VLAN

You need to set the priority per-vlan, as shown here:

```
Switch B(config)#spanning-tree vlan 1 priority ?
  <0-61440>  bridge priority in increments of 4096
Switch B(config)#spanning-tree vlan 1 priority 4096
```

You can set the priority to any value from 0 through 61440. Setting it to zero (0) means the switch will always be the root, and the highest setting means it never will. The bridge priority is set in increments of 4096. If you want to set a switch to be the root bridge for every VLAN in your network, then you have to change the priority for each VLAN.

Check out the following output—now that I've changed the priority of Switch B for VLAN 1 to the lowest possible priority, I've successfully forced this switch to become the root:

```
SwitchB#show spanning-tree
VLAN0001
  Spanning tree enabled protocol ieee
  Root ID    Priority    4097
             Address     0012.7f52.0280
             This bridge is the root
             Hello Time   2 sec  Max Age 20 sec  Forward Delay 15 sec
```

```
 Bridge ID  Priority    4097   (priority 4096 sys-id-ext 1)
            Address     0012.7f52.0280
            Hello Time   2 sec  Max Age 20 sec  Forward Delay 15 sec
            Aging Time 15
[output cut]
```

Optimizing Spanning-Tree Operations

There are a couple of enhancements that have been made to the original STP standard. A few of these started out as Cisco proprietary features and then later were changed and made into the new version of STP called *Rapid STP* (RSTP).

Table 5.9 lists the options, which are pretty simple.

TABLE 5.9   Options for RSTP

Option	Meaning
portfast	Configures a switch port to immediately transition to forwarding and not wait for the STP timer
interface range	Allows you to choose a range of interfaces to configure
bpdufilter	Filters BPDUs from entering a switch port
bpduguard	Shuts down a switch port if it receives a BPDU
uplinkfast	Configures spanning tree to find and maintain a secondary link to the root bridge
backbonefast	Configures spanning tree to maintain an alternate path to the root bridge in case there is an indirect link failure.
mode	Configures the spanning tree mode to either MST, PVST, or rapid-pvst

Spanning-Tree PortFast

If you have a server or other devices connected into your switch that you're totally sure won't create a switching loop if STP is disabled, you can use something called PortFast on these ports. Using it means the port won't spend the usual 50 seconds to come up into forwarding mode while STP is converging.

```
Switch(config-if)#spanning-tree portfast ?
  disable  Disable portfast for this interface
```

```
    trunk    Enable portfast on the interface even in trunk mode
    <cr>
```

Let's take a look at the message I get when I turn PortFast on an interface:

```
Switch(config-if)#spanning-tree portfast
%Warning: portfast should only be enabled on ports connected to a
    single host. Connecting hubs, concentrators, switches, bridges,
    etc... to this interface  when portfast is enabled, can cause
    temporary bridging loops.
 Use with CAUTION
%Portfast has been configured on FastEthernet0/1 but will only
 have effect when the interface is in a non-trunking mode.
Switch(config-if)#
```

Interface Range

A helpful interface command is the range command; you can use it on switches to help you configure multiple ports at the same time. Here's an example that allows you to configure 12 interfaces at one time!

```
Switch(config)#int range fastEthernet 0/1 - 12
Switch(config-if-range)#spanning-tree portfast
```

BPDUFilter

Another helpful command to use with PortFast is BPDUFilter. Since a switch port that has PortFast enabled will still receive BPDUs by default, you can use the BPDUFilter to stop BPDUs coming into that port completely. BPDU filtering not only blocks just the BPDUs, but it takes the port out of PortFast status and forces the port to be a part of the STP topology again.

```
S1(config-if-range)#spanning-tree bpdufilter ?
  disable  Disable BPDU filtering for this interface
  enable   Enable BPDU filtering for this interface
S1(config-if-range)#spanning-tree bpdufilter enable
```

BPDUGuard

I talked about this a bit earlier—if you turn on PortFast for a switch port, turning on BPDUGuard is a really good idea. If a switch port that has PortFast enabled receives a BPDU on that port, it will shut that port down and put it into an error-disabled state.

```
S1(config-if-range)#spanning-tree bpduguard ?
  disable  Disable BPDU guard for this interface
```

```
  enable   Enable BPDU guard for this interface
S1(config-if-range)#spanning-tree bpduguard enable
```

UplinkFast

UplinkFast allows a switch to find alternate paths to the root bridge before the primary link fails. What this means is that if the primary link fails, the secondary link would come up more quickly—the port wouldn't wait for the normal STP convergence time of 50 seconds.

```
Switch(config)#spanning-tree uplinkfast ?
  max-update-rate  Rate at which station address updates are sent
  <cr>
UplinkFast is enabled

Station update rate set to 150 packets/sec.

UplinkFast statistics
-----------------------
Number of transitions via uplinkFast (all VLANs)         : 1
Number of proxy multicast addresses transmitted (all VLANs) : 8

Name                Interface List
------------------- -----------------------------------
VLAN0001            Fa0/1(fwd), Fa0/2
S1(config)#
```

The uplinkfast command is a global command, and it's enabled on every port.

BackboneFast

Unlike UplinkFast that's used to determine and quickly fix link failures on the local switch, another Cisco-propriety STP extension called BackboneFast is used for speeding up convergence when a link that's not directly connected to the switch fails. If a switch running BackboneFast receives an inferior BPDU (one that indicates a higher cost to the root) from its designated bridge (the bridge chosen as the path to the root for a particular segment), it knows that a link on the path to the root has failed. Once enabled on all switches of a bridge network, BackboneFast can save a switch up to 20 seconds (max_age) when it recovers from an indirect link failure.

```
Switch(config)#spanning-tree backbonefast ?
  <cr>
BackboneFast is enabled
```

```
BackboneFast statistics
-----------------------
Number of transition via backboneFast (all VLANs)        : 0
Number of inferior BPDUs received (all VLANs)            : 2
Number of RLQ request PDUs received (all VLANs)          : 0
Number of RLQ response PDUs received (all VLANs)         : 1
Number of RLQ request PDUs sent (all VLANs)              : 1
Number of RLQ response PDUs sent (all VLANs)             : 0
S2(config)#
```

RSTP (802.1w)

Configuring RSTP is as easy as it is for any of the other 802.1d extensions. Considering how much better it is than 802.1d, you'd think the configuration would be more complex, but you're in luck—it's not. So let's turn in on the Core switch now and see what happens:

```
Core#config t
Core(config)#spanning-tree mode ?
  mst         Multiple spanning tree mode
  pvst        Per-Vlan spanning tree mode
  rapid-pvst  Per-Vlan rapid spanning tree mode
Core(config)#spanning-tree mode rapid-pvst
Core(config)#
1d02h: %LINEPROTO-5-UPDOWN: Line protocol on Interface Vlan1, changed state to down
1d02h: %LINEPROTO-5-UPDOWN: Line protocol on Interface Vlan1, changed state to up
```

Sweet! The Core switch is now running the 802.1w STP. Let's verify that:

```
Core#show spanning-tree
VLAN0001
  Spanning tree enabled protocol rstp
  Root ID    Priority    32769
             Address     000d.29bd.4b80
             This bridge is the root
             Hello Time    2 sec  Max Age 20 sec  Forward Delay 15 sec

  Bridge ID  Priority    32769   (priority 32768 sys-id-ext 1)
             Address     000d.29bd.4b80
             Hello Time    2 sec  Max Age 20 sec  Forward Delay 15 sec
             Aging Time 300
```

```
Interface         Role Sts Cost      Prio.Nbr Type
----------------  ---- --- --------- -------- ------------
Fa0/5             Desg FWD 19         128.5    P2p Peer(STP)
Fa0/6             Desg FWD 19         128.6    P2p Peer(STP)
Fa0/7             Desg FWD 19         128.7    P2p Peer(STP)
Fa0/8             Desg FWD 19         128.8    P2p Peer(STP)
```

EtherChannel

There are two versions of EtherChannel, the Cisco version and the IEEE version. I'll show how to use the Cisco version in this section and bundle the links between the S1 switch and the Core.

PAgP

I'll use the interface port-channel global command and the channel-group and channel-protocol interface commands on the S1 and Core switches. Here (in Table 5.10) are the commands we'll use for etherchannel:

TABLE 5.10 PAgP Commands

Command	Meaning
interface port-channel	Configures the virtual port or interface that will serve as the new single-bundled interface
channel-group	Configures the virtual link that binds the physical interfaces to the virtual interface bundle
channel-protocol	Configures the EtherChannel protocol to be used

Here's what that looks like:

```
S1#config t
S1(config)#int port-channel 1
S1(config-if)#int range f0/1-2
S1(config-if-range)#switchport mode trunk
1d03h: %SPANTREE_FAST-7-PORT_FWD_UPLINK: VLAN0001 FastEthernet0/2 moved to
Forwarding (UplinkFast).
S1(config-if-range)#switchport nonegotiate
S1(config-if-range)#channel-group 1 mode desirable
S1(config-if-range)#do sh int fa0/1 etherchannel
Port state    = Up Sngl-port-Bndl Mstr Not-in-Bndl
```

```
Channel group = 1        Mode = Desirable-Sl    Gcchange = 0
Port-channel  = null     GC   = 0x00010001      Pseudo port-channel = Po1
Port index    = 0        Load = 0x00            Protocol =   PAgP
[output cut]
```

```
Core#config t
Core(config)#int port-channel 1
Core(config-if)#int range f0/7-8
Core(config-if-range)#switchport trunk encap dot1q
Core(config-if-range)#switchport mode trunk
1d03h: %SPANTREE_FAST-7-PORT_FWD_UPLINK: VLAN0001 FastEthernet0/2 moved to
Forwarding (UplinkFast).
Core(config-if-range)#switchport nonegotiate
Core(config-if-range)#channel-group 1 mode desirable
1d04h: %SPANTREE_FAST-7-PORT_FWD_UPLINK: VLAN0001 FastEthernet0/2 moved to
Forwarding (UplinkFast).
1d04h: %SPANTREE_FAST-7-PORT_FWD_UPLINK: VLAN0001 FastEthernet0/2 moved to
Forwarding (UplinkFast).
1d04h: %LINK-3-UPDOWN: Interface Port-channel1, changed state to up
1d04h: %LINEPROTO-5-UPDOWN: Line protocol on Interface Port-channel1, changed
state to up
Core(config-if-range)#do show int port-channel 1
Port-channel1 is up, line protocol is up (connected)
  Hardware is EtherChannel, address is 001b.2b55.7501 (bia 001b.2b55.7501)
  MTU 1500 bytes, BW 200000 Kbit, DLY 100 usec,
     reliability 255/255, txload 1/255, rxload 1/255
  Encapsulation ARPA, loopback not set
  Full-duplex, 100Mb/s, link type is auto, media type is unknown
[output cut]
```

I added the `switchport nonegotiate` interface command to stop the switches from trying to autodetect the link types and to automatically set up trunking. Instead, I statically configured my trunk links. The two links between the S1 and the Core are now bundled using the Cisco EtherChannel version of Port Aggregation Protocol (PAgP).

LACP

Link Aggregation Control Protocol (LACP) is an IEE 802.3ad standard. It use slightly different commands as shown in Table 5.11. When LACP is configured one end of the link is specified as active and the other as passive.

TABLE 5.11 Command and Meaning

Command	Meaning
interface range *interface*	Specifies the interfaces that will compose the Etherchannel group
channel-group *number* mode {active | passive}	Assigns the interface to a port channel group and sets the LACP mode

Verifying Cisco Catalyst Switches

Table 5.12 lists the most important basic commands you can use on a switch for verification purposes:

TABLE 5.12 Command and Meaning

Command	Meaning
show interface	Displays statistics for a given interface
show mac address-table	Displays the cache table of learned hardware addresses
show spanning-tree	Displays the spanning tree statistics, including information about the root bridge and port status

show interface

To verify the IP address set on a switch, you can use the show interface command. Here is the output:

```
S1#sh int vlan 1
Vlan1 is up, line protocol is up
   Hardware is EtherSVI, address is 001b.2b55.7540 (bia 001b.2b55.7540)
   Internet address is 192.168.10.17/28
   MTU 1500 bytes, BW 1000000 Kbit, DLY 10 usec,
      reliability 255/255, txload 1/255, rxload 1/255
   Encapsulation ARPA, loopback not set, reliability 255/255, txload 1/255,
rxload 1/255
   [output cut]
```

show mac address-table

I'm sure you remember being shown the show mac address-table command earlier in the chapter. Using it displays the forward filter table also called a *content addressable memory* (CAM) table. Here's the output from the S1 switch:

```
S1#sh mac address-table
        Mac Address Table
-------------------------------------------

Vlan    Mac Address      Type        Ports
----    -----------      --------    -----
 All    0100.0ccc.cccc   STATIC      CPU
 All    ffff.ffff.ffff   STATIC      CPU
[output cut]
   1    0002.1762.b235   DYNAMIC     Po1
   1    0009.b79f.c080   DYNAMIC     Po1
   1    000d.29bd.4b87   DYNAMIC     Po1
   1    000d.29bd.4b88   DYNAMIC     Po1
   1    0016.4662.52b4   DYNAMIC     Fa0/4
   1    0016.4677.5eab   DYNAMIC     Po1
   1    001a.2f52.49d8   DYNAMIC     Po1
   1    001a.2fe7.4170   DYNAMIC     Fa0/8
   1    001a.e2ce.ff40   DYNAMIC     Po1
   1    0050.0f02.642a   DYNAMIC     Fa0/3
Total Mac Addresses for this criterion: 31
S1#
```

The switches use what are called *base MAC addresses* that are assigned to the CPU, and the 2960s use 20. From the previous output, you can see that I have seven MAC addresses dynamically assigned to EtherChannel port 1. Ports Fa0/3, Fa0/8, and Fa0/4 have only one MAC address assigned, and all ports are assigned to VLAN 1. This code has been described many times in this chapter.

```
S2#sh mac address-table
        Mac Address Table
-------------------------------------------

Vlan    Mac Address      Type        Ports
----    -----------      --------    -----
 All    0008.205a.85c0   STATIC      CPU
 All    0100.0ccc.cccc   STATIC      CPU
 All    0100.0ccc.cccd   STATIC      CPU
```

```
 All     0100.0cdd.dddd    STATIC    CPU
[output cut]
   1     0002.1762.b235    DYNAMIC   Fa0/3
   1     000d.29bd.4b80    DYNAMIC   Fa0/1
   1     000d.29bd.4b85    DYNAMIC   Fa0/1
   1     0016.4662.52b4    DYNAMIC   Fa0/1
   1     0016.4677.5eab    DYNAMIC   Fa0/4
   1     001b.2b55.7540    DYNAMIC   Fa0/1
Total Mac Addresses for this criterion: 26
S2#
```

You can see in the previous output that I have four MAC addresses assigned to Fa0/1. And of course, you can also see that you have one connection for each host on ports 3 and 4. But where's port 2? Port 2 is a redundant link, so STP placed fa0/2 into blocking mode.

show spanning-tree

By this time you know that the show spanning-tree command is important. With it, you can see who the root bridge is and what the priorities are set to for each VLAN.

Understand that Cisco switches run what is called *Per-VLAN Spanning-Tree* (PVST), which basically means that each VLAN runs its own instance of STP. If you typed **show spanning-tree**, you'd receive information for each VLAN, starting with VLAN 1. So, say you have multiple VLANs and you want to see what's up with VLAN 2—you'd type the command **show spanning-tree vlan 2**.

Here is an output from the show spanning-tree command from switch S1. Since I'm using only VLAN 1, I don't need to add the VLAN number to the command:

```
S1#sh spanning-tree
VLAN0001
  Spanning tree enabled protocol ieee
  Root ID    Priority    32769
             Address     000d.29bd.4b80
             Cost        3012
             Port        56 (Port-channel1)
             Hello Time   2 sec  Max Age 20 sec  Forward Delay 15 sec

  Bridge ID  Priority    49153  (priority 49152 sys-id-ext 1)
             Address     001b.2b55.7500
             Hello Time   2 sec  Max Age 20 sec  Forward Delay 15 sec
             Aging Time 15
  Uplinkfast enabled
```

```
Interface          Role Sts Cost      Prio.Nbr Type
---------------- ---- --- --------- -------- ----------
Fa0/3              Desg FWD 3100      128.3    Edge Shr
Fa0/4              Desg FWD 3019      128.4    Edge P2p
Fa0/8              Desg FWD 3019      128.8    P2p
Po1                Root FWD 3012      128.56   P2p
```

Since I have only VLAN 1 configured, there's no more output for this command, but if I had more, I would get another page for each VLAN configured on the switch. The default priority is 32768, but there's something called the *system ID extension* (sys-id-ext), which is the VLAN identifier. The bridge ID priority is incremented by the number of that VLAN. And since I have only VLAN 1, I increment by 1 to 32769. Understand, by default, BackboneFast raises the default priority to 49152 to help prevent the bridge from becoming the root.

The top of the output shows you who the root bridge is:

```
VLAN0001
    Root ID  Priority     32769
             Address      000d.29bd.4b80
             Cost         3012
             Port         56 (Port-channel1)
             Hello Time   2 sec  Max Age 20 sec  Forward Delay 15 sec
```

EtherChannel Port 1 is the root port, which means that it's the chosen path to the root bridge, and it has an identifier of 000d.29bd.4b80. That can be either the Core switch or S2 only, and you'll find out which one it is in a minute.

The last output from the command displays the ports that are running STP and have a connection to another device. Because I'm running EtherChannel, I have no blocked ports. One way to determine whether your bridge is the root is to look to see whether there are any Altn BLK ports (meaning a blocked port that is an alternate). A root bridge would never have a blocked port on any interface, but all the ports on S1 show Forwarding (FWD) because of the EtherChannel configuration.

Determining the Root Bridge

To determine your root bridge, you would obviously use the show spanning-tree command. Let's take a look at the other two switches and see which switch is the default root bridge. Make a mental note of the bridge ID MAC address as well as the priority of the S1 switch. Here's the S2 output:

S2#**sh spanning-tree**

```
VLAN0001
  Spanning tree enabled protocol ieee
  Root ID    Priority     32769
             Address      000d.29bd.4b80
```

```
            Cost        3019
            Port        2 (FastEthernet0/1)
            Hello Time  2 sec  Max Age 20 sec  Forward Delay 15 sec

  Bridge ID  Priority    49153 (priority 49152 sys-id-ext 1)
             Address     001a.e2ce.ff00
             Hello Time  2 sec  Max Age 20 sec  Forward Delay 15 sec
             Aging Time 300
  Uplinkfast enabled

Interface        Role Sts Cost      Prio.Nbr Type
---------------- ---- --- --------- -------- ------------
Fa0/1            Root FWD 3019      128.2    P2p
Fa0/2            Altn BLK 3019      128.3    P2p
Fa0/3            Desg FWD 3100      128.4    Edge Shr
Fa0/4            Desg FWD 3019      128.5    Edge P2p
S2#
```

You can see that port Fa0/2 is blocked, so this cannot be your root bridge! A root bridge cannot have blocked ports. Again, pay special attention to the bridge ID MAC address and the priority. Here's the output from the Core switch:

```
Core#sh spanning-tree
VLAN0001
  Spanning tree enabled protocol rstp
  Root ID    Priority    32769
             Address     000d.29bd.4b80
             This bridge is the root
             Hello Time   2 sec  Max Age 20 sec  Forward Delay 15 sec

  Bridge ID  Priority    32769 (priority 32768 sys-id-ext 1)
             Address     000d.29bd.4b80
             Hello Time   2 sec  Max Age 20 sec  Forward Delay 15 sec
             Aging Time 300

Interface        Role Sts Cost      Prio.Nbr Type
---------------- ---- --- --------- -------- --------------
Fa0/5            Desg FWD 19        128.5    P2p Peer(STP)
Fa0/6            Desg FWD 19        128.6    P2p Peer(STP)
Po1              Desg FWD 12        128.66   P2p Peer(STP)
```

Well there you have it. "This bridge is the root."

But think about this—why does the Core switch have just the default of 32768 and not 49152 like the other switches? Well, it's running the 802.1w version of STP and BackboneFast is disabled by default.

Let's take a look at the bridge MAC address of each switch:

- *S1 address:* 001b.2b55.7500
- *S2 address:* 001a.e2ce.ff00
- *Core address:* 000d.29bd.4b80

If all switches are set to the default priority, which switch do you think will be the root switch? Start reading the MAC addresses from the left, moving toward the right. Core is obviously the lowest MAC address, and by looking at the output of the show spanning-tree command, you can see that it is, indeed, the root bridge (even if all switches had the same priority). It's just good practice to figure out the root bridge by comparing the MAC addresses of the switches once in awhile.

Setting the Root Bridge

Commands used to specify a particular switch as the root bridge are contained in Table 5.13.

TABLE 5.13 Command and Meaning

Command	Meaning
spanning-tree vlan *vlan* priority *priority*	Changes the STP priority of the PVST
spanning-tree vlan *vlan* root primary	Sets the switch to be the primary root bridge of the PVST
spanning-tree vlan *vlan* root secondary	Sets the switch to be the secondary root of the PVST

```
S1(config)#spanning-tree vlan 1 root ?
  primary    Configure this switch as primary root for this spanning tree
  secondary  Configure switch as secondary root
S1(config)#spanning-tree vlan 1 root primary
```

It's kind of convenient that the Core switch is the root bridge by default because that's right where I'd typically choose to set the root. But just for fun, let's change it. Here's how you can do that:

```
S1#config t
S1(config)#spanning-tree vlan 1 priority ?
  <0-61440>  bridge priority in increments of 4096
```

```
S1(config)#spanning-tree vlan 1 priority 16384
S1(config)#do show spanning-tree
VLAN0001
Spanning tree enabled protocol ieee
  Root ID     Priority     16385
              Address      001b.2b55.7500
              This bridge is the root
              Hello Time    2 sec  Max Age 20 sec  Forward Delay 15 sec

  Bridge ID   Priority     16385  (priority 16384 sys-id-ext 1)
              Address      001b.2b55.7500
              Hello Time    2 sec  Max Age 20 sec  Forward Delay 15 sec
              Aging Time 300

Interface          Role Sts Cost      Prio.Nbr Type
---------------- ---- --- --------- -------- -----------
Fa0/3              Desg FWD 100       128.3    Edge Shr
Fa0/4              Desg FWD 19        128.4    Edge P2p
Fa0/8              Desg FWD 19        128.8    P2p
Po1                Desg FWD 12        128.56   P2p
```

By lowering the S1 priority to 16384, the S1 switch immediately became the root bridge. You can set your priorities all the way from 0 to 61440. Zero (0) means that the switch will always be the root bridge, and 61440 means the switch will never be a root.

There's one last command I want to tell you about; if you want to skip all this verification and configuration of the root bridge stuff—and no, you don't get to skip all that if you want to pass the Cisco exams—here's a simple command you can run on a switch to set it as a root bridge:

```
S1(config)#spanning-tree vlan 1 root ?
  primary    Configure this switch as primary root for this spanning tree
  secondary  Configure switch as secondary root
S1(config)#spanning-tree vlan 1 root primary
```

Understand that this does not override a low-priority switch; this command would work for you only if all your switches had the same priority, or higher, set.

Chapter 6

Virtual LANs (VLANs)

In this chapter, you'll learn the commands on how to create VLANs, put ports into VLANs, configure trunks and trunking protocols, configure VTP and all its options, configure inter-VLAN routing, and look at VLAN verification information.

For up-to-the minute updates for this chapter, please see www.lammle.com.

Understanding VLAN Basics

Here's a short list of ways that configuring VLANs can help simplify network management:

- Network adds, moves, and changes are achieved with ease by just configuring a port into the appropriate VLAN.
- A group of users that needs an unusually high level of security can be put into their own VLAN so that users outside the VLAN can't communicate with them.
- As a logical grouping of users by function, VLANs can be considered independent from their physical or geographic locations.
- VLANs greatly enhance network security.
- VLANs increase the number of broadcast domains while decreasing their size.

Configuring VLANs

It may come as a surprise to you, but configuring VLANs is actually pretty easy. Figuring out which users you want in each VLAN is not. It's time-consuming, but once you've decided on the number of VLANs you want to create and established which users you want to belong to each one, it's time to bring your first VLAN into the world!

To configure VLANs on a Cisco Catalyst switch, use the global configuration vlan command. In the following example, I'll demonstrate how to configure VLANs on the S1 switch by creating three VLANs for three different departments—again, remember that VLAN 1 is the native and administrative VLAN by default.

Creating VLANs is very simple. Here in Table 6.1 is the command:

TABLE 6.1   Creating A VLAN

Command	Meaning
vlan	Creates or allows the modification of a VLAN in the VLAN database
name	Configures a name for a given VLAN from the VLAN configuration mode

Here is how you simply create VLANs on a switch:

```
S1#config t
S1(config)#vlan ?
  WORD      ISL VLAN IDs 1-4094
  internal  internal VLAN
S1(config)#vlan 2
S1(config-vlan)#name Sales
S1(config-vlan)#vlan 3
S1(config-vlan)#name Marketing
S1(config-vlan)#vlan 4
S1(config-vlan)#name Accounting
S1(config-vlan)#^Z
S1#
```

From the previous output, you can see that you can create VLANs from 2-4094. This is only mostly true. Like I said, VLANs can really be created only up to 1005, and you can't use, change, rename, or delete VLANs 1 and 1002 through 1005 because they're reserved. The previous VLAN numbers are called *extended* VLANs and won't be saved in the database unless your switch is set to VTP Transparent mode. You won't see these VLAN numbers used too often in production. Here's an example of setting my S1 switch to VLAN 4000 when my switch is set to VTP Server mode (the default VTP mode):

```
S1#config t
S1(config)#vlan 4000
S1(config-vlan)#^Z
% Failed to create VLANs 4000
Extended VLAN(s) not allowed in current VTP mode.
%Failed to commit extended VLAN(s) changes.
```

Verifying VLAN Creation

Once the VLANs are created, verify your configuration with the show vlan command in Table 6.2 (sh vlan for short):

TABLE 6.2   Verifying a VLAN

Command	Meaning
show vlan	Displays the contents or list of VLANs stored in the VLAN database file. (The VLAN database file is called vlan.dat and can be seen with the show flash command.)

Here is the output:

```
S1#sh vlan

VLAN Name                             Status    Ports
---- -------------------------------- --------- ---------------------------------
1    default                          active    Fa0/3, Fa0/4, Fa0/5, Fa0/6
                                                 Fa0/7, Fa0/8, Gi0/1
2    Sales                            active
3    Marketing                        active
4    Accounting                       active
 [output cut]
```

Assigning Switch Ports to VLANs

You configure a port to belong to a VLAN by assigning a membership mode that specifies the kind of traffic the port carries, plus the number of VLANs to which it can belong. You can configure each port on a switch to be in a specific VLAN (access port) by using the interface switchport command. You can also configure multiple ports at the same time with the interface range command.

Here in Table 6.3 are the basic switch VLAN commands used on a switch port:

TABLE 6.3   Assigning Switch Port Memberships

Command	Meaning
interface	Enters the interface configuration mode and allows the configuration of a specific interface.

Command	Meaning
`interface range`	Allows the selection of multiple ports for the purpose of configuring the same functions on all of those ports.
`switchport mode`	The `switchport` command is used to modify most layer-2 properties of a switch port. The mode option allows the modification of how a switch port will handle traffic for a specific VLAN or set of VLANs.
`switchport access`	Configures the port into a specific VLAN for the purpose of allowing only traffic from that VLAN to pass to and from that port.

Here's an example of setting a switch port assignment to VLAN 3:

```
S1#config t
S1(config)#int fa0/3
S1(config-if)#switchport ?
  access        Set access mode characteristics of the interface
  backup        Set backup for the interface
  block         Disable forwarding of unknown uni/multi cast addresses
  host          Set port host
  mode          Set trunking mode of the interface
  nonegotiate   Device will not engage in negotiation protocol on this
                interface
  port-security Security related command
  priority      Set appliance 802.1p priority
  protected     Configure an interface to be a protected port
  trunk         Set trunking characteristics of the interface
  voice         Voice appliance attributes
S1(config-if)#switchport mode ?
  access   Set trunking mode to ACCESS unconditionally
  dynamic  Set trunking mode to dynamically negotiate access or
trunk mode
  trunk    Set trunking mode to TRUNK unconditionally

S1(config-if)#switchport mode access
S1(config-if)#switchport access vlan 3
```

Configuring Trunk Ports

The 2960 switch runs the IEEE 802.1q encapsulation method only. To configure trunking on a Fast Ethernet port, use the interface command trunk [*parameter*]. It's a tad different on the 3560 switch, and I'll show you that in the next section.

The following switch output shows the trunk configuration on interface fa0/8 as set to trunk on:

```
S1#config t
S1(config)#int fa0/8
S1(config-if)#switchport mode trunk
```

Table 6.4 lists the trunk commands you can use:

TABLE 6.4   Configuring Trunk Ports

Mode	Meaning
access	This places a port into permanent nontrunking mode.
dynamic auto	This port state is able to convert to a trunk link if the neighbor interface is set to become a trunk and can negotiate with DTP.
dynamic desirable	Through the use of dynamic trunking protocol (DTP) this port mode attempts to convert the link into a trunk.
trunk	This sets the port state to permanent trunking mode and negotiates to make the neighbor interface a trunk port as well.
nonegotiate	This command can be used with access and trunk modes. It disables the sending of DTP packets out the interface, thereby disabling the ability to negotiate the trunk status.

Here is a list of the various trunk modes on a switch port:

switchport mode access   This puts the interface (access port) into permanent nontrunking mode and negotiates to convert the link into a nontrunk link. The interface becomes a nontrunk interface regardless of whether the neighboring interface is a trunk interface. This port would be a dedicated layer-2 port.

switchport mode dynamic auto   This mode makes the interface able to convert the link to a trunk link. The interface becomes a trunk interface if the neighboring interface is set to trunk or desirable mode. This is now the default switchport mode for all Ethernet interfaces on all new Cisco switches.

switchport mode dynamic desirable This one makes the interface actively attempt to convert the link to a trunk link. The interface becomes a trunk interface if the neighboring interface is set to trunk, desirable, or auto mode. I used to see this mode as the default on some older switches, but not any longer. The default is dynamic auto now.

switchport mode trunk This puts the interface into permanent trunking mode and negotiates to convert the neighboring link into a trunk link. The interface becomes a trunk interface even if the neighboring interface isn't a trunk interface.

switchport nonegotiate This prevents the interface from generating DTP frames. You can use this command only when the interface switchport mode is access or trunk. You must manually configure the neighboring interface as a trunk interface to establish a trunk link.

Trunking with the Cisco Catalyst 3560 Switch

In this section, you'll look at one more switch—the Cisco Catalyst 3560. The configuration is pretty much the same as it is for a 2960 with the exception being that the 3560 can provide layer-3 services and the 2960 can't. Plus, the 3560 can run both the ISL and the IEEE 802.1Q trunking encapsulation methods—the 2960 can run 802.1Q only. With all this in mind, let's just take a quick look at the VLAN encapsulation difference regarding the 3560 switch.

With a higher end switch, you have the option to set the encapsulation method, as highlighted in Table 6.5:

TABLE 6.5 Configuring Trunk Encapsulations

Command	Meaning
switchport trunk encapsulation	Allows the configuration of an encapsulation type. The type of encapsulation used can vary depending on the device or the type used on the other end of the trunk link.

For the 3560, you have the encapsulation command that the 2960 switch doesn't:

```
Core(config-if)#switchport trunk encapsulation ?
  dot1q      Interface uses only 802.1q trunking encapsulation
 when trunking
  isl        Interface uses only ISL trunking encapsulation
 when trunking
  negotiate  Device will negotiate trunking encapsulation with peer on
             interface
Core(config-if)#switchport trunk encapsulation dot1q
Core(config-if)#switchport mode trunk
```

Here in Table 6.6 are the two options:

TABLE 6.6   Encapsulation options

Command	Meaning
dot1q	Specifies the IEEE specification 802.1q encapsulation. This type of encapsulation is an open standard and is supported by almost all switches.
ISL	Specifies the ISL standard of encapsulation that is a Cisco proprietary standard of encapsulation. This encapsulation type is being phased out of use. Cisco doesn't even support it on their lower-level switches any more.

As you can see, we have the option to add either the IEEE 802.1Q (dot1q) encapsulation or the ISL encapsulation to the 3560 switch. After you set the encapsulation, you still have to set the interface mode to trunk.

Defining the Allowed VLANs on a Trunk

As I've mentioned, trunk ports send and receive information from all VLANs by default, and if a frame is untagged, it's sent to the management VLAN. This applies to the extended range VLANs as well.

But you can remove VLANs from the allowed list to prevent traffic from certain VLANs from traversing a trunked link. Table 6.7 lists the command for how you'd do that:

TABLE 6.7   Removing VLANs from Traversing a Trunk

Command	Meaning
switchport trunk allowed	Allows the configuration of a specific list of VLANs to be carried over a trunk link

Here is an example of using the command:

```
S1#config t
S1(config)#int f0/1
S1(config-if)#switchport trunk allowed vlan ?
  WORD    VLAN IDs of the allowed VLANs when this port is in
trunking mode
  add     add VLANs to the current list
  all     all VLANs
  except  all VLANs except the following
```

```
  none    no VLANs
  remove  remove VLANs from the current list
S1(config-if)#switchport trunk allowed vlan remove ?
  WORD  VLAN IDs of disallowed VLANS when this port is in trunking mode
S1(config-if)#switchport trunk allowed vlan remove 4
```

The previous command stopped VLAN 4 traffic from traversing the trunk link config-ured on S1 port f0/1, causing it to drop all traffic sent and received for VLAN 4.

Changing or Modifying the Trunk Native VLAN

Cisco doesn't recommend that you change the trunk port native VLAN from VLAN 1, but you can, and some people do it for security reasons. To change the native VLAN, use the command in Table 6.8:

TABLE 6.8   Changing the native VLAN

Command	Meaning
switchport trunk native	Allows the configuration of the native VLAN on a trunk link. The native VLAN is important for the proper opera-tion of 802.1q encapsulation because it specifies what VLAN will carry any traffic that is not tagged.

Because nontagged traffic is considered a security threat, the recommended configura-tion for the native VLAN is a parked VLAN. A parked VLAN is a real VLAN that exists in the VLAN database but is not used to carry any enterprise data. This means you create the VLAN and assign no ports or data to it. This way, if there is any untagged data, it will be placed in this parked VLAN and go nowhere, causing no harm.

```
S1#config t
S1(config)#int f0/1
S1(config-if)#switchport trunk ?
  allowed  Set allowed VLAN characteristics when interface is
in trunking mode
  native   Set trunking native characteristics when interface
is in trunking mode
  pruning  Set pruning VLAN characteristics when interface is
in trunking mode
S1(config-if)#switchport trunk native ?
  vlan  Set native VLAN when interface is in trunking mode
S1(config-if)#switchport trunk native vlan ?
  <1-4094>  VLAN ID of the native VLAN when this port is in
 trunking mode
```

```
S1(config-if)#switchport trunk native vlan 40
S1(config-if)#^Z
```

Configuring Inter-VLAN Routing

By default, only hosts that are members of the same VLAN can communicate. To change this and allow inter-VLAN communication to be possible, you need a router or a layer-3 switch.

To support ISL or 802.1Q routing on a Fast Ethernet interface, the router's interface is divided into logical interfaces—one for each VLAN. These are called *subinterfaces*. Anyway, from a Fast Ethernet or Gigabit interface, you can set the interface to trunk with the encapsulation command.

The configuration of the switch would look something like this:

```
2960#config t
2960(config)#int f0/1
2960(config-if)#switchport mode trunk
2960(config-if)#int f0/2
2960(config-if)#switchport access vlan 1
2960(config-if)#int f0/3
2960(config-if)#switchport access vlan 1
2960(config-if)#int f0/4
2960(config-if)#switchport access vlan 3
2960(config-if)#int f0/5
2960(config-if)#switchport access vlan 3
2960(config-if)#int f0/6
2960(config-if)#switchport access vlan 2
```

Before you configure the router, you need to design your logical network:

VLAN 1: 192.168.10.16/28

VLAN 2: 192.168.10.32/28

VLAN 3: 192.168.10.48/28

The configuration of the router would then look like this:

```
ISR#config t
ISR(config)#int f0/0
ISR(config-if)#no ip address
ISR(config-if)#no shutdown
ISR(config-if)#int f0/0.1
ISR(config-subif)#encapsulation dot1q 1
ISR(config-subif)#ip address 192.168.10.17 255.255.255.240
ISR(config-subif)#int f0/0.2
ISR(config-subif)#encapsulation dot1q 2
```

```
ISR(config-subif)#ip address 192.168.10.33 255.255.255.240
ISR(config-subif)#int f0/0.3
ISR(config-subif)#encapsulation dot1q 3
ISR(config-subif)#ip address 192.168.10.49 255.255.255.240
```

The hosts in each VLAN would be assigned an address from their subnet range, and the default gateway would be the IP address assigned to the router's subinterface in that VLAN.

Configuring VTP

All Cisco switches are configured to be VTP servers by default. To configure VTP, first you have to configure the domain name you want to use. And of course, once you configure the VTP information on a switch, you need to verify it.

When you create the VTP domain, you have a bunch of options, including setting the domain name, password, operating mode, and pruning capabilities of the switch. Use the vtp global configuration mode command to set all this information. In the following example, I'll set the S1 switch to a vtp server, the VTP domain to Lammle, and the VTP password to todd.

Here in Table 6.9 are the commands you need:

TABLE 6.9 VTP Commands

Command	Meaning
vtp mode server	Configures a switch to be a VTP server. In Server mode, the VLAN database is allowed to be modified. VLANs can be added, deleted, modified or changed. Server is the default vtp mode for a Cisco switch. Changing the server option to client or transparent would configure the switch to that mode.
vtp domain	Configures the VTP domain name for a group of switches in the layer-2 switch fabric.
vtp password	Configures a password to be used by the switches in a VTP domain. The password serves two purposes. It allows updates to be authenticated, ensuring the update came from the correct server. With that authentication, it then adds a step in preventing an incorrect server from joining the domain and wiping out the VLAN database.
show vtp status	Displays all the configured options for VTP on the current switch. This is one of the most useful commands when troubleshooting VTP, because it allows the domain name, revision number, and other settings to easily be verified.

Let's take a look at an example on how to use these commands:

```
S1#config t
S1#(config)#vtp mode server
Device mode already VTP SERVER.
S1(config)#vtp domain Lammle
Changing VTP domain name from null to Lammle
S1(config)#vtp password todd
Setting device VLAN database password to todd
S1(config)#do show vtp password
VTP Password: todd
S1(config)#do show vtp status
VTP Version                     : 2
Configuration Revision          : 0
Maximum VLANs supported locally : 255
Number of existing VLANs        : 8
VTP Operating Mode              : Server
VTP Domain Name                 : Lammle
VTP Pruning Mode                : Disabled
VTP V2 Mode                     : Disabled
VTP Traps Generation            : Disabled
MD5 digest                      : 0x15 0x54 0x88 0xF2 0x50 0xD9 0x03 0x07
Configuration last modified by 192.168.24.6 at 3-14-93 15:47:32
Local updater ID is 192.168.24.6 on interface Vl1 (lowest numbered VLAN
interface found)
```

Let's go to the Core and S2 switches and set them into the Lammle VTP domain. It is important to remember that the VTP domain name is case sensitive! VTP is not forgiving—one teeny small mistake, and it just won't work!

```
Core#config t
Core(config)#vtp mode client
Setting device to VTP CLIENT mode.
Core(config)#vtp domain Lammle
Changing VTP domain name from null to Lammle
Core(config)#vtp password todd
Setting device VLAN database password to todd
Core(config)#do show vtp status
VTP Version                     : 2
Configuration Revision          : 0
Maximum VLANs supported locally : 1005
Number of existing VLANs        : 5
```

```
VTP Operating Mode              : Server
VTP Domain Name                 : Lammle
VTP Pruning Mode                : Disabled
VTP V2 Mode                     : Disabled
VTP Traps Generation            : Disabled
MD5 digest                      : 0x2A 0x6B 0x22 0x17 0x04 0x4F 0xB8 0xC2
Configuration last modified by 192.168.10.19 at 3-1-93 03:13:16
Local updater ID is 192.168.24.7 on interface Vl1 (first interface found)
```

Here's how to use the show vlan brief command on the Core and S2 switch:

```
Core#sh vlan brief
VLAN Name               Status    Ports
---- ------------------ --------- ---------------------
1    default            active    Fa0/1,Fa0/2,Fa0/3,Fa0/4
                                  Fa0/9,Fa0/10,Fa0/11,Fa0/12
                                  Fa0/13,Fa0/14,Fa0/15,Fa0/16,Fa0/17, Fa0/18,
                                  Fa0/19, Fa0/20,Fa0/21,
                                  Fa0/22, Fa0/23, Fa0/24, Gi0/1, Gi0/2

2    Sales              active
3    Marketing          active
4    Accounting         active
[output cut]
```

Telephony: Configuring Voice VLANs

The voice VLAN feature enables access ports to carry IP voice traffic from an IP phone. When a switch is connected to a Cisco IP Phone, the phone sends voice traffic with layer-3 IP precedence and layer-2 class of service (CoS) values, which are both set to 5 for voice traffic; all other traffic defaults to 0. Because the sound quality of an IP phone call can deteriorate if the data is unevenly sent, the switch supports quality of service (QoS) based on IEEE 802.1p CoS (802.1p provides a mechanism for implementing QoS at the MAC level). The 802.1p field is carried in the 802.1q trunk header. If you look at the fields in an 802.1q tag, you will see a field called the *priority field*, which is where the 802.1p information goes. QoS uses classification and scheduling to send network traffic from the switch in an organized, predictable manner.

The Cisco IP Phone is a configurable device, and you can configure it to forward traffic with an IEEE 802.1p priority. You can also configure the switch to either trust or override the traffic priority assigned by a Cisco IP Phone—which is exactly what I'll show how to do here. The Cisco phone basically has a three-port switch: one to connect to the Cisco switch, one to a PC device, and one to the actual phone, which is internal.

You can also configure an access port with an attached Cisco IP Phone to use one VLAN for voice traffic and another VLAN for data traffic from a device attached to the phone—like a PC. You can configure access ports on the switch to send Cisco Discovery Protocol (CDP) packets that instruct an attached Cisco IP Phone to send voice traffic to the switch in any of these ways:

- In the voice VLAN, tagged with a layer-2 CoS priority value
- In the access VLAN, tagged with a layer-2 CoS priority value
- In the access VLAN, untagged (no layer-2 CoS priority value)

The switch can also process tagged data traffic (traffic in IEEE 802.1Q or IEEE 802.1p frame types) from the device attached to the access port on the Cisco IP Phone. You can configure layer-2 access ports on the switch to send CDP packets that instruct the attached Cisco IP Phone to configure the phone access port in one of these modes:

- In trusted mode, all traffic received through the access port on the Cisco IP Phone passes through the phone unchanged.
- In untrusted mode, all traffic in IEEE 802.1Q or IEEE 802.1p frames received through the access port on the Cisco IP Phone receive a configured layer-2 CoS value. The default layer-2 CoS value is 0. Untrusted mode is the default.

Configuring the Voice VLAN

By default, the voice VLAN feature is disabled, and you enable it by using the interface command `switchport voice vlan`. When the voice VLAN feature is enabled, all untagged traffic is sent according to the default CoS priority of the port. The CoS value is not trusted for IEEE 802.1p or IEEE 802.1Q tagged traffic.

These are the voice VLAN configuration guidelines:

- You should configure voice VLAN on switch access ports; voice VLAN isn't supported on trunk ports, even though you can actually configure it!
- The voice VLAN should be present and active on the switch for the Cisco IP Phone to correctly communicate on it. Use the `show vlan` privileged exec command to see whether the VLAN is present—if it is, it'll be listed in the display.
- Before you enable the voice VLAN, it's recommend you enable QoS on the switch by entering the `mls qos` global configuration command and set the port trust state to trust by entering the `mls qos trust cos` interface configuration command.
- You must make sure that CDP is enabled on the switch port connected to the Cisco IP Phone to send the configuration. This is on by default, so unless you disabled it, you shouldn't have a problem.
- The PortFast feature is automatically enabled when the voice VLAN is configured, but when you disable the voice VLAN, the PortFast feature isn't automatically disabled.

- To return the port to its default setting, use the no `switchport voice vlan` interface configuration command.

Here in Table 6.10 are the commands you need:

TABLE 6.10 Configuring Voice Switch Ports

Command	Meaning
`mls qos`	Configured from global configuration mode, this command enables globally on the switch the feature set to run QOS.
`switchport voice vlan`	This configures a switch port association into a voice VLAN. The voice VLAN used to be called an *auxiliary VLAN* and allows an access port to be associated to a data and voice VLAN simultaneously.
`mls qos trust cos`	This configures a switch port to trust the frame's COS priority tag. If a frame is untagged, then the port's default COS value will be used.
`switchport priority extend cos`	Configures the switchport to override or rewrite the 802.1p (COS) value that is in an incoming frame's header. This is establishing your QOS policy at the edge or your network. With regard to QOS, the edge of the network is also called the *trust boundary*.
`switchport priority extend trust`	This configures the switchport to trust or leave the 802.1p (COS) value that is in an incoming frame's header. This is establishing your QOS policy at the edge or your network. With regard to QOS, the edge of the network is also called the *trust boundary*.
`mls qos trust device cisco-phone`	This configures the switchport to trust the priority marking coming from the Cisco phone. This configuration will work only with a Cisco phone because the switch and the phone communicate using CDP.

OK, here goes, this is the hardest part of the book, but take a look at how I did it and try it for yourself if possible:

```
Switch#configure t
Switch(config)#mls qos
```

```
Switch(config)#interface f0/1
Switch(config-if)#switchport priority extend ?
  cos    Override 802.1p priority of devices on appliance
  trust  Trust 802.1p priorities of devices on appliance
Switch(config-if)#switchport priority extend trust
Switch(config-if)#mls qos trust cos
Switch(config-if)#switchport voice vlan dot1p
Switch(config-if)#switchport mode access
Switch(config-if)#switchport access vlan 3
Switch(config-if)#switchport voice vlan 10
```

The command mls qos trust cos will configure the interface to classify incoming traffic packets by using the packet CoS value. For untagged packets, the port's default CoS value will be used. But before configuring the port trust state, you must first globally enable QoS by using the mls qos global configuration command.

Security

In this chapter, you'll learn a lot about deterring the most commonly attempted threats to your network's security with Cisco routers and IOS firewalls that together offer quite a powerful, integrated detection package against many types of invasion. I'll cover how Cisco IOS Firewall puts actual security and policy enforcement for your internal and external networking needs. I'll also show you how to create secure connections to any remote locations you may have living on the fringes, too!

Access lists are an integral part of Cisco's security solution, and I'll show you the keys of both simple and advanced access lists that will equip you with the ability to ensure internetwork security as well as mitigate most security-oriented network threats.

 For up-to-the minute updates for this chapter, please see www.lammle.com.

Perimeter Routers, Firewalls, and Internal Routers

Typically, medium to large enterprise networks base their various strategies for security on some recipe of internal and perimeter routers plus firewall devices. Internal routers provide additional security to the network by screening traffic to various parts of the protected corporate network, and they do this using access lists. Figure 7.1 shows where you can find each of these types of devices.

I'll first discuss the security threats a typical secured internetwork faces, and then I'll provide some ways of protecting the internetwork using the Cisco IOS Firewall feature set and access lists.

Recognizing Security Threats

You see, it all comes down to planning—or, rather, a lack thereof. Basically, the vital tool that the Internet has become to us today was absolutely unforeseen by those who brought it into being. This is a big reason why security is now such an issue—most IP implementations are innately insecure. No worries, though. Cisco can help us with this. But first, let's examine some common attack profiles:

- Application-layer attacks
- Autorooters
- Backdoors
- Denial of Service (DoS) and Distributed Denial of Service (DDoS) attacks
  - TCP SYN flood
  - "Ping of Death" attacks
  - Tribe Flood Network (TFN) and Tribe Flood Network 2000 (TFN2K)
  - Stacheldraht
- IP spoofing
- Man-in-the-middle attacks
- Network reconnaissance
- Packet sniffers
- Password attacks
- Brute-force attack
- Port redirection attacks
- Trojan horse attacks and viruses
- Trust exploitation attacks

FIGURE 7.1   A typical secured network

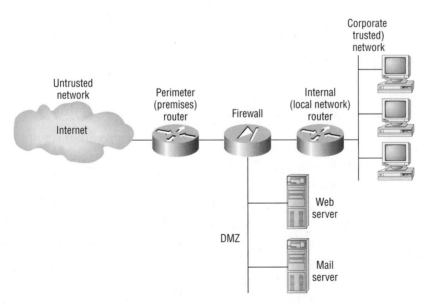

Using Cisco IOS Firewall

Here's where you'll find out how to mitigate some of the more common security threats on the list in the previous section using the following Cisco IOS Firewall features:

Stateful IOS firewall inspection engine   This is your perimeter protection feature, because it gives your internal users secure access control on a per-application basis. People often call it *context-based access control* (CBAC).

Intrusion detection   This is a deep packet inspection tool that lets you monitor, intercept, and respond to abuse in real-time by referencing 102 of the most common attack and intrusion detection signatures.

Firewall voice traversal   This is an application-level feature based on the protocol's understanding of call flow, as well as the relevant open channels. It supports both the H.323v2 and Session Initiation Protocol (SIP) voice protocols.

ICMP inspection   Basically, this permits responses to ICMP packets such as `ping` and `traceroute` that come from inside your firewall while denying other ICMP traffic.

Authentication proxy   This is a feature that makes users authenticate any time they want to access the network's resources through HTTP, HTTPS, FTP, and Telnet. It keeps personal network access profiles for users, and it automatically gets them for you from a RADIUS or TACACS+ server and applies them as well.

Destination URL policy management   This is a buffet of features that's commonly referred to as *URL filtering*.

Per-user firewalls   These are basically personalized, user-specific, downloadable firewalls obtained through service providers. You can also get personalized ACLs and other settings via AAA server profile storage.

Cisco IOS router and firewall provisioning   This allows for no-touch router provisioning, version updates, and security policies.

DoS detection and prevention   This is a feature that checks packet headers and drops any packets it finds suspicious.

Dynamic port mapping   This is a sort of adapter that permits applications supported by firewalls on nonstandard ports.

Java applet blocking   This protects you from any strange, unrecognized Java applets.

Policy-based, multi-interface support   This allows you to control user access by IP address and interface depending on your security policy.

Network Address Translation (NAT)   This conceals the internal network from the outside, which increases security.

Time-based access lists   This determines security policies based upon the exact time of day and the particular day of week.

Peer router authentication   This guarantees that routers are getting dependable routing information from actual, trusted sources. (For this to work, you need a routing protocol that supports authentication such as RIPv2, EIGRP, or OSPF.)

Introduction to Access Lists

Creating access lists is really a lot like programming a series of if-then statements—if a given condition is met, then a given action is taken. If the specific condition isn't met, nothing happens, and the next statement is evaluated. Access-list statements are basically packet filters that packets are compared against, categorized by, and acted upon accordingly. Once the lists are built, they can be applied to either inbound or outbound traffic on any interface. Applying an access list causes the router to analyze every packet crossing that interface in the specified direction and take the appropriate action.

A packet follows a few important rules when it's being compared to an access list:

- It's always compared to each line of the access list in sequential order; in other words, it'll always start with the first line of the access list, then go to line 2, then line 3, and so on.
- It's compared to lines of the access list only until a match is made. Once the packet matches the condition on a line of the access list, the packet is acted upon, and no further comparisons take place.
- There is an implicit "deny" at the end of each access list; this means that if a packet doesn't match the condition on any of the lines in the access list, the packet will be discarded.

There are two main types of access lists:

Standard access lists   These use only the source IP address in an IP packet as the condition test. All decisions are made based on the source IP address. This means standard access lists basically permit or deny an entire suite of protocols. They don't distinguish between any of the many types of IP traffic such as WWW, Telnet, UDP, and so on.

Extended access lists   Extended access lists can evaluate many of the other fields in the layer-3 and layer-4 headers of an IP packet. They can evaluate source and destination IP addresses, the protocol field in the Network layer header, and the port number at the Transport layer header. This gives extended access lists the ability to make much more granular decisions when controlling traffic.

Named access lists   Hey, wait a minute—I said two types of access lists but listed three! Well, technically there really are only two since *named access lists* are either standard or extended and not actually a new type. I'm just distinguishing them because they're created and referred to differently than standard and extended access lists. But they're functionally the same.

Here's a list of the many security threats you can mitigate with ACLs:

- IP address spoofing—inbound

- IP address spoofing—outbound
- DoS TCP SYN attacks—blocking external attacks
- DoS TCP SYN attacks—using TCP intercept
- DoS smurf attacks
- Filtering ICMP messages—inbound
- Filtering ICMP messages—outbound
- Filtering `traceroute`

It's generally wise not to allow any IP packets coming into a private network that contain the source address of any internal hosts or networks—just don't do it!

Here's a list of rules to live by when configuring ACLs from the Internet to your production network to mitigate security problems:

- Deny any addresses from your internal networks.
- Deny any local host addresses (127.0.0.0/8).
- Deny any reserved private addresses.
- Deny any addresses in the IP multicast address range (224.0.0.0/4).

Standard Access Lists

Standard IP access lists filter network traffic by examining the source IP address in a packet. You create a *standard IP access list* by using the access-list numbers 1–99 or 1300–1999 (expanded range). Access-list types are generally differentiated using a number. Based on the number used when the access list is created, the router knows which type of syntax to expect as the list is entered. By using numbers 1–99 or 1300–1999, you're telling the router you want to create a standard IP access list, so the router will expect syntax specifying only the source IP address in the test lines.

Here in Table 7.1 are the basic access-list commands that will get your configuration started:

TABLE 7.1 Creating an Access-list and Applying it to an Interface

Command	Meaning
`access-list`	Configures a single access-list statement into a router's memory for use in a complete access list that will be applied to an interface
`ip access-group`	Places an access list on a device's physical interface

Table 7.2 lists the options for these commands:

TABLE 7.2　Access-list Command Options

Option	Meaning
`<ID number>`	Identifies an access list by number as a standard or extended list. Also allows the creation and separation of multiple access lists.
`permit` or `deny`	Specifies the effect of the access-list statement as allowing or blocking the traffic specified.
`hostname` or `IP address`	Specifies the hostname or device's IP address that will be acted upon in the access-list statement.
`host`	Specifies a single specific host for the statement.
`any`	Specifies that regardless of the host or device IP, it will match the statement.

The following is an example of the many access-list number ranges that you can use to filter traffic on your network (the protocols for which you can specify access lists depend on your IOS version):

```
Corp(config)#access-list ?
  <1-99>            IP standard access list
  <100-199>         IP extended access list
  <1100-1199>       Extended 48-bit MAC address access list
  <1300-1999>       IP standard access list (expanded range)
  <200-299>         Protocol type-code access list
  <2000-2699>       IP extended access list (expanded range)
  <700-799>         48-bit MAC address access list
  compiled          Enable IP access-list compilation
  dynamic-extended  Extend the dynamic ACL absolute timer
  rate-limit        Simple rate-limit specific access list
```

Let's take a look at the syntax used when creating a standard access list:

```
Corp(config)#access-list 10 ?
  deny    Specify packets to reject
  permit  Specify packets to forward
  remark  Access list entry comment
```

As I said, by using the access-list numbers between 1–99 or 1300–1999, you're telling the router that you want to create a standard IP access list.

After you choose the access-list number, you need to decide whether you're creating a permit or deny statement. For this example, you will create a deny statement:

```
Corp(config)#access-list 10 deny ?
  Hostname or A.B.C.D  Address to match
  any                  Any source host
  host                 A single host address
```

The next step requires a more detailed explanation. Three options are available. You can use the any parameter to permit or deny any host or network, you can use an IP address to specify either a single host or a range of them, or you can use the host command to specify a specific host only. The any command is pretty obvious—any source address matches the statement, so every packet compared against this line will match. The host command is relatively simple. Here's an example of how to use it:

```
Corp(config)#access-list 10 deny host ?
  Hostname or A.B.C.D  Host address
Corp(config)#access-list 10 deny host 172.16.30.2
```

This tells the list to deny any packets from host 172.16.30.2. The default parameter is host. In other words, if you type **access-list 10 deny 172.16.30.2**, the router assumes you mean host 172.16.30.2.

Wildcard Masking

Wildcards are used with access lists to specify an individual host, a network, or a certain range of a network or networks. To understand a *wildcard*, you need to understand what a *block size* is; it's used to specify a range of addresses. Some of the different block sizes available are 64, 32, 16, 8, and 4.

The following example tells the router to match the first three octets exactly but that the fourth octet can be anything:

```
Corp(config)#access-list 10 deny 172.16.10.0 0.0.0.255
```

The next example tells the router to match the first two octets and that the last two octets can be any value:

```
Corp(config)#access-list 10 deny 172.16.0.0 0.0.255.255
```

Try to figure out this next line:

```
Corp(config)#access-list 10 deny 172.16.16.0 0.0.3.255
```

The previous configuration tells the router to start at network 172.16.16.0 and use a block size of 4. The range would then be 172.16.16.0 through 172.16.19.0.

Controlling VTY (Telnet) Access

You'll probably have a difficult time trying to stop users from telnetting to a large router because any active interface on a router is fair game for VTY access. You could try to create an extended IP access list that limits Telnet access to every IP address on the router. But if you did that, you'd have to apply it inbound on every interface, and that really wouldn't scale well to a large router with dozens, even hundreds, of interfaces, would it? Here's a much better solution: use a standard IP access list to control access to the VTY lines themselves.

Why does this work? Well, when you apply an access list to the VTY lines, you don't need to specify the Telnet protocol, since access to the VTY implies terminal access. You also don't need to specify a destination address, since it really doesn't matter which interface address the user used as a target for the Telnet session. You really need only to control where the user is coming from—their source IP address.

To perform this function, follow these steps:

1. Create a standard IP access list that permits only the host or hosts you want to be able to telnet into the routers.

2. Apply the access list to the VTY line with the `access-class` command. Here in Table 7.3 is the command you can configure on the VTY lines:

TABLE 7.3   Assigning and Access List to a VTY Line

Command	Meaning
access-class	Places an access list on the VTY lines of a device

Here is an example of allowing only host 172.16.10.3 to telnet into a router:

```
Lab_A(config)#access-list 50 permit 172.16.10.3
Lab_A(config)#line vty 0 4
Lab_A(config-line)#access-class 50 in
```

Because of the implied deny any at the end of the list, the access list stops any host from telnetting into the router except the host 172.16.10.3, regardless of which individual IP address on the router is used as a target.

Extended Access Lists

What if you needed sales to gain access to a certain server on the finance LAN but not to other network services for security reasons? With a standard IP access list, you can't allow users to get to one network service and not another. Said another way, when you need to make decisions based on both source and destination addresses, a standard access list won't allow you to do that since it makes decisions based on source address only.

But an *extended access list* will hook you up. That's because extended access lists allow you to specify source and destination addresses as well as the protocol and port number that identify the upper-layer protocol or application. By using extended access lists, you can effectively allow users access to a physical LAN and stop them from accessing specific hosts—or even specific services on those hosts.

Table 7.4 lists your basic access-list commands:

TABLE 7.4   Creating an Access List and Applying it to an Interface

Command	Meaning
access-list	Configures a single access-list statement into a router's memory for use in a complete access list that will be applied to an interface
ip access-group	Places an access list on a device's physical interface

Choose a number to identify the list as standard or extended, then add your options (see Table 7.5):

TABLE 7.5   Extended Access List Options

Option	Meaning
<ID number>	Identifies an access list by number as a standard or extended list. Also allows the creation and separation of multiple access lists.
permit or deny	Specifies the effect of the access-list statement as allowing or blocking the traffic specified.
protocol	Specifies the protocol to be filtered in the access-list statement.
hostname or IP address	Specifies the hostname or device's IP address that will be acted upon in the access-list statement. In an extended access list, this field will be entered for both the source and destination host or device.
host	Specifies a single specific host for the statement.

Option	Meaning
any	Specifies that regardless of the host or device IP, it will match the statement.
eq	Means equal to, and specifies the application protocol to be filtered by the statement.
<port # or ID>	Lists the actual port number or protocol for filtering.

Here's an example of an extended IP access list:

```
Corp(config)#access-list ?
  <1-99>             IP standard access list
  <100-199>          IP extended access list
  <1100-1199>        Extended 48-bit MAC address access list
  <1300-1999>        IP standard access list (expanded range)
  <200-299>          Protocol type-code access list
  <2000-2699>        IP extended access list (expanded range)
  <700-799>          48-bit MAC address access list
  compiled           Enable IP access-list compilation
  dynamic-extended   Extend the dynamic ACL absolute timer
  rate-limit         Simple rate-limit specific access list
```

The first command shows the access-list numbers available. You'll use the extended access-list range from 100 to 199. Be sure to notice that the range 2000–2699 is also available for extended IP access lists.

At this point, you need to decide what type of list entry you are making. For this example, you'll choose a deny list entry:

```
Corp(config)#access-list 110 ?
  deny     Specify packets to reject
  dynamic  Specify a DYNAMIC list of PERMITs or DENYs
  permit   Specify packets to forward
  remark   Access list entry comment
```

Once you choose the access-list type, you then need to select a protocol field entry:

```
Corp(config)#access-list 110 deny ?
  <0-255>  An IP protocol number
  ahp      Authentication Header Protocol
  eigrp    Cisco's EIGRP routing protocol
  esp      Encapsulation Security Payload
```

```
gre       Cisco's GRE tunneling
icmp      Internet Control Message Protocol
igmp      Internet Gateway Message Protocol
ip        Any Internet Protocol
ipinip    IP in IP tunneling
nos       KA9Q NOS compatible IP over IP tunneling
ospf      OSPF routing protocol
pcp       Payload Compression Protocol
pim       Protocol Independent Multicast
tcp       Transmission Control Protocol
udp       User Datagram Protocol
```

Here, you'll choose to filter an Application-layer protocol that uses TCP by selecting TCP as the protocol. You'll specify the specific TCP port later. Next, you will be prompted for the source IP address of the host or network (you can choose the any command to allow any source address):

```
Corp(config)#access-list 110 deny tcp ?
  A.B.C.D  Source address
  any      Any source host
  host     A single source host
```

After the source address is selected, the destination address is chosen:

```
Corp(config)#access-list 110 deny tcp any ?
  A.B.C.D  Destination address
  any      Any destination host
  eq       Match only packets on a given port number
  gt       Match only packets with a greater port number
  host     A single destination host
  lt       Match only packets with a lower port number
  neq      Match only packets not on a given port number
  range    Match only packets in the range of port numbers
```

In the following example, any source IP address that has a destination IP address of 172.16.30.2 has been denied:

```
Corp(config)#access-list 110 deny tcp any host 172.16.30.2 ?
  ack          Match on the ACK bit
  dscp         Match packets with given dscp value
  eq           Match only packets on a given port number
  established  Match established connections
  fin          Match on the FIN bit
```

```
fragments       Check non-initial fragments
gt              Match only packets with a greater port number
log             Log matches against this entry
log-input       Log matches against this entry, including input interface
lt              Match only packets with a lower port number
neq             Match only packets not on a given port number
precedence      Match packets with given precedence value
psh             Match on the PSH bit
range           Match only packets in the range of port numbers
rst             Match on the RST bit
syn             Match on the SYN bit
time-range      Specify a time-range
tos             Match packets with given TOS value
urg             Match on the URG bit
<cr>
```

You can press Enter here and leave the access list as is. But if you do that, all TCP traffic to host 172.16.30.2 will be denied, regardless of the destination port. You can be even more specific: once you have the host addresses in place, just specify the type of service you are denying. The following help output shows you the available options. You can choose a port number or use the application or protocol name:

```
Corp(config)#access-list 110 deny tcp any host 172.16.30.2 eq ?
  <0-65535>     Port number
  bgp           Border Gateway Protocol (179)
  chargen       Character generator (19)
  cmd           Remote commands (rcmd, 514)
  daytime       Daytime (13)
  discard       Discard (9)
  domain        Domain Name Service (53)
  drip          Dynamic Routing Information Protocol (3949)
  echo          Echo (7)
  exec          Exec (rsh, 512)
  finger        Finger (79)
  ftp           File Transfer Protocol (21)
  ftp-data      FTP data connections (20)
  gopher        Gopher (70)
  hostname      NIC hostname server (101)
  ident         Ident Protocol (113)
  irc           Internet Relay Chat (194)
  klogin        Kerberos login (543)
```

```
kshell        Kerberos shell (544)
login         Login (rlogin, 513)
lpd           Printer service (515)
nntp          Network News Transport Protocol (119)
pim-auto-rp   PIM Auto-RP (496)
pop2          Post Office Protocol v2 (109)
pop3          Post Office Protocol v3 (110)
smtp          Simple Mail Transport Protocol (25)
sunrpc        Sun Remote Procedure Call (111)
syslog        Syslog (514)
tacacs        TAC Access Control System (49)
talk          Talk (517)
telnet        Telnet (23)
time          Time (37)
uucp          Unix-to-Unix Copy Program (540)
whois         Nicname (43)
www           World Wide Web (HTTP, 80)
```

At this point, let's block Telnet (port 23) to host 172.16.30.2 only. If the users want to FTP, fine—that's allowed. The log command is used to log messages every time the access list is hit. This can be an extremely cool way to monitor inappropriate access attempts. Here is how to do this:

```
Corp(config)#access-list 110 deny tcp any host 172.16.30.2 eq 23 log
```

You need to keep in mind that the next line is an implicit deny any by default. If you apply this access list to an interface, you might as well just shut the interface down, since by default there is an implicit deny all at the end of every access list. You have to follow up the access list with the following command:

```
Corp(config)#access-list 110 permit ip any any
```

Remember, 0.0.0.0 255.255.255.255 is the same command as any, so the command could look like this:

```
Corp(config)#access-list 110 permit ip 0.0.0.0 255.255.255.255 0.0.0.0
255.255.255.255
```

Once the access list is created, you need to apply it to an interface (it's the same command as the IP standard list), like so:

```
Corp(config-if)#ip access-group 110 in
```

or like so:

```
Corp(config-if)#ip access-group 110 out
```

Named Access Lists

Named access lists allow you to use names to both create and apply either standard or extended access lists. There is nothing new or different about these access lists aside from being able to refer to them in a way that makes sense to humans. But the syntax has some subtle changes so let's take a look at the commands in Table 7.6:

TABLE 7.6   Named Access List Commands

Command	Meaning
ip access-list	Configures a named access list
ip access-group	Places an access list on a device's physical interface

Here in Table 7.7 are the options you can use:

TABLE 7.7   Named Access List Options

Option	Meaning
standard or extended	In a named access list, the type must be specified because there is no number used for identification.
permit or deny	Specifies the effect of the access-list statement as allowing or blocking the traffic specified.
hostname or IP address	Specifies the hostname or device's IP address that will be acted upon in the access list statement.
host	Specifies a single specific host for the statement.
any	Specifies that regardless of the host or device IP, it will match the statement.

Let's take a look at an example using all the commands and options:

```
Lab_A#config t
Enter configuration commands, one per line.  End with CNTL/Z.
Lab_A(config)#ip access-list ?
  extended  Extended Acc
  logging   Control access list logging
  standard  Standard Access List
```

Notice that I started by typing **ip access-list**, not **access-list**. This allows me to enter a named access list. Next, I'll need to specify that it's to be a standard access list:

```
Lab_A(config)#ip access-list standard ?
  <1-99>  Standard IP access-list number
  WORD    Access-list name
```

```
Lab_A(config)#ip access-list standard BlockSales
Lab_A(config-std-nacl)#
```

I specified a standard access list and then added a name: BlockSales. Notice that I could have used a number for a standard access list, but instead, I chose to use a descriptive name. Also, notice that after entering the name, I hit Enter, and the router prompt changed. I'm now in named access list configuration mode and am entering the named access list:

```
Lab_A(config-std-nacl)#?
Standard Access List configuration commands:
  default  Set a command to its defaults
  deny     Specify packets to reject
  exit     Exit from access-list configuration mode
  no       Negate a command or set its defaults
  permit   Specify packets to forward
```

```
Lab_A(config-std-nacl)#deny 172.16.40.0 0.0.0.255
Lab_A(config-std-nacl)#permit any
Lab_A(config-std-nacl)#exit
Lab_A(config)#^Z
Lab_A#
```

I enter the access list and then exit out of configuration mode. Next, I'll take a look at the running configuration to verify that the access list is indeed in the router:

```
Lab_A#show running-config

!
ip access-list standard BlockSales
 deny    172.16.40.0 0.0.0.255
 permit any
!
```

The BlockSales access list has truly been created and is in the running-config file of the router. Next, I'll need to apply the access list to an interface:

```
Lab_A#config t
Enter configuration commands, one per line.  End with CNTL/Z.
```

```
Lab_A(config)#int e1
Lab_A(config-if)#ip access-group BlockSales out
Lab_A(config-if)#^Z
Lab_A#
```

Switch Port ACLs

You can apply port ACLs to only layer-2 interfaces on your switches. Why? They're supported only on physical interfaces, that's why. Another good thing to keep in mind is that you can apply them only as inbound lists on your interfaces as well.

Port ACLs control IP traffic via IP access lists. Any non-IP traffic is filtered through the use of MAC addresses. And even though you can apply both types of filter to a single interface, you get to apply only one of each. If you try a put an additional ACL of either type on an interface that already has them in place, the new one will override the one you had there before. So, it's a good idea to be careful here—look before you leap.

Let's check out the access list in Table 7.8 that we can use on a switch port:

TABLE 7.8   Switch Access List Commands

Command	Meaning
mac access-list	Configures a MAC access-list statement
mac access-group	Places a MAC access list on a device's physical interface

Table 7.9 lists the options:

TABLE 7.9   Switch Access List Options

Option	Meaning
<word> name	Identifies an access list by name. Also allows the creation and separation of multiple access lists.
permit or deny	Specifies the effect of the access-list statement as allowing or blocking the traffic specified.
h.h.h mac address	Specifies the device by MAC address that will be acted upon in the access-list statement.
Host	Specifies a single specific host for the statement
Any	Specifies that regardless of the host or device IP, it will match the statement.

Here's an example of this command:

```
S1#config t
S1(config)#mac access-list ?
  extended  Extended Access List
S1(config)#mac access-list extended ?
  WORD   access-list name
S1(config)#mac access-list extended Todd_MAC_List
S1(config-ext-macl)#deny ?
  H.H.H  48-bit source MAC address
  any    any source MAC address
  host   A single source host
S1(config-ext-macl)#deny any ?
  H.H.H  48-bit destination MAC address
  any    any destination MAC address
  host   A single destination host
S1(config-ext-macl)#deny any host ?
  H.H.H  48-bit destination MAC address
S1(config-ext-macl)#deny any host 000d.29bd.4b85
S1(config-ext-macl)#permit ?
  H.H.H  48-bit source MAC address
  any    any source MAC address
  host   A single source host
S1(config-ext-macl)#permit any any
S1(config-ext-macl)#do show access-list
Extended MAC access list Todd_MAC_List
    deny    any host 000d.29bd.4b85
    permit any any
S1(config-ext-macl)#
```

You can see that you can create only an extended named access list. You have no other options. And don't forget to add the permit any any at the end!

Here is how you would apply the list to a switch port:

```
S1(config-ext-macl)#int f0/6
S1(config-if)#mac access-group Todd_MAC_List in
```

This is pretty much the same as it is with an IP list, except you start with the command mac.

Although it's true there are special circumstances where you would deny based on MAC address, there is another option, and I think it's usually the better one: just deny access based on the `ether-type` field in the Ethernet frame header instead. Take a look at all the options you have here:

```
S1(config-ext-macl)#deny any any ?
  <0-65535>      An arbitrary EtherType in decimal, hex, or octal
  aarp           EtherType: AppleTalk ARP
  amber          EtherType: DEC-Amber
  appletalk      EtherType: AppleTalk/EtherTalk
  cos            CoS value
  dec-spanning   EtherType: DEC-Spanning-Tree
  decnet-iv      EtherType: DECnet Phase IV
  diagnostic     EtherType: DEC-Diagnostic
  dsm            EtherType: DEC-DSM
  etype-6000     EtherType: 0x6000
  etype-8042     EtherType: 0x8042
  lat            EtherType: DEC-LAT
  lavc-sca       EtherType: DEC-LAVC-SCA
  lsap           LSAP value
  mop-console    EtherType: DEC-MOP Remote Console
  mop-dump       EtherType: DEC-MOP Dump
  msdos          EtherType: DEC-MSDOS
  mumps          EtherType: DEC-MUMPS
  netbios        EtherType: DEC-NETBIOS
  vines-echo     EtherType: VINES Echo
  vines-ip       EtherType: VINES IP
  xns-idp        EtherType: XNS IDP
  <cr>
```

Time-Based ACLs

Time-based ACLs work a lot like extended ACLs do, but their type of access control is totally time-oriented. Basically, you specify a certain time of day and week and then identify that particular period by giving it a name referenced by a task. So, by necessity, the reference function will fall under whatever time constraints you've dictated. The time period is based upon the router's clock, but I highly recommend using it in conjunction with Network Time Protocol (NTP) synchronization.

Here's an example of the command in Table 7.10:

TABLE 7.10 Timed Access List Commands

Command	Meaning
time-range	Configures a time range value to be added to an access list as an option to control traffic and access by time

and the options (see Table 7.11):

TABLE 7.11 Timed Access List Options

Option	Meaning
<ID name>	Identifies the time range by name for use in an access-list statement
Periodic	Specifies how the time range will act or be created, allowing specific time values to be set
hh:mm	Specifies time values for when the range will start and stop on specific days

Here is an example of the time-based ACL's:

```
Corp#config t
Corp(config)#time-range no-http
Corp(config-time-range)#periodic we?
Wednesday  weekdays  weekend
Corp(config-time-range)#periodic weekend ?
  hh:mm  Starting time
Corp(config-time-range)#periodic weekend 06:00 to 12:00
Corp(config-time-range)#exit
Corp(config)#time-range tcp-yes
Corp(config-time-range)#periodic weekend 06:00 to 12:00
Corp(config-time-range)#exit
Corp(config)#ip access-list extended Time
Corp(config-ext-nacl)#deny tcp any any eq www time-range no-http
Corp(config-ext-nacl)#permit tcp any any time-range tcp-yes
Corp(config-ext-nacl)#interface f0/0
Corp(config-if)#ip access-group Time in
Corp(config-if)#do show time-range
```

```
time-range entry: no-http (inactive)
   periodic weekdays 8:00 to 15:00
   used in: IP ACL entry
time-range entry: tcp-yes (inactive)
   periodic weekend 8:00 to 13:00
   used in: IP ACL entry
Corp(config-if)#
```

The time-range command is pretty flexible and will drive users crazy if you deny them access to basic network access or the Internet during off-hours. Be careful with the previous commands; make sure you test your list on a nonproduction network before you implement the lists on your production network.

Monitoring Access Lists

Again, it's always good to be able to verify a router's configuration. Table 7.12 lists the commands you can use:

TABLE 7.12   Access List Verification Commands

Command	Meaning
show access-list	Displays all access lists and their parameters configured on the router. This command does not show you which interface the list is set on.
show access-list 110	Shows only the parameters for the access list 110. This command does not show you the interface the list is set on.
show ip access-list	Shows only the IP access lists configured on the router.
show ip interface	Shows which interfaces have access lists set.
show running-config	Shows the access lists and which interfaces have access lists set.
show mac access-group	Displays MAC access lists applied to all layer-2 interfaces or the specified layer-2 interface (used on layer-2 switches only).

You've already seen how to use the show running-config command to verify that a named access list was in the router as well as a MAC access list on a layer-2 switch. So now I'll show the output from some of the other commands.

The show access-list command will list all access lists on the router, whether or not they have been applied to an interface:

```
Lab_A#show access-list
Standard IP access list 10
    deny   172.16.40.0, wildcard bits 0.0.0.255
    permit any
Standard IP access list BlockSales
    deny   172.16.40.0, wildcard bits 0.0.0.255
    permit any
Extended IP access list 110
    deny tcp any host 172.16.30.5 eq ftp
    deny tcp any host 172.16.30.5 eq telnet
    permit ip any any
Lab_A#
```

First, notice that both access list 10 and the named access list appear on this list. Second, notice that even though I entered actual numbers for TCP ports in access list 110, the show command gives you the protocol names rather than TCP ports for readability (hey, not everyone has them all memorized!).

Here's the output of the show ip interface command:

```
Lab_A#show ip interface e1
Ethernet1 is up, line protocol is up
  Internet address is 172.16.30.1/24
  Broadcast address is 255.255.255.255
  Address determined by non-volatile memory
  MTU is 1500 bytes
  Helper address is not set
  Directed broadcast forwarding is disabled
  Outgoing access list is BlockSales
  Inbound  access list is not set
  Proxy ARP is enabled
  Security level is default
  Split horizon is enabled
  ICMP redirects are always sent
  ICMP unreachables are always sent
  ICMP mask replies are never sent
  IP fast switching is disabled
```

```
        IP fast switching on the same interface is disabled
        IP Null turbo vector
        IP multicast fast switching is disabled
        IP multicast distributed fast switching is disabled
        Router Discovery is disabled
        IP output packet accounting is disabled
        IP access violation accounting is disabled
        TCP/IP header compression is disabled
        RTP/IP header compression is disabled
        Probe proxy name replies are disabled
        Policy routing is disabled
        Network address translation is disabled
        Web Cache Redirect is disabled
        BGP Policy Mapping is disabled
Lab_A#
```

Be sure to notice the bold line indicating that the outgoing list on this interface is BlockSales, but the inbound access list isn't set.

As I've already mentioned, you can use the show running-config command to see all access lists. However, on a layer-2 switch, you can verify your interface configurations with the show mac access-group command:

```
S1#sh mac access-group
Interface FastEthernet0/1:
   Inbound access-list is not set
   Outbound access-list is not set
Interface FastEthernet0/2:
   Inbound access-list is not set
   Outbound access-list is not set
S1#
```

Depending on how many interfaces you set your MAC access lists on, you can use the interface command to view individual interfaces:

```
S1#sh mac access-group interface f0/6
Interface FastEthernet0/6:
   Inbound access-list is Todd_MAC_List
   Outbound access-list is not set
```

Chapter 8

Network Address Translation (NAT)

In this chapter, I'll give you the skinny on Network Address Translation (NAT); Dynamic NAT; and Port Address Translation (PAT), which is also known as NAT Overload.

It will be helpful for you to read Chapter 7 before reading this chapter since you need to use access lists in your NAT configurations.

 For up-to-the minute updates for this chapter, please see www.lammle.com.

When Do We Use NAT?

Similar to Classless Inter-Domain Routing (CIDR), the original intention for NAT was to slow the depletion of available IP address space by allowing many private IP addresses to be represented by some smaller number of public IP addresses.

Since then, it has been discovered that NAT is also a useful tool for network migrations and mergers, server load sharing, and virtual server creation. So in this chapter, I'll describe the basics of NAT functionality and the terminology common to NAT.

At times, NAT really decreases the overwhelming amount of public IP addresses required in your networking environment. And NAT really comes in handy when two companies that have duplicate internal addressing schemes merge. NAT is also great to have around when an organization changes its Internet service provider (ISP) and the networking manager doesn't want the hassle of changing the internal address scheme.

Here are some situations when it's best to have NAT on your side:

- You need to connect to the Internet, and your hosts don't have globally unique IP addresses.

- You change to a new ISP that requires you to renumber your network.

- You need to merge two intranets with duplicate addresses.

You typically use NAT on a border router, called Corporate in this example. For an illustration of this, see Figure 8.1.

Now you may be thinking, "NAT's totally cool. It's the grooviest, greatest network gadget, and I just gotta have it." Well, hang on a minute. There are truly some serious snags related to NAT use. Oh, don't get me wrong—it really can save you sometimes, but it has a dark side you need to know about, too. For some of the pros and cons linked to using NAT, check out Table 8.1.

FIGURE 8.1   Where to configure NAT

TABLE 8.1   Advantages and Disadvantages of Implementing NAT

Advantages	Disadvantages
Conserves legally registered addresses.	Translation introduces switching path delays.
Reduces address overlap occurrence.	Loss of end-to-end IP traceability.
Increases flexibility when connecting to Internet.	Certain applications will not function with NAT enabled.
Eliminates address renumbering as network changes.	

Types of Network Address Translation

In this section, I'll go over the three types of NAT with you:

Static NAT   This type of NAT is designed to allow one-to-one mapping between local and global addresses. Keep in mind that the static version requires you to have one real Internet IP address for every host on your network.

Dynamic NAT This version gives you the ability to map an unregistered IP address to a registered IP address from out of a pool of registered IP addresses. You don't have to statically configure your router to map an inside to an outside address as you would using static NAT, but you do need to have enough real, bona fide IP addresses for everyone who is going to be sending packets to and receiving them from the Internet.

Overloading This is the most popular type of NAT configuration. Understand that overloading really is a form of dynamic NAT that maps multiple unregistered IP addresses to a single registered IP address—many-to-one—by using different ports. Now, why is this so special? Well, it's also known as Port Address Translation (PAT). And by using PAT (NAT Overload), you get to have thousands of users connect to the Internet using only one real global IP address—pretty slick, yeah? Seriously, NAT Overload is the real reason we haven't run out of valid IP address on the Internet. Really, I'm not joking.

NAT Names

The names we use to describe the addresses used with NAT are pretty simple. Addresses used after NAT translations are called *global* addresses. These are usually the public addresses used on the Internet, but remember, you don't need public addresses if you aren't going on the Internet.

Local addresses are the ones we use before NAT translation. So, the inside local address is actually the private address of the sending host that's trying to get to the Internet, while the outside local address is the address of the destination host. The latter is usually a public address (web address, mail server, and so on) and is how the packet begins its journey.

After translation, the inside local address is then called the *inside global address*, and the outside global address becomes the name of the destination host. Check out Table 8.2, which lists all this terminology, for a clear picture of the various names used with NAT.

TABLE 8.2 NAT Terms

Names	Meaning
Inside local	IP address of inside host before translation
Outside local	IP address as your known to the Internet, typically your router interface connected to the ISP
Inside global	IP address of inside host after translation
Outside global	Name of outside destination host after translation

Static NAT Configuration

OK, let's start looking at some actual commands (see Table 8.3) used with NAT:

TABLE 8.3   Basic NAT Commands

Command	Meaning
ip nat inside source static *inside_local inside_global*	Statically maps a host with a private IP address to a global Internet address
ip nat inside	Sets the interface as an inside interface
ip nat outside	Sets the interface as an outside interface

Let's take a look at a simple basic static NAT configuration:

```
ip nat inside source static 10.1.1.1 170.46.2.2
!
interface Ethernet0
 ip address 10.1.1.10 255.255.255.0
 ip nat inside
!
interface Serial0
 ip address 170.46.2.1 255.255.255.0
 ip nat outside
!
```

In the preceding router output, the ip nat inside source command identifies which IP addresses will be translated. In this configuration example, the ip nat inside source command configures a static translation between the inside local IP address 10.1.1.1 to the inside global IP address 170.46.2.2.

If you look further down in the configuration, you can see an ip nat command under each interface. The ip nat inside command identifies that interface as the inside interface. The ip nat outside command identifies that interface as the outside interface. When you look back at the ip nat inside source command, you see that the command is referencing the inside interface as the source or starting point of the translation. The command could also be used like this—ip nat outside source—which is referencing the interface you designated as the outside interface to be the source or starting point for the translation.

Dynamic NAT Configuration

Table 8.4 lists the commands you'll need to create dynamic NAT:

TABLE 8.4 Dynamic NAT Commands

Command	Meaning
ip nat pool *pool_name* *starting_ address ending_ address mask*	Creates a pool of inside global addresses for the inside local hosts to use
ip nat inside source list *list_number* pool *pool_name*	Sets the inside local hosts that match the access-list number to use the pool of addresses configured by the ip nat pool command
ip nat inside	Sets the inside local interface
ip nat ouside	Sets the inside global interface
access-list *list_number* permit *network inverse_mask*	Creates an access list that permits the inside local hosts to use the global pool of addresses

Dynamic NAT means we have a pool of addresses that we will use to provide real IP addresses to a group of users on the inside. We do not use port numbers, so we need to have real IP addresses for every user trying to get outside the local network.

Here is a sample output of a dynamic NAT configuration:

```
ip nat pool todd 170.168.2.2 170.168.2.254
    netmask 255.255.255.0
ip nat inside source list 1 pool todd
!
interface Ethernet0
 ip address 10.1.1.10 255.255.255.0
 ip nat inside
!
interface Serial0
 ip address 170.168.2.1 255.255.255.0
 ip nat outside
!
access-list 1 permit 10.1.1.0 0.0.0.255
 !
```

The `ip nat inside source list 1 pool todd` command tells the router to translate IP addresses that match `access-list 1` to an address found in the IP NAT pool named todd. The access list in this case is not being used to permit or deny traffic as we would use it for security reasons to filter traffic. It is being used in this case to select or designate what we often call "interesting" traffic. When interesting traffic has been matched with the access list, it is pulled into the NAT process to be translated. This is a common use for access lists; they don't always have the dull job of just blocking traffic at an interface.

The `ip nat pool todd 170.168.2.2 192.168.2.254` command creates a pool of addresses that will be distributed to those hosts that require NAT.

PAT (Overloading) Configuration

As you'll see in Table 8.5, the commands used for PAT are similar to what we used for dynamic NAT:

TABLE 8.5 PAT Commands

Command	Meaning
`ip nat pool` *pool_name starting_ address ending_address* `mask`	Creates a pool of inside global addresses for the inside local hosts to use.
`ip nat inside source list` *list_ number* `pool` *pool_name* `overload`	Sets the inside local hosts that match the access-list number to use the pool of addresses configured by the `ip nat pool` command. The Overload command configures PAT.
`ip nat inside`	Sets the inside local interface.
`ip nat ouside`	Sets the inside global interface.
`access-list` *list_number* `permit network` *inverse_mask*	Creates an access list that permits the inside local hosts to use the global pool of addresses.

This example shows how to configure inside global address overloading. This is the typical NAT you would use today. It is rare you would use static or dynamic NAT unless you were statically mapping an internal server, for example.

Here is a sample output of a PAT configuration:

```
ip nat pool globalnet 170.168.2.1 170.168.2.1
   netmask 255.255.255.0
ip nat inside source list 1 pool globalnet overload
!
interface Ethernet0/0
```

```
 ip address 10.1.1.10 255.255.255.0
 ip nat inside
!
interface Serial0/0
 ip address 170.168.2.1 255.255.255.0
 ip nat outside
!
access-list 1 permit 10.1.1.0 0.0.0.255
```

The nice feature of PAT is that the only differences between this configuration and the previous dynamic NAT configuration is that the pool of addresses has shrunk to only one IP address and at the end of the ip nat inside source command I included the overload command.

Notice in the example that the one IP address that is in the pool for you to use is the IP address of the outside interface. This is perfect if you are configuring NAT Overload for yourself at home or for a small office that has only one IP from your ISP. You could, however, use an additional address such as 170.168.2.2 if you had the address available to you. This could be helpful in a large implementation where you may have so many internal users that you need more than one overloaded IP address on the outside.

Simple Verification of NAT

Table 8.6 is a list of commands you can use to verify NAT on your router:

TABLE 8.6 NAT Verification Commands

Command	Meaning
show ip nat translation	Shows the basic translation table. This is probably one of the most important NAT command for verification.
debug ip nat	Shows the sending address, the translation, and the destination address on each debug line.
show ip nat statistics	Shows a summary of your configuration, your active translations, and the inside and outside interfaces that are being used.

Once you have configured the type of NAT you are going to use, typically Overload (PAT), you need to be able to verify the configuration.

To see basic IP address translation information, use the following command:

Router#**show ip nat translation**

When looking at the IP NAT translations, you may see many translations from the same host to the same host at the destination. This is typical of many connections to the Web. Here is an example:

```
Router#sh ip nat trans
Pro Inside global      Inside local       Outside local      Outside global
icmp 64.1.1.5:271      10.1.9.2:271       64.1.1.10:271      64.1.1.10:271
tcp 64.1.1.5:11000     10.1.9.2:11000     64.1.1.10:23       64.1.1.10:23
Corp#
```

In addition, you can verify your NAT configuration with the debug ip nat command. This output will show the sending address, the translation, and the destination address on each debug line:

```
Router#debug ip nat
*May  9 22:57:47.679: NAT*: TCP s=11000->1024, d=23
*May  9 22:57:47.679: NAT*: s=10.1.6.2->64.1.1.5, d=64.1.1.10 [0]
*May  9 22:57:47.683: NAT*: TCP s=23, d=1024->11000
*May  9 22:57:47.683: NAT*: s=64.1.1.10, d=64.1.1.5->10.1.6.2 [0]
*May  9 22:57:47.699: NAT*: TCP s=11000->1024, d=23
*May  9 22:57:47.699: NAT*: s=10.1.6.2->64.1.1.5, d=64.1.1.10 [1]
*May  9 22:57:47.703: NAT*: TCP s=23, d=1024->11000
*May  9 22:57:47.703: NAT*: s=64.1.1.10, d=64.1.1.5->10.1.6.2 [1]
*May  9 22:57:47.707: NAT*: TCP s=11000->1024, d=23
*May  9 22:57:47.707: NAT*: s=10.1.6.2->64.1.1.5, d=64.1.1.10 [2]
*May  9 22:57:47.711: NAT*: TCP s=11000->1024, d=23
*May  9 22:57:47.711: NAT*: s=10.1.6.2->64.1.1.5, d=64.1.1.10 [3]
*May  9 22:57:47.719: NAT*: TCP s=23, d=1024->11000
*May  9 22:57:47.719: NAT*: s=64.1.1.10, d=64.1.1.5->10.1.6.2 [2]
*May  9 22:57:47.723: NAT*: TCP s=23, d=1024->11000
*May  9 22:57:47.723: NAT*: s=64.1.1.10, d=64.1.1.5->10.1.6.2 [3]
*May  9 22:57:47.723: NAT*: TCP s=11000->1024, d=23
*May  9 22:57:47.723: NAT*: s=10.1.6.2->64.1.1.5, d=64.1.1.10 [4]
*May  9 22:57:47.731: NAT*: TCP s=11000->1024, d=23
*May  9 22:57:47.731: NAT*: s=10.1.6.2->64.1.1.5, d=64.1.1.10 [5]
*May  9 22:57:47.735: NAT*: TCP s=23, d=1024->11000
*May  9 22:57:47.735: NAT*: s=64.1.1.10, d=64.1.1.5->10.1.6.2 [4]
*May  9 22:57:47.735: NAT*: TCP s=11000->1024, d=23
*May  9 22:57:47.735: NAT*: s=10.1.6.2->64.1.1.5, d=64.1.1.10 [6]
*May  9 22:57:47.747: NAT*: TCP s=11000->1024, d=23
*May  9 22:57:47.747: NAT*: s=10.1.6.2->64.1.1.5, d=64.1.1.10 [7]
*May  9 22:57:47.951: NAT*: TCP s=11000->1024, d=23
```

```
*May  9 22:57:47.951: NAT*: s=10.1.6.2->64.1.1.5, d=64.1.1.10 [8]
*May  9 22:57:48.103: NAT*: TCP s=23, d=1024->11000
*May  9 22:57:48.103: NAT*: s=64.1.1.10, d=64.1.1.5->10.1.6.2 [5]
Corp#
```

Now, let's use the command show ip nat statistics on the router:

```
Corp#sh ip nat stat
Total active translations: 2 (0 static, 2 dynamic; 2 extended)
Outside interfaces:
  Serial0/2/0
Inside interfaces:
  FastEthernet0/1, Serial0/0/0, Serial0/0/1, Serial0/1/0
Hits: 269  Misses: 13
CEF Translated packets: 227, CEF Punted packets: 0
Expired translations: 27
Dynamic mappings:
-- Inside Source
[Id: 1] access-list 1 pool Todd refcount 2
 pool Todd: netmask 255.255.255.252
        start 64.1.1.5 end 64.1.1.5
        type generic, total addresses 1, allocated 1 (100%), misses 0
Queued Packets: 0
Corp#
```

What you can see here is a summary of the configuration, the two active translations, and the inside and outside interfaces that are being used. The pool is listed right there toward the bottom of the output.

Chapter 9

Internet Protocol Version 6 (IPv6)

People refer to IPv6 as the "next-generation Internet protocol," and it was originally created as the answer to IPv4's inevitable, looming address-exhaustion crisis. Though you've probably heard a thing or two about IPv6 already, it has been improved even further in the quest to bring you the flexibility, efficiency, capability, and optimized functionality that can truly meet your ever-increasing needs. The capacity of its predecessor, IPv4, pales in comparison—and that's the reason it will eventually fade into history completely.

The IPv6 header and address structure has been completely overhauled, and many of the features that were basically just afterthoughts and addendums in IPv4 are now included as full-blown standards in IPv6. It's seriously well equipped, poised, and ready to manage the mind-blowing demands of the Internet to come.

For up-to-the-minute updates for this chapter, check out www.lammle.com.

Why Do We Need IPv6?

Well, the short answer is, we need to communicate, and our current system isn't really cutting it anymore—kind of like how the Pony Express can't compete with airmail. Just look at how much time and effort we've invested in coming up with slick new ways to conserve bandwidth and IP addresses. We've even come up with variable-length subnet masks (VLSMs) in our struggle to overcome the worsening address drought.

It's reality—the amount of people and devices that connect to networks increases every day. That's not a bad thing at all—we're finding new and exciting ways to communicate to more people all the time, and that's a good thing. In fact, it's a basic human need. But the forecast isn't exactly blue skies and sunshine because IPv4, upon which our ability to communicate is currently dependent, is going to run out of addresses for us to use. IPv4 has only about 4.3 billion addresses available—that's in theory, and we know that we don't even get to use all of those. There really are only about 250 million addresses that can be assigned to devices. Sure, Classless Inter-Domain Routing (CIDR) and Network Address Translation (NAT) have helped to extend the inevitable dearth of addresses, but we will run out of them, and it's going to happen within a few years. China is barely online, and we know there's a huge population of people and corporations there that surely want to be. Many reports give us all kinds of numbers, but all you really need to think about to convince yourself that I'm not just being an alarmist is the fact that there are about 6.5 billion people in the world today, and it's estimated that just more than 10 percent of that population is connected to the Internet—wow!

That statistic is basically screaming at us the ugly truth that, based on IPv4's capacity, every person can't even have a computer—let alone all the other devices we use with them. I have more than one computer, and it's pretty likely you do too. And I'm not even including in the mix phones, laptops, game consoles, fax machines, routers, switches, and a mother lode of other devices we use every day! So I think I've made it pretty clear that we have to do something before we run out of addresses and lose the ability to connect with each other as we know it. And that "something" just happens to be implementing IPv6.

IPv6 Addressing and Expressions

Just as understanding how IP addresses are structured and used is critical with IPv4 addressing, it's also vital when it comes to IPv6. You already know that at 128 bits, an IPv6 address is much larger than an IPv4 address. Because of this, as well as the new ways the addresses can be used, you've probably guessed that IPv6 will be more complicated to manage. But no worries! As I said, I'll break down the basics and show you what the address looks like, how you can write it, and what many of its common uses are. It's going to be a little weird at first, but before you know it, you'll have it nailed!

So let's take a look at Figure 9.1, which has a sample IPv6 address broken down into sections.

FIGURE 9.1   IPv6 address example

```
2001:0db8:3c4d:0012:0000:0000:1234:56ab
_____|___|_____
Global prefix   Subnet        Interface ID
```

So as you can now see, the address is truly much larger—but what else is different? Well, first, notice that it has eight groups of numbers instead of four and also that those groups are separated by colons instead of periods. And, hey, wait a second... there are letters in that address! Yep, the address is expressed in hexadecimal just like a MAC address is, so you could say this address has eight 16-bit hexadecimal colon-delimited blocks. That's already quite a mouthful, and you probably haven't even tried to say the address out loud yet!

When you use a web browser to make an HTTP connection to an IPv6 device, you have to type the address into the browser with brackets around the literal address. Why? Well, the browser is already using a colon for specifying a port number. So basically, if you don't enclose the address in brackets, the browser will have no way to identify the information.

Here's an example of how this looks:

```
http://[2001:0db8:3c4d:0012:0000:0000:1234:56ab]/default.html
```

Now obviously, if you can, you would rather use names to specify a destination (such as www.lammle.com). However, even though it's definitely going to be a pain in the rear, we just have to accept the fact that sometimes we have to type the address number. So, it should be pretty clear that DNS is going to become extremely important when implementing IPv6.

Shortened Expression

The good news is there are a few tricks to help rescue us when writing these monster addresses. For one thing, you can actually omit parts of the address to abbreviate it, but to get away with doing that you have to follow a couple of rules. First, you can drop any leading zeros in each of the individual blocks. After you do that, the sample address from earlier would then look like this:

```
2001:db8:3c4d:12:0:0:1234:56ab
```

OK, that's a definite improvement—at least we don't have to write all of those extra zeros! But what about whole blocks that don't have anything in them except zeros? Well, we can kind of lose those too—at least some of them. Again referring to our sample address, we can remove the two blocks of zeros by replacing them with double colons, like this:

```
2001:db8:3c4d:12::1234:56ab
```

Cool—we replaced the blocks of all zeros with double colons. The rule you have to follow to get away with this is that you can replace only one contiguous block of zeros in an address. So if my address has four blocks of zeros and each of them were separated, I just don't get to replace them all. Check out this example:

```
2001:0000:0000:0012:0000:0000:1234:56ab
```

And just know that you *can't* do this:

```
2001::12::1234:56ab
```

Instead, this is the best you can do:

```
2001::12:0:0:1234:56ab
```

The reason why the previous example is your best shot is that if you remove two sets of zeros, the device looking at the address will have no way of knowing where the zeros go back in. Basically, the router would look at the incorrect address and say, "Well, do I place two blocks into the first set of double colons and two into the second set, or do I place three blocks into the first set and one block into the second set?" And on and on it would go because the information the router needs just isn't there.

Configuring Cisco Routers with IPv6

Look at Table 9.1.

TABLE 9.1   Basic IPv6 Cisco Router Commands

Command	Meaning
(config)#**ipv6 unicast-routing**	Starts the IPv6 routing on a router.
(config-if)#**ipv6 address** *ipv6-prefix/ prefix-length* **[eui-64]**	Configures a router interface with the IPv6 routed protocol. With the EUI-64 option the last 64 bits are derived from an expansion of the 48-bit interface MAC address.
(config-if)#**ipv6 enable**	Enables IPv6 on a LAN link only.

To enable IPv6 on a router, you have to use the ipv6 unicast-routing global configuration command:

Corp(config)#**ipv6 unicast-routing**

By default, IPv6 traffic forwarding is disabled, so using this command enables it. Also, as you've probably guessed, IPv6 isn't enabled by default on any interfaces either, so we have to go to each interface individually and enable it.

You can do this in a few different ways, but a really easy way is to just add an address to the interface. You use the interface configuration command ipv6 address <ipv6prefix>/<prefix-length> [eui-64]to get this done.

Here's an example:

Corp(config-if)#**ipv6 address 2001:db8:3c4d:1:0260.d6FF.FE73.1987/64**

You can specify the entire 128-bit global IPv6 address, or you can use the eui-64 option. Remember, the eui-64 format allows the device to use its MAC address and pad it to make the interface ID. Check it out:

Corp(config-if)#**ipv6 address 2001:db8:3c4d:1::/64 eui-64**

As an alternative to typing an IPv6 address on a router, you can enable the interface instead to permit the application of an automatic link-local address.

To configure a router so that it uses only link-local addresses, use the `ipv6 enable` interface configuration command:

```
Corp(config-if)#ipv6 enable
```

Stateless Auto Configuration

It's actually not necessary to have a DHCP server provide IP configurations to the devices. If all you need to provide to the devices is an IPv6 address and prefix, you can use a feature called stateless auto configuration. This feature allows the router, through the use of multicast packets called router advertisements, to provide the devices with a network prefix (functions like a network ID in IPv4) to which the devices will append a 64-bit host identifier. This identifier is derived by the expansion of the interface's 48-bit MAC address to 64-bit. The result is unique IPv6 address that resides in the proper network.

To configure this functionality the router must be instructed to perform this function with the following single command on any interface that needs to provide this functionality:

```
Router(config-if)#ipv6 address autoconfig [default]
```

The default parameter can be used to also provide devices with a default route if one is configured on the router.

IPv6 Static Routing

Creating static routes can be done as easily with IPv6 as with IPv4. The only difference is the use of IPv6 addressing. The command to create a static route using IPv6 is

```
Router(config)#ipv6 route ipv6_network/ipv6_mask outgoing interface ipv6_next_hop
```

For example, the command to configure a route to the 2001:DB8:B01::/48 network using the Fa0/5 interface as the outgoing interface and the IPv6 address 2001:DB8:D1A7:D800::2 address as the next hop is

```
Router(config)#ipv6 route 2001:DB8:B01::/48 Fa0/5  2001:DB8:D1A7:D800::2
```

Moreover, you can also configure a default route in a similar fashion. The command is as follows:

```
Router(config)#ipv6 route ::/0 outgoing interface ipv6_next_hop
```

For example, to configure a default route that sends traffic to a next hop address of 2001:DB8:D1A7:D800::2, use the following command:

```
Router(config)#ipv6 route ::/0 Fa0/5 2001:DB8:D1A7:D800::2
```

To verify a static route configuration the following command can be used to verify the static route exists in the routing table:

Show ipv6 route static

IPv6 Routing Protocols

Most of the routing protocols I've already discussed have been upgraded for use in IPv6 networks. Also, many of the functions and configurations you've already learned will be used in almost the same way as they're used now. Knowing that broadcasts have been eliminated in IPv6, it follows that any protocols that use entirely broadcast traffic will go the way of the dodo—but unlike the dodo, it'll be good to say goodbye to these bandwidth-hogging, performance-annihilating little gremlins!

The routing protocols you'll still use in IPv6 have gotten a new name and a facelift. I'll talk about a few of them now.

First on the list is *RIPng* (next generation). If you've been in IT for a while, you know that RIP has worked well on smaller networks, which happens to be the reason it didn't get whacked and will still be around in IPv6. And you still have EIGRPv6 because it already had protocol-dependent modules, and all you have to do was add a new one to it for the IPv6 protocol. Rounding out the group of protocol survivors is OSPFv3—that's not a typo; it really is v3. OSPF for IPv4 was actually v2, so when it got its upgrade to IPv6, it became OSPFv3.

RIPng

Table 9.2 lists IPv6 RIP Commands. To be honest, the primary features of RIPng are the same as they were with RIPv2. It is still a distance-vector protocol; has a max hop count of 15; and uses split horizon, poison reverse, and other loop avoidance mechanisms. However, it now uses UDP port 521.

TABLE 9.2   IPv6 RIP Commands

Command	Meaning
(config-if)#**ipv6 rip 1 enable**	Enables RIP on the router interface
(config)#**ipv6 router rip 1**	Enters router configuration mode

It still uses multicast to send its updates too, but in IPv6, it uses FF02::9 for the transport address. This is actually kind of cool since in RIPv2, the multicast address was 224.0.0.9, so the address still has a 9 at the end in the new IPv6 multicast range. In fact, most routing protocols got to keep a little bit of their IPv4 identities like that.

But of course there are differences in the new version, or it wouldn't be a new version, would it? We know that routers keep the next-hop addresses of their neighbor routers for every destination network in their routing table. The difference is that with RIPng, the router keeps track of this next-hop address using the link-local address, not a global address.

Probably one of the biggest changes with RIPng (and all of the IPv6 routing protocols for that matter) is that you configure or enable the advertisement of a network from interface configuration mode instead of with a network command in router configuration mode. So in RIPng's case, if you enable it directly on an interface without going into router configuration mode and starting a RIPng process, a new RIPng process will simply be started for you. It will look something like this:

```
Router1(config-if)#ipv6 rip 1 enable
```

That 1 you see in this command is a tag that identifies the process of RIPng that's running, and as I said, this will start a process of RIPng so you don't have to go into router configuration mode.

But if you need to go to router configuration mode to configure something else like redistribution, you still can. If you do that, it will look like this on your router:

```
Router1(config)#ipv6 router rip 1
Router1(config-rtr)#
```

So, just remember that RIPng will pretty much work the same way as with IPv4, with the biggest difference being that it uses the network itself instead of using the network command you used to use to enable the interface to route the connected network.

EIGRPv6

As with RIPng, EIGRPv6 works much the same as its IPv4 predecessor does (see Table 9.3)—most of the features that EIGRP provided before EIGRPv6 will still be available.

TABLE 9.3 IPv6 EIGRP Commands

Command	Meaning
(config)#ipv6 router eigrp AS	Enables EIGRP on the router
(config-rtr)#no shutdown	Is required for EIGRP to be enabled on the router
(config-if)#ipv6 eigrp 10	Enables EIGRP on each interface you want to use
(config)#ipv6 unicast routing	Enables IPv6 traffic forwarding

EIGRPv6 is still an advanced distance-vector protocol that has some link-state features. The neighbor discovery process using hellos still happens, and it still provides reliable communication with reliable transport protocol that gives you loop-free fast convergence using the Diffusing Update Algorithm (DUAL).

Hello packets and updates are sent using multicast transmission, and as with RIPng, EIGRPv6's multicast address stayed almost the same. In IPv4 it was 224.0.0.10; in IPv6, it's FF02::A (A = 10 in hexadecimal notation).

But obviously, there are differences between the two versions. Most notably, and just as with RIPng, the use of the network command is gone, and the network and interface to be advertised must be enabled from interface configuration mode. But you still have to use the router configuration mode to enable the routing protocol in EIGRPv6 because the routing process must be turned on like an interface with the no shutdown command—interesting!

The configuration for EIGRPv6 is going to look like this:

```
Router1(config)#ipv6 router eigrp 10
```

The 10 in this case is still the autonomous system (AS) number. The prompt changes to (config-rtr), and from here you must perform a no shutdown:

```
Router1(config-rtr)#no shutdown
```

Other options also can be configured in this mode, such as redistribution.

So now, let's go to the interface and enable IPv6:

```
Router1(config-if)#ipv6 eigrp 10
```

The 10 in the interface command again references the AS number that was enabled in the configuration mode.

Last to check out in this group is what OSPF looks like in the IPv6 routing protocol.

OSPFv3

Take a look at Table 9.4.

TABLE 9.4   IPv6 OSPF Commands

Command	Meaning
(config)#**ipv6 router ospf** *process_id*	Enables the OSPF database on the router
(config-rtr)#**router-id** *a.b.c.d*	Sets the RID of the router
(config-if)#**ipv6 ospf** *process_id* **area** *area*	Configures the area for the interface

TABLE 9.4   IPv6 OSPF Commands *(continued)*

Command	Meaning
(config-if)#**ipv6 ospf priority** *priority value*	Assigns a priority number to this interface for the purpose of electing a DR
(config-if)#**ipv6 ospf cost** *cost value*	Assigns a cost to this interface for the purpose of calculating best route

The new version of OSPF continues the trend of the routing protocols having many similarities with their IPv4 versions.

The foundation of OSPF remains the same—it is still a link-state routing protocol that divides an entire internetwork or autonomous system into areas, making a hierarchy. And just trust me—be really thankful that multiarea OSPF is out of scope for the CCNA objectives—at least, for now!

In OSPF version 2, the router ID (RID) is determined by the highest IP addresses assigned to the router (or you could assign it). In version 3, you assign the RID, area ID, and link-state ID, which are all still 32-bit values. Changes regarding how these values are assigned, along with the removal of the IP address information from OSPF packet headers, makes the new version of OSPF capable of being routed over almost any Network layer protocol—cool!

Adjacencies and next-hop attributes now use link-local addresses, and OSPFv3 still uses multicast traffic to send its updates and acknowledgments, with the addresses FF02::5 for OSPF routers and FF02::6 for OSPF-designated routers. These new addresses are the replacements for 224.0.0.5 and 224.0.0.6, respectively.

Other, less flexible IPv4 protocols don't give you the ability that OSPFv2 does to assign specific networks and interfaces into the OSPF process—however, this is something that is still configured under the router configuration process. And with OSPFv3, just as with the other IPv6 routing protocols we've talked about, the interfaces and therefore the networks attached to them are configured directly on the interface in interface configuration mode.

The configuration of OSPFv3 is going to look like this:

```
Router1(config)#ipv6 router osfp 10
Router1(config-rtr)#router-id 1.1.1.1
```

You get to perform some configurations from router configuration mode such as summarization and redistribution, but you don't even need to configure OSPFv3 from this prompt if you configure OSPFv3 from the interface.

When the interface configuration is completed, the router configuration process is added automatically. and the interface configuration looks like this:

```
Router1(config-if)#ipv6 ospf 10 area 0.0.0.0
```

So, if you just go to each interface and assign a process ID and area, poof, you're done! With all that behind you, it's now time to move on and learn about how to verify these routing protocols!

Verifying RIPng

Now take a look at Table 9.5.

TABLE 9.5   Verifying IPv6 RIP

Command	Meaning
show ipv6 route	Displays the IPv6 routing table on a router
show ipv6 protocols	Doesn't display much, but it does show up the IPv6 routing protocols that are enabled
Show ipv6 rip	Displays the administrative distance, plus the multicast group, maximum paths, and timers
show ipv6 interface *interface*	Displays the IPv6 address, unicast address, and other interface information regarding IPv6
debug ipv6 rip	Displays the IPv6 RIP updates sent and received on a router

I'll start with the usual show ipv6 route command. Here's the output from the R3 router:

```
R3#sh ipv6 route
R    2001:DB8:3C4D:11::/64 [120/2]
      via FE80::21A:2FFF:FE55:C9E8, Serial0/0/1
R    2001:DB8:3C4D:12::/64 [120/2]
      via FE80::21A:2FFF:FE55:C9E8, Serial0/0/1
R    2001:DB8:3C4D:13::/64 [120/2]
      via FE80::21A:2FFF:FE55:C9E8, Serial0/0/1
R    2001:DB8:3C4D:14::/64 [120/2]
      via FE80::21A:2FFF:FE55:C9E8, Serial0/0/1
C    2001:DB8:3C4D:15::/64 [0/0]
      via ::, Serial0/0/1
L    2001:DB8:3C4D:15:21A:6DFF:FE37:A44E/128 [0/0]
      via ::, Serial0/0/1
L    FE80::/10 [0/0]
```

```
     via ::, Null0
L   FF00::/8 [0/0]
     via ::, Null0
R3#
```

Wow, it looks just like the regular IPv4 RIP table, including the administrative distance and hop count. I can see subnets 11, 12, 13, 14, and 15.

Let's take a look at a few more verification commands:

```
R3#sh ipv6 protocols
IPv6 Routing Protocol is "connected"
IPv6 Routing Protocol is "static"
IPv6 Routing Protocol is "rip 1"
  Interfaces:
    Serial0/0/1
  Redistribution:
    None
R3#
```

Not too much information is provided with the show ipv6 protocols command. Let's try the show ipv6 rip command:

```
R3#sh ipv6 rip
RIP process "1", port 521, multicast-group FF02::9, pid 60
     Administrative distance is 120. Maximum paths is 16
     Updates every 30 seconds, expire after 180
     Holddown lasts 0 seconds, garbage collect after 120
     Split horizon is on; poison reverse is off
     Default routes are not generated
     Periodic updates 44, trigger updates 19
  Interfaces:
    Serial0/0/1
  Redistribution:
    None
```

Now we're talking! You can see that the administrative distance is still 120, plus the multicast group, maximum paths, and timers. So, let's try two more verification commands, beginning with the show ipv6 interface s0/0/1 command:

```
R3#sh ipv6 interface serial 0/0/1
Serial0/0/1 is up, line protocol is up
  IPv6 is enabled, link-local address is FE80::21A:6DFF:FE37:A44E
  Global unicast address(es):
    2001:DB8:3C4D:1:21A:6DFF:FE37:A44E, subnet is 2001:DB8:3C4D:1::/64 [EUI]
```

```
Joined group address(es):
  FF02::1
  FF02::2
  FF02::9
  FF02::1:FF37:A44E
MTU is 1500 bytes
ICMP error messages limited to one every 100 milliseconds
ICMP redirects are enabled
ND DAD is enabled, number of DAD attempts: 1
ND reachable time is 30000 milliseconds
Hosts use stateless autoconfig for addresses.
```

This got us some pretty good information too. But wait, the best is yet to come: the debug ipv6 rip command. This should be good:

```
R3#debug ipv6 rip
*May 24 18:31:11.959: RIPng: Sending multicast update on Serial0/0/1 for 1
*May 24 18:31:11.959:        src=FE80::21A:6DFF:FE37:A44E
*May 24 18:31:11.959:        dst=FF02::9 (Serial0/0/1)
*May 24 18:31:11.959:        sport=521, dport=521, length=32
*May 24 18:31:11.959:        command=2, version=1, mbz=0, #rte=1
*May 24 18:31:11.959:        tag=0, metric=1, prefix=2001:DB8:3C4D:1::/64
*May 24 18:40:44.079: %LINEPROTO-5-UPDOWN: Line protocol on Interface
   Serial0/0/0, changed state to down
*May 24 18:31:24.959: RIPng: response received from
  FE80::21A:2FFF:FE55:C9E8 on Serial0/0/1 for 1
*May 24 18:31:24.959:        src=FE80::21A:2FFF:FE55:C9E8 (Serial0/0/1)
*May 24 18:31:24.959:        dst=FF02::9
*May 24 18:31:24.959:        sport=521, dport=521, length=32
*May 24 18:31:24.959:        command=2, version=1, mbz=0, #rte=1
*May 24 18:31:24.959:        tag=0, metric=16,
   prefix=2001:DB8:3C4D:12::/64
*May 24 18:31:24.959: RIPng: 2001:DB8:3C4D:12::/64, path
  FE80::21A:2FFF:FE55:C9E8/Serial0/0/1 unreachable
*May 24 18:31:24.959: RIPng: 2001:DB8:3C4D:12::/64, expired, ttg is 120
*May 24 18:31:24.959: RIPng: Triggered update requested
*May 24 18:31:25.959: RIPng: generating triggered update for 1
*May 24 18:31:25.959: RIPng: Suppressed null multicast update on
   Serial0/0/1 for 1
```

Now this is interesting. You can see that the source and destination ports used are 521 (yes, I'm still using UDP) and that network/subnet 12 is unreachable. This is because the s0/0/0 interface of my Corp router has just decided to go bad. (I swear, writing this book is just like being at work!) Either way, you can see that RIPng still has some basic IPv4 RIP characteristics. Let's add OSPFv3 to the routers.

Verifying EIGRPv6

The commands used to verify EIGRPv6 and an explanation of their use are contained in Table 9.6. Following the table is an example of partial output from each command.

TABLE 9.6 Commands to Verify EIGRPv6

Command	Meaning
Show ipv6 eigrp interfaces	Display the interfaces configure for EIGRPv6
Show ipv6 eigrp neighbors	Displays a list of EIGRP neighbors
Show ipv6 eigrp topology	Displays the list of routes contained in the topology table
Show ipv6 route eigrp	Displays EGRP derived routes only

```
Router# show ipv6 interface ethernet 0/0
Ethernet0 is up, line protocol is up
  IPv6 is enabled, link-local address is 2001:0DB8::/29
  Global unicast address(es):
    2000:0DB8::2, subnet is 2001:0DB8::/64
  Joined group address(es):
    FF02::1
    FF02::2
    FF02::1:FF11:6770
  MTU is 1500 bytes
<output omitted>
```

```
Router# show ipv6 eigrp neighbors
IPv6-EIGRP neighbors for process 1
H Address Interface  Hold     Uptime    SRTT  RTO  Q    Seq
                     (Sec)              (ms)       Cnt  Num
0 Link-local  Et0/0  14       00:00:13  11    00   0    2
```

```
address
FE80::A8BB:CCFF:FE00:200


Router# show ipv6 eigrp topology
IPv6-EIGRP Topology Table for AS(1)/ID(2001:0DB8:10::/64)


Codes: P - Passive, A - Active, U - Update, Q - Query, R - Reply,
r - reply Status, s - sia Status


P 2001:0DB8:3::/64, 1 successors, FD is 281600
via Connected, Ethernet1/0

R1#show ipv6 route eigrp
IPv6 Routing Table - 12 entries
Codes: C - Connected, L - Local, S - Static, R - RIP, B - BGP
       U - Per-user Static route, M - MIPv6
       I1 - ISIS L1, I2 - ISIS L2, IA - ISIS interarea, IS -   ISIS summary
       O - OSPF intra, OI - OSPF inter, OE1 - OSPF ext 1, OE2 - OSPF ext 2
       ON1 - OSPF NSSA ext 1, ON2 - OSPF NSSA ext 2
       D - EIGRP, EX - EIGRP external
D   1000:AB8::/64 [90/2297856]
     via FE80::2, Serial0/0
D   2000:AB8::/64 [90/2297856]
     via FE80::2, Serial0/0
D   3000:AB8::/64 [90/2297856]
     via FE80::2, Serial0/0
```

Verifying OSPFv3

Note the information in Table 9.7.

TABLE 9.7   Verifying IPv6 OSPF

Command	Meaning
debug ipv6 ospf adjacencies	Display debug messages about the adjacency process
show ipv6 interface	Display the interfaces configured for OSPFv3

TABLE 9.7 Verifying IPv6 OSPF *(continued)*

Command	Meaning
show ipv6 ospf	Displays general OSPFv3 information (processes ID, router ID, etc.)
show ipv6 route	Displays the IPv6 routing table on the router
show ipv6 protocols	Displays minimal routing protocol information
show ipv6 ospf neighbor	Displays the OSPF "neighborship" table
debug ipv6 ospf packet	Displays the events that occur if an update takes place
debug ipv6 ospf hello	Displays the updates between neighbor routers

I'll start as usual with the show ipv6 route command:

```
R3#sh ipv6 route
IPv6 Routing Table - 7 entries
O    2001:DB8:3C4D:11::/64 [110/65]
     via FE80::21A:2FFF:FE55:C9E8, Serial0/0/1
O    2001:DB8:3C4D:13::/64 [110/128]
     via FE80::21A:2FFF:FE55:C9E8, Serial0/0/1
O    2001:DB8:3C4D:14::/64 [110/128]
     via FE80::21A:2FFF:FE55:C9E8, Serial0/0/1
C    2001:DB8:3C4D:15::/64 [0/0]
     via ::, Serial0/0/1
L    2001:DB8:3C4D:15:21A:6DFF:FE37:A44E/128 [0/0]
     via ::, Serial0/0/1
L    FE80::/10 [0/0]
     via ::, Null0
L    FF00::/8 [0/0]
     via ::, Null0
R3#
```

Perfect. I see all the subnets (except 12, which is down because of that bad interface). Let's take a look at the show ipv6 protocols command:

```
R3#sh ipv6 protocols
IPv6 Routing Protocol is "connected"
IPv6 Routing Protocol is "static"
```

```
IPv6 Routing Protocol is "rip 1"
  Interfaces:
    Serial0/0/1
  Redistribution:
    None
IPv6 Routing Protocol is "ospf 1"
  Interfaces (Area 0):
    Serial0/0/1
  Redistribution:
    None
```

For the next command, I want to go back to the Corp router so can I see more connections by using the show ipv6 ospf neighbor command:

```
Corp#sh ipv6 ospf neighbor
Neighbor ID    Pri   State      Dead Time   Interface ID   Interface
172.16.10.4     1    FULL/  -  00:00:36     6              Serial0/2/0
172.16.10.3     1    FULL/  -  00:00:33    16              Serial0/1/0
172.16.10.2     1    FULL/  -  00:00:30     6              Serial0/0/1
Corp#
```

Wait! I need to do the debugging commands. I'll use two of them: debug ipv6 ospf packet and debug ipv6 ospf hello (almost the same commands I used with IPv4):

```
Corp#debug ipv6 ospf packet
  OSPFv3 packet debugging is on
Corp#
*May 24 19:38:12.283: OSPFv3: rcv. v:3 t:1 l:40 rid:172.16.10.3
      aid:0.0.0.0 chk:E1D2 inst:0 from Serial0/1/0
Corp#
*May 24 19:38:15.103: OSPFv3: rcv. v:3 t:1 l:40 rid:172.16.10.4
      aid:0.0.0.0 chk:7EBB inst:0 from Serial0/2/0
Corp#
*May 24 19:38:18.875: OSPFv3: rcv. v:3 t:1 l:40 rid:172.16.10.2
      aid:0.0.0.0 chk:192D inst:0 from Serial0/0/1
Corp#
*May 24 19:38:22.283: OSPFv3: rcv. v:3 t:1 l:40 rid:172.16.10.3
      aid:0.0.0.0 chk:E1D2 inst:0 from Serial0/1/0
Corp#un all
All possible debugging has been turned off
Corp#debug ipv6 ospf hello
  OSPFv3 hello events debugging is on
```

```
Corp#
*May 24 19:38:32.283: OSPFv3: Rcv hello from 172.16.10.3 area 0 from
    Serial0/1/0 FE80::213:60FF:FE20:4E4C interface ID 16
*May 24 19:38:32.283: OSPFv3: End of hello processing
Corp#
*May 24 19:38:35.103: OSPFv3: Rcv hello from 172.16.10.4 area 0 from
    Serial0/2/0 FE80::21A:6DFF:FE37:A44E interface ID 6
*May 24 19:38:35.103: OSPFv3: End of hello processing
Corp#
*May 24 19:38:38.875: OSPFv3: Rcv hello from 172.16.10.2 area 0 from
    Serial0/0/1 FE80::21A:6DFF:FE64:9B2 interface ID 6
*May 24 19:38:38.875: OSPFv3: End of hello processing
Corp#un all
All possible debugging has been turned off
Corp#
```

Chapter 10

Wide Area Networks (WANs)

The Cisco IOS supports a ton of different wide area network (WAN) protocols that help you extend your local LANs to other LANs at remote sites. And I don't think I have to tell you how positively essential information exchange between disparate sites is these days—it's vital! But even so, it wouldn't exactly be cost effective or efficient to install your own cable and connect all of your company's remote locations yourself, now would it? A much better way to go about doing this is to simply lease the existing installations that service providers already have in place—and then save big time.

So it follows that I'm going to discuss the various types of connections, technologies, and devices used in accordance with WANs in this chapter. I'll also get into how to implement and configure High-Level Data-Link Control (HDLC), Point-to-Point Protocol (PPP), cable, DSL, and Frame Relay. I'll also introduce you to WAN security concepts, tunneling, and virtual private network basics.

Just so you know, I'm not going to cover every type of Cisco WAN support here—again, the focus of this book is to equip you with everything you need to successfully meet the CCNA objectives.

But first things first—let's begin with an exploration into WAN basics.

For up-to-the-minute updates for this chapter, check out www.lammle.com.

Introduction to Wide Area Networks

So what, exactly, is it that makes something a *wide area network (WAN)* instead of a local area network (LAN)? Well, there's obviously the distance thing, but these days, wireless LANs can cover some serious turf. What about bandwidth? Well, here again, some really big pipes can be had for a price in many places, so that's not it either. So, what the heck is it then?

One of the main ways a WAN differs from a LAN is that while you generally own a LAN infrastructure, you usually lease WAN infrastructure from a service provider. To be honest, modern technologies even blur this definition, but it still fits neatly into the context of Cisco's exam objectives.

Anyway, I've already talked about the data link that you usually own (Ethernet), but now you're going to find out about the kind you usually don't own—the type most often leased from a service provider.

The key to understanding WAN technologies is to be familiar with the different WAN terms and connection types commonly used by service providers to join your networks together.

Defining WAN Terms

Before you run out and order a WAN service type from a provider, it would be a really good idea to understand the following terms that service providers typically use:

Customer premises equipment (CPE)   Equipment that's owned by the subscriber and located on the subscriber's premises.

Demarcation point   The precise spot where the service provider's responsibility ends and the CPE begins. It's generally a device in a telecommunications closet owned and installed by the telecommunications company (telco). It's your responsibility to add cable (extended demarc) from this box to the CPE, which is usually a connection to a CSU/DSU or ISDN interface.

Local loop   Connects the demarc to the closest switching office, which is called a *central office*.

Central office (CO)   Connects the customer's network to the provider's switching network. Good to know is that a CO is sometimes referred to as a *point of presence (POP)*.

Toll network   A trunk line inside a WAN provider's network. This network is a collection of switches and facilities owned by the ISP.

Definitely familiarize yourself with these terms because they're crucial to understanding WAN technologies.

WAN Support

First, take a look at Table 10.1.

TABLE 10.1   Setting the Encapsulation on an Interface

Command	Meaning
configure terminal	Takes you to global configuration mode
interface *interface*	Chooses your interface to configure
encapsulation *encapsulation*	Sets the WAN encapsulation type

Basically, Cisco just supports HDLC, PPP, and Frame Relay on its serial interfaces, and you can see this with the encapsulation ? command from any serial interface (your output may vary depending on the IOS version you are running):

```
Corp#config t
Corp(config)#int s0/0/0
Corp(config-if)#encapsulation ?
  atm-dxi      ATM-DXI encapsulation
  frame-relay  Frame Relay networks
  hdlc         Serial HDLC synchronous
  lapb         LAPB (X.25 Level 2)
  ppp          Point-to-Point protocol
  smds         Switched Megabit Data Service (SMDS)
  x25          X.25
```

Understand that if I had other types of interfaces on my router, I would have other encapsulation options, such as ISDN or ADSL. And remember, you can't configure Ethernet or Token Ring encapsulation on a serial interface.

Next, I'm going to define the most prominently known WAN protocols used today: Frame Relay, ISDN, HDLC, PPP, PPPoE, cable, DSL, and ATM. Just so you know, the only WAN protocols you'll usually find configured on a serial interface are HDLC, PPP, and Frame Relay, but who said we're stuck with using only serial interfaces for wide area connections?

Frame Relay   A packet-switched technology that made its debut in the early 1990s, *Frame Relay* is a high-performance Data Link and Physical layer specification. It's pretty much a successor to X.25, except that much of the technology in X.25 that used to compensate for physical errors (noisy lines) has been eliminated. An upside to Frame Relay is that it can be more cost effective than point-to-point links; plus, it typically runs at speeds of 64Kbps up to 45Mbps (T3). Another Frame Relay benefit is that it provides features for dynamic bandwidth allocation and congestion control.

ISDN   *Integrated Services Digital Network (ISDN)* is a set of digital services that transmit voice and data over existing phone lines. ISDN offers a cost-effective solution for remote users who need a higher-speed connection than analog dial-up links can give them, and it's also a good choice to use as a backup link for other types of links such as Frame Relay or T1 connections.

HDLC   *High-Level Data-Link Control (HDLC)* was derived from Synchronous Data Link Control (SDLC), which was created by IBM as a Data Link connection protocol. HDLC works at the Data Link layer and creates very little overhead compared to LAPB.

It wasn't intended to encapsulate multiple Network layer protocols across the same link—the HDLC header doesn't contain any identification about the type of protocol being carried inside the HDLC encapsulation. Because of this, each vendor that uses HDLC has its own way of identifying the Network layer protocol, meaning each vendor's HDLC is proprietary with regard to its specific equipment.

PPP   *Point-to-Point Protocol (PPP)* is a pretty famous, industry-standard protocol. Because all multiprotocol versions of HDLC are proprietary, PPP can be used to create point-to-point links between different vendors' equipment. It uses a Network Control Protocol field in the Data Link header to identify the Network layer protocol and allows authentication and multi-link connections to be run over asynchronous and synchronous links.

ATM   *Asynchronous Transfer Mode* (ATM) was created for time-sensitive traffic, providing simultaneous transmission of voice, video, and data. ATM uses cells that are a fixed 53 bytes long instead of packets. It also can use isochronous clocking (external clocking) to help the data move faster. Typically, if you are running Frame Relay today, you will be running Frame Relay over ATM.

Ethernet   The abundance of new fiber deployments to business areas has resulted in the emergence of Ethernet as a method of providing point-to-point and multipoint services. This technology is not only familiar to enterprise customers but can provide connections up to 100 Gb/s.

Broadband   Broadband connections send multiple pieces of data at once to increase the effective rate of transmission. A variety of these connection types are available.

PPPoE / PPPoA   Point-to-Point Protocol over Ethernet encapsulates PPP frames in Ethernet frames and is usually used in conjunction with ADSL services. It gives you a lot of the familiar PPP features such as authentication, encryption, and compression, but there's a downside—it has a lower maximum transmission unit (MTU) than standard Ethernet does, and if your firewall isn't solidly configured, this little attribute can really give you some grief!

Still somewhat popular in the United States, PPPoE on Ethernet's main feature is that it adds a direct connection to Ethernet interfaces while providing DSL support as well. It's often used by many hosts on a shared Ethernet interface for opening PPP sessions to various destinations via at least one bridging modem.

Point-to-Point Protocol over ATM encapsulates PPP frames in ATM Adaptation Layer 5 (AAL5) frames and is usually used in conjunction with cable modems and DSL modems.

Cable   In a modern HFC network, typically 500 to 2,000 active data subscribers are connected to a certain cable network segment, all sharing the upstream and downstream bandwidth. (*Hybrid fiber-coaxial*, or HFC, is a telecommunications industry term for a network that incorporates both optical fiber and coaxial cable to create a broadband network.) The actual bandwidth for Internet service over a cable TV (CATV) line can be up to about 27Mbps on the download path to the subscriber, with about 2.5Mbps of bandwidth on the upload path. Typically users get an access speed from 256Kbps to 6Mbps. This data rate varies greatly throughout the United States.

DSL   *Digital subscriber line* is a technology used by traditional telephone companies to deliver advanced services (high-speed data and sometimes video) over twisted-pair copper telephone wires. It typically has lower data carrying capacity than HFC networks, and data speeds can range by line lengths and quality. DSL is not a complete end-to-end solution but rather a Physical layer transmission technology like dial-up, cable, or wireless. DSL connections are deployed in the last mile of a local telephone network—the local loop. The connection is set up between a pair of modems on either end of a copper wire that is between the CPE and the DSLAM. A DSLAM is the device located at the provider's CO and concentrates connections from multiple DSL subscribers.

Point-to-Point Serial Links

Point-to-point serial connections can be used to provide direct connections between two routers in a LAN and to support a WAN connection type called Ethernet emulation. The configuration of the customer routers in both cases is the same with the exception of the configuration of a clock rate, which is required only when connecting two routers directly in a LAN. The clock rate does not need to be configured in Ethernet emulation as it is usually provided by the service providers CSU/DSU.

Service providers can offer a connection called Ethernet emulation. This connection appears to each router in the customers remote offices as a direct Ethernet connection to the router in the other office. The provider's network is transparent to the customer routers. When this type of service is provided, the configuration of the customer routers at each end of one of these links is as follows:

```
RouterA(config)#interface fa0/1
RouterA(config-if)ip address 192.168.5.3 255.255.255.0
RouterA(config)#no shutdown

RouterB(config)#interface fa0/1
RouterB(config-if)ip address 192.168.5.4 255.255.255.0
RouterB(config)#no shutdown
```

That's all there is to it! It is just like configuring a direct connection between two routers in a LAN. The only additional item to configure when connecting two routers directly in a LAN is the clock command on the router with the DCE end of the V.35 cable; you can do this as follows. Here, router A has the DCE end of the V.35 cable.

```
RouterA(config)#interface fa0/1
RouterA(config-if)#ip address 192.168.5.3 255.255.255.0
RouterA(config-if)#clock rate 64000
RouterA(config)#no shutdown

RouterB(config)#interface fa0/1
RouterB(config-if)#ip address 192.168.5.4 255.255.255.0
RouterB(config)#no shutdown
```

V.35 cables have the DTE and DCE ends of the cable indicated on the cable. In cases where you are managing routers remotely and cannot physically determine the end to which a router is connected, you can use the show controllers command to determine this, as shown here. The cable type is indicated in the seventh line of the output; in this case it is the DTE end.

```
Router#show controllers serial
MK5 unit 0, NIM slot 1, NIM type code 7, NIM version 1
idb = 0x6150, driver structure at 0x34A878, regaddr = 0x8100300
IB at 0x6045500: mode=0x0108, local_addr=0, remote_addr=0
N1=1524, N2=1, scaler=100, T1=1000, T3=2000, TP=1
buffer size 1524
DTE V.35 serial cable attached
RX ring with 32 entries at 0x45560 : RLEN=5, Rxhead 0
<output omitted>
```

High-Level Data-Link Control (HDLC) Protocol

HDLC is a popular ISO-standard, bit-oriented, Data Link layer protocol. It specifies an encapsulation method for data on synchronous serial data links using frame characters and checksums. HDLC is a point-to-point protocol used on leased lines. No authentication can be used with HDLC.

In *byte-oriented protocols*, control information is encoded using entire bytes. On the other hand, *bit-oriented protocols* use single bits to represent the control information. Some common bit-oriented protocols include SDLC, LLC, HDLC, TCP, and IP.

HDLC is the default encapsulation used by Cisco routers over synchronous serial links. And Cisco's HDLC is proprietary—it won't communicate with any other vendor's HDLC implementation. But don't give Cisco grief for it—*everyone's* HDLC implementation is proprietary. Figure 10.1 shows the Cisco HDLC format.

In cases where the default encapsulation on an interface has been changed and you would like to use HDLC, use the following command to enable HDLC on an interface.

```
Router(config-if)#encapsulation hdlc
```

As shown in the figure, the reason that every vendor has a proprietary HDLC encapsulation method is that each vendor has a different way for the HDLC protocol to encapsulate multiple Network layer protocols. If the vendors didn't have a way for HDLC to communicate the different layer-3 protocols, then HDLC would be able to carry only one protocol. This proprietary header is placed in the data field of the HDLC encapsulation.

FIGURE 10.1 Cisco HDLC frame format

Cisco HDLC

Flag	Address	Control	Proprietary	Data	FCS	Flag

- Each vendor's HDLC has a proprietary data field to support multiprotocol environments.

HDLC

Flag	Address	Control	Data	FCS	Flag

- Supports only single-protocol environments

Point-to-Point Protocol (PPP)

Let's spend a little time on PPP. Remember that it's a Data Link layer protocol that can be used over either asynchronous serial (dial-up) or synchronous serial (ISDN) media. It uses Link Control Protocol (LCP) to build and maintain data-link connections. Network Control Protocol (NCP) is used to allow multiple Network layer protocols (routed protocols) to be used on a point-to-point connection.

Since HDLC is the default serial encapsulation on Cisco serial links and it works great, why and when would you choose to use PPP? Well, the basic purpose of PPP is to transport layer-3 packets across a Data Link layer point-to-point link, and it's nonproprietary. So unless you have all Cisco routers, you need PPP on your serial interfaces—the HDLC encapsulation is Cisco proprietary, remember? Plus, since PPP can encapsulate several layer-3 routed protocols and provide authentication, dynamic addressing, and callback, PPP could be the best encapsulation solution for you instead of HDLC.

Figure 10.2 shows the protocol stack compared to the OSI reference model.

PPP contains four main components:

EIA/TIA-232-C, V.24, V.35, and ISDN   A Physical layer international standard for serial communication.

HDLC   A method for encapsulating datagrams over serial links.

LCP   A method of establishing, configuring, maintaining, and terminating the point-to-point connection.

NCP   A method of establishing and configuring different Network layer protocols. NCP is designed to allow the simultaneous use of multiple Network layer protocols. Some examples of protocols here are Internet Protocol Control Protocol (IPCP) and Internetwork Packet Exchange Control Protocol (IPXCP).

FIGURE 10.2   PPP stack

Burn it into your mind that the PPP protocol stack is specified at the Physical and Data Link layers only. NCP is used to allow communication of multiple Network layer protocols by encapsulating the protocols across a PPP data link.

Configuring PPP on Cisco Routers

Configuring PPP encapsulation (see Table 10.2) on an interface is really pretty straightforward.

TABLE 10.2   Configuring PPP Encapsulation

Command	Meaning
bandwidth	Used to set a bandwidth value to be used by routing protocols for the purpose of calculating route cost
clock rate	Sets the clock rate to be provided by the DCE end of the connection
configure terminal	Takes you to global configuration mode
interface *interface*	Chooses your interface to configure
encapsulation ppp/hdlc	Sets the WAN encapsulation type to ppp or hdlc

To configure PPP from the CLI, follow these simple router commands:

```
Router#config t
Enter configuration commands, one per line. End with CNTL/Z.
Router(config)#int s0
Router(config-if)#encapsulation ppp
Router(config-if)#^Z
Router#
```

Of course, PPP encapsulation has to be enabled on both interfaces connected to a serial line in order to work, and several additional configuration options are available to you via the help command.

Configuring PPP Authentication

After you configure your serial interface to support PPP encapsulation, you can configure authentication using PPP between routers (see Table 10.3). First, you need to set the hostname of the router, if it's not already. Then you set the username and password for the remote router that will be connecting to your router.

TABLE 10.3 PPP Authentication Commands

Command	Meaning
configure terminal	Takes you to global configuration mode
hostname *hostname*	Configures the hostname of the local router
username *username* password *password*	Configures the hostname of the remote router that your local router will authenticate with and the password that both routers will use for authentication
ppp authentication *chap/pap*	Configures the PPP authentication method under the physical interface to either chap or pap, typically just chap

Here's an example:

```
Router#config t
Enter configuration commands, one per line. End with CNTL/Z.
Router(config)#hostname RouterA
RouterA(config)#username RouterB password cisco
```

When using the `hostname` command, remember that the username is the hostname of the remote router that's connecting to your router. And it's case sensitive too. Also, the password on both routers must be the same. It's a plain-text password that you can see with a `show run` command; you can encrypt the password by using the command `service password-encryption`. You must have a username and password configured for each remote system to which you plan to connect. The remote routers must also be configured with usernames and passwords.

Now, after you've set the hostname, usernames, and passwords, choose the authentication type, either chap or pap:

```
RouterA#config t
Enter configuration commands, one per line. End with CNTL/Z.
RouterA(config)#int s0
RouterA(config-if)#ppp authentication chap pap
RouterA(config-if)#^Z
RouterA#
```

If both methods are configured on the same line, as shown here, then only the first method will be used during link negotiation—the second acts as a backup just in case the first method fails.

Verifying PPP Encapsulation

Now that PPP encapsulation is enabled, I'll show you how to verify that it's up and running (see Table 10.4) connected with either a point-to-point serial or ISDN connection.

TABLE 10.4 Verifying PPP

Command	Meaning
`show interface` *interface*	Verifies the interface configuration and encapsulation set on each interface
`debug ppp authentication`	Displays the CHAP authentication process as it occurs between two routers in the network
`show cdp neighbors detail`	Displays a detailed output of all directly connected Cisco devices, which includes the IP addresses of each device and their hostname

FIGURE 10.3   PPP authentication example

hostname Pod1R1
username Pod1R2 password cisco
  interface serial 0
    ip address 10.0.1.1 255.255.255.0
    encapsulation ppp
    ppp authentication chap

hostname Pod1R2
username Pod1R1 password cisco
  interface serial 0
    ip address 10.0.1.2 255.255.255.0
    encapsulation ppp
    ppp authentication chap

You can start verifying the configuration shown in Figure 10.3 with the show interface command:

```
Pod1R1#sh int s0/0
Serial0/0 is up, line protocol is up
  Hardware is PowerQUICC Serial
  Internet address is 10.0.1.1/24
  MTU 1500 bytes, BW 1544 Kbit, DLY 20000 usec,
     reliability 239/255, txload 1/255, rxload 1/255
  Encapsulation PPP
  loopback not set
  Keepalive set (10 sec)
  LCP Open
  Open: IPCP, CDPCP
[output cut]
```

Notice that the sixth line lists encapsulation as PPP and the eighth line shows that the LCP is open. This means it has negotiated the session establishment and all is good! The ninth line tells you that NCP is listening for the protocols IP and CDP.

But what will you see if everything isn't perfect? I'm going to type in the configuration shown in Figure 10.4 and find out.

FIGURE 10.4   Failed PPP authentication

hostname Pod1R1
username Pod1R2 password Cisco
  interface serial 0
    ip address 10.0.1.1 255.255.255.0
    encapsulation ppp
    ppp authentication chap

hostname Pod1R2
username Pod1R1 password cisco
  interface serial 0
    ip address 10.0.1.2 255.255.255.0
    encapsulation ppp
    ppp authentication chap

What's wrong here? Take a look at the usernames and passwords. Do you see the problem now? That's right, the C is capitalized on the Pod1R2 username command found in the configuration of router Pod1R1. This is wrong because the usernames and passwords are case sensitive, remember? Let's take a look at the show interface command and see what happens:

```
Pod1R1#sh int s0/0
Serial0/0 is up, line protocol is down
  Hardware is PowerQUICC Serial
  Internet address is 10.0.1.1/24
  MTU 1500 bytes, BW 1544 Kbit, DLY 20000 usec,
     reliability 243/255, txload 1/255, rxload 1/255
  Encapsulation PPP, loopback not set
  Keepalive set (10 sec)
  LCP Closed
  Closed: IPCP, CDPCP
```

First, notice in the first line of output that Serial0/0 is up, line protocol is down. This is because there are no keepalives coming from the remote router. Second, notice that the LCP is closed because the authentication failed.

Debugging PPP Authentication

To display the CHAP authentication process as it occurs between two routers in the network, just use the command debug ppp authentication.

If your PPP encapsulation and authentication are set up correctly on both routers and if your usernames and passwords are all good, then the debug ppp authentication command will display output that looks like this:

```
d16h: Se0/0 PPP: Using default call direction
1d16h: Se0/0 PPP: Treating connection as a dedicated line
1d16h: Se0/0 CHAP: O CHALLENGE id 219 len 27 from "Pod1R1"
1d16h: Se0/0 CHAP: I CHALLENGE id 208 len 27 from "Pod1R2"
1d16h: Se0/0 CHAP: O RESPONSE id 208 len 27 from "Pod1R1"
1d16h: Se0/0 CHAP: I RESPONSE id 219 len 27 from "Pod1R2"
1d16h: Se0/0 CHAP: O SUCCESS id 219 len 4
1d16h: Se0/0 CHAP: I SUCCESS id 208 len 4
```

But if you have the username wrong, as we did previously in the PPP authentication failure example in Figure 11.4, the output would look something like this:

```
1d16h: Se0/0 PPP: Using default call direction
1d16h: Se0/0 PPP: Treating connection as a dedicated line
1d16h: %SYS-5-CONFIG_I: Configured from console by console
1d16h: Se0/0 CHAP: O CHALLENGE id 220 len 27 from "Pod1R1"
1d16h: Se0/0 CHAP: I CHALLENGE id 209 len 27 from "Pod1R2"
```

```
1d16h: Se0/0 CHAP: O RESPONSE id 209 len 27 from "Pod1R1"
1d16h: Se0/0 CHAP: I RESPONSE id 220 len 27 from "Pod1R2"
1d16h: Se0/0 CHAP: O FAILURE id 220 len 25 msg is "MD/DES compare failed"
```

PPP with CHAP authentication is a three-way authentication, and if the username and passwords are not configured exactly the way they should be, then the authentication will fail and the link will be down.

Mismatched WAN Encapsulations

If you have a point-to-point link but the encapsulations aren't the same, the link will never come up. Figure 10.5 shows one link with PPP and one with HDLC.

FIGURE 10.5   Mismatched WAN encapsulations

```
                  Pod1R1                        Pod1R2

        hostname Pod1R1                    hostname Pod1R2
        username Pod1R2 password Cisco     username Pod1R1 password cisco
          interface serial 0                 interface serial 0
          ip address 10.0.1.1 255.255.255.0  ip address 10.0.1.2 255.255.255.0
          encapsulation ppp                  encapsulation HDLC
```

Look at router Pod1R1 in this output:

```
Pod1R1#sh int s0/0
Serial0/0 is up, line protocol is down
  Hardware is PowerQUICC Serial
  Internet address is 10.0.1.1/24
  MTU 1500 bytes, BW 1544 Kbit, DLY 20000 usec,
     reliability 254/255, txload 1/255, rxload 1/255
  Encapsulation PPP, loopback not set
  Keepalive set (10 sec)
  LCP REQsent
Closed: IPCP, CDPCP
```

The serial interface is down, and LCP is sending requests but will never receive any responses because router Pod1R2 is using the HDLC encapsulation. To fix this problem, you would have to go to router Pod1R2 and configure the PPP encapsulation on the serial interface. One more thing—even though the usernames are configured and they're wrong, it doesn't matter because the command ppp authentication chap isn't used under the serial interface configuration and the username command isn't relevant in this example.

Mismatched IP Addresses

A tricky problem to spot is if you have HDLC or PPP configured on your serial interface but your IP addresses are wrong. Things seem to be just fine because the interfaces will show that they are up. Take a look at Figure 10.6, and see whether you can see what I mean; the two routers are connected with different subnets—router Pod1R1 with 10.0.1.1/24 and router Pod1R2 with 10.2.1.2/24.

FIGURE 10.6 Mismatched IP addresses

hostname Pod1R1
username Pod1R2 password cisco
  interface serial 0
  ip address 10.0.1.1 255.255.255.0
  encapsulation ppp
  ppp authentication chap

hostname Pod1R2
username Pod1R1 password cisco
  interface serial 0
  ip address 10.2.1.2 255.255.255.0
  encapsulation ppp
  ppp authentication chap

This will never work. But as I said, take a look at the output:

```
Pod1R1#sh int s0/0
Serial0/0 is up, line protocol is up
  Hardware is PowerQUICC Serial
  Internet address is 10.0.1.1/24
  MTU 1500 bytes, BW 1544 Kbit, DLY 20000 usec,
     reliability 255/255, txload 1/255, rxload 1/255
  Encapsulation PPP, loopback not set
  Keepalive set (10 sec)
  LCP Open
  Open: IPCP, CDPCP
```

See that? The IP addresses between the routers are wrong, but the link looks like it's working fine. This is because PPP, like HDLC and Frame Relay, is a layer-2 WAN encapsulation and doesn't care about IP addresses at all. So yes, the link is up, but you can't use IP across this link since it's misconfigured.

To find and fix this problem, you can use the show running-config or show interfaces command on each router, or you can the show cdp neighbors detail command:

```
Pod1R1#sh cdp neighbors detail
-------------------------
Device ID: Pod1R2
Entry address(es):
  IP address: 10.2.1.2
```

You can view and verify the directly connected neighbor's IP address and then solve your problem.

Now let's move on to Frame Relay.

Introduction to Frame Relay Technology

As a CCNA, you'll need to understand the basics of the Frame Relay technology and be able to configure it in simple scenarios. First, understand that Frame Relay is a packet-switched technology. From everything you've learned so far, just telling you this should make you immediately realize several things about it:

- You won't be using the encapsulation hdlc or encapsulation ppp command to configure it.

- Frame Relay doesn't work like a point-to-point leased line (although it can be made to look and act like one).

- Frame Relay is usually less expensive than leased lines are, but there are some sacrifices to make to get that savings.

So, why would you even consider using Frame Relay? Take a look at Figure 10.7 to get an idea of what a network looked like before Frame Relay.

FIGURE 10.7   Before Frame Relay

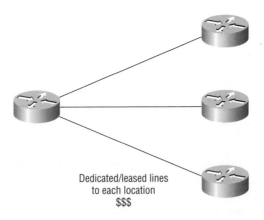

Dedicated/leased lines
to each location
$$$

Now check out Figure 10.8. You can see that there's now only one connection between the Corporate router and the Frame Relay switch. That saves some major cash!

If, for example, you had to add seven remote sites to the corporate office and had only one free serial port on your router, it's Frame Relay to the rescue! Of course, I should probably mention that you now also have one single point of failure, which is not so good. But Frame Relay is used to save money, not to make a network more resilient.

Coming up, I'm going to cover the Frame Relay technology information you need to know about when studying the CCNA objectives.

FIGURE 10.8　After Frame Relay

Frame Relay creates a cost-effective mesh network.

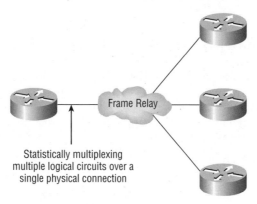

Statistically multiplexing
multiple logical circuits over a
single physical connection

Frame Relay Encapsulation Types

Note the Frame-Relay encapsulation commands in Table 10.5.

TABLE 10.5　Frame-Relay Encapsulation Commands

Command	Meaning
interface *interface*	Chooses your interface
encapsulation frame-relay	Sets the Frame Relay encapsulation to Cisco
encapsulation frame-relay ietf	Sets the Frame Relay encapsulation to IETF

　　When configuring Frame Relay on Cisco routers, you need to specify it as an encapsulation on serial interfaces. As I said earlier, you can't use HDLC or PPP with Frame Relay. When you configure Frame Relay, you specify an encapsulation of Frame Relay (as shown in the following output). But unlike HDLC or PPP, with Frame Relay there are two encapsulation types: Cisco and Internet Engineering Task Force (IETF). The following router output shows these two different encapsulation methods when Frame Relay is chosen on your Cisco router:

```
RouterA(config)#int s0
RouterA(config-if)#encapsulation frame-relay ?
  ietf  Use RFC1490 encapsulation
  <cr>
```

The default encapsulation is Cisco unless you manually type in **ietf**, and Cisco is the type to use when connecting two Cisco devices. You'd opt for the IETF-type encapsulation if you needed to connect a Cisco device to a non-Cisco device with Frame Relay. Whichever you choose, make sure the Frame Relay encapsulation is the same on both ends.

Data Link Connection Identifiers (DLCIs)

Table 10.6 lists the command for configuring and verifying DLCIs.

TABLE 10.6   Configuring and Verifying Your DLCIs

Command	Meaning
show frame-relay map	Displays the Network layer–to–DLCI mappings.
show frame-relay pvc	Provides you with a list of all configured PVCs and DLCI numbers. It provides the status of each PVC connection and traffic statistics too.
frame-relay interface-dlci *dlci-number*	Configures the DLCI number for the interface.

Frame Relay PVCs are identified to DTE end devices by *Data Link Connection Identifiers (DLCIs)*. A Frame Relay service provider typically assigns DLCI values, which are used on Frame Relay interfaces to distinguish between different virtual circuits. Because many virtual circuits can be terminated on one multipoint Frame Relay interface, many DLCIs are often affiliated with it.

Let me explain—suppose you have a central HQ with three branch offices. If you were to connect each branch office to HQ using a T1, you would need three serial interfaces on your router at HQ, one for each T1. Simple, right? Well, suppose you use Frame Relay PVCs instead. You could have a T1 at each branch connected to a service provider and only a *single* T1 at HQ. There would be three PVCs on the single T1 at HQ, one going to each branch. And even though there's only a single interface and a single CSU/DSU, the three PVCs function as three separate circuits.

Before I continue, I want to define Inverse ARP (IARP) and discuss how it's used with DLCIs in a Frame Relay network. Yes, it is somewhat similar to ARP in that it maps a DLCI to an IP address—kind of like ARP does with MAC addresses to IP addresses. And even though you can't configure IARP, you can disable it. It runs on a Frame Relay router and maps the DLCI to an IP address for Frame Relay so it knows how to get to the Frame Relay switch. You can see IP-to-DLCI mappings with the show frame-relay map command.

But if you have a non-Cisco router living in your network and it doesn't support IARP, then you're stuck with having to statically provide IP-to-DLCI mappings with the `frame-relay map` command—something I'll demonstrate in a bit.

Let's talk about DLCIs a bit more. They're locally significant—global significance requires the entire network to use the LMI extensions that offer global significance. This is why you'll mostly find global DLCIs only in private networks.

To discover why DLCIs are considered locally significant, take a look at Figure 10.9. In the figure, DLCI 100 is considered locally significant to RouterA and identifies the circuit between RouterA and its ingress Frame Relay switch. DLCI 200 would identify the circuit between RouterB and its ingress Frame Relay switch.

FIGURE 10.9   DLCIs are local to your router

RouterA   DLCI 100   DLCI 200   RouterB

DLCI numbers that are used to identify a PVC are typically assigned by the provider and start at 16.

You configure a DLCI number to be applied to an interface like this:

```
RouterA(config-if)#frame-relay interface-dlci ?
  <16-1007> Define a DLCI as part of the current
            subinterface
RouterA(config-if)#frame-relay interface-dlci 16
```

> DLCIs identify the logical circuit between the local router and a Frame Relay switch.

Local Management Interface (LMI)

Take a look at Table 10.7.

TABLE 10.7   Configuring the LMI

Command	Meaning
`frame-relay lmi-type` *type*	Sets the LMI type on the Frame Relay interface

Local Management Interface (LMI) is a signaling standard used between your router and the first Frame Relay switch to which it's connected. It allows for passing information about the operation and status of the virtual circuit between the provider's network and the DTE (your router). It communicates information about the following:

Keepalives   These verify that data is flowing.

Multicasting   This is an optional extension of the LMI specification that allows, for example, the efficient distribution of routing information and ARP requests over a Frame Relay network. Multicasting uses the reserved DLCIs from 1019 through 1022.

Global addressing   This provides global significance to DLCIs, allowing the Frame Relay cloud to work exactly like a LAN.

Status of virtual circuits   This provides DLCI status. The status inquiries and messages are used as keepalives when there is no regular LMI traffic to send.

But remember, LMI is not communication between your routers; it's communication between your router and the nearest Frame Relay switch. So, it's entirely possible that the router on one end of a PVC is actively receiving LMI while the router on the other end of the PVC is not. And of course, PVCs won't work with one end down. (I say this to clarify the local nature of LMI communications.)

There are three different types of LMI message formats: Cisco, ANSI, and Q.933A. The different kinds in use depend on both the type and the configuration of the telco's switching gear, so it's imperative that you configure your router for the correct format, which should be provided by the telco.

On Cisco equipment, the default type is, surprise, Cisco, but you still might have to change to ANSI or Q.933A depending on what your service provider tells you. The three different LMI types are shown in the following router output:

```
RouterA(config-if)#frame-relay lmi-type ?
  cisco
  ansi
  q933a
```

As shown in the output, all three standard LMI signaling formats are supported. Here's a description of each:

Cisco   LMI was defined by the Gang of Four (default). The Local Management Interface (LMI) was developed in 1990 by Cisco Systems, StrataCom, Northern Telecom, and Digital Equipment Corporation and became known as the Gang-of-Four LMI, or Cisco LMI.

ANSI   Annex D is included with ANSI standard T1.617.

ITU-T (Q.933A)   Annex A is included in the ITU-T standard and defined by using the Q.933a command keyword.

Routers receive LMI information from the service provider's Frame Relay switch on a frame-encapsulated interface and update the virtual circuit status to one of three different states:

Active state   Everything is up, and routers can exchange information.

Inactive state   The router's interface is up and working with a connection to the switching office, but the remote router isn't up.

Deleted state   No LMI information is being received on the interface from the switch, which could be because of a mapping problem or a line failure.

Troubleshooting Using Frame Relay Congestion Control

TABLE 10.8   Verifying Your PVC

Command	Meaning
show frame-relay pvc	Provides you with a list of all configured PVCs and DLCI numbers. It provides the status of each PVC connection and traffic statistics too.

Now let's say all your users are whining that their Frame Relay connection to the corporate site is super slow. Because you strongly suspect that the link is overloaded, you verify (see Table 10.8) the Frame Relay congestion control information with the show frame-relay pvc command and get this:

```
RouterA#sh frame-relay pvc

PVC Statistics for interface Serial0/0 (Frame Relay DTE)

              Active      Inactive      Deleted       Static
  Local         1            0             0             0
  Switched      0            0             0             0
  Unused        0            0             0             0

DLCI = 100, DLCI USAGE = LOCAL, PVC STATUS = ACTIVE, INTERFACE = Serial0/0
  input pkts 1300         output pkts 1270       in bytes 21212000
  out bytes 21802000      dropped pkts 4         in pkts dropped 147
  out pkts dropped 0      out bytes dropped 0     in FECN pkts 147
   in BECN pkts 192       out FECN pkts 147
  out BECN pkts 259       in DE pkts 0            out DE pkts 214
  out bcast pkts 0        out bcast bytes 0
```

```
    pvc create time 00:00:06, last time pvc status changed 00:00:06
Pod1R1#
```

What you want to look for is the in BECN pkts 192 output because this is what's telling the local router that traffic sent to the corporate site is experiencing congestion. BECN means that the path that a frame took to "return" to you is congested.

Frame Relay Implementation and Monitoring

TABLE 10.9   Implementing Frame-Relay

Command	Meaning
configure terminal	Takes you to global configuration mode
interface *interface*	Chooses your interface
encapsulation frame-relay	Sets the Frame Relay encapsulation to Cisco
encapsulation frame-relay ietf	Sets the Frame Relay encapsulation to IETF
ip address *address* mask	Sets the IP address and mask for the Frame Relay interface
frame-relay lmi-type *type*	Sets the LMI type for the Frame Relay interface
frame-relay interferface-dlci *dlci-number*	Configures the DLCI number for the interface

As I've said, there are a ton of Frame Relay commands and configuration options (see Table 10.9), but I'm going to zero in on the ones you really need to know when studying for the CCNA exam objectives. I'm going to start with one of the simplest configuration options—two routers with a single PVC between them. Next, I'll show you a more complex configuration using subinterfaces and demonstrate some of the monitoring commands available to verify the configuration.

Single Interface

Let's get started by looking at a simple example. Say that you just want to connect two routers with a single PVC. Here's how that configuration would look:

```
RouterA#config t
Enter configuration commands, one per line.  End with CNTL/Z.
```

```
RouterA(config)#int s0/0
RouterA(config-if)#encapsulation frame-relay
RouterA(config-if)#ip address 172.16.20.1 255.255.255.0
RouterA(config-if)#frame-relay lmi-type ansi
RouterA(config-if)#frame-relay interface-dlci 101
RouterA(config-if)#^Z
RouterA#
```

The first step is to specify the encapsulation as Frame Relay. Notice that since I didn't specify a particular encapsulation type—either Cisco or IETF—the Cisco default type was used. If the other router were non-Cisco, I would've specified IETF. Next, I assigned an IP address to the interface and then specified the LMI type of ANSI (the default being Cisco) based on information provided by the telecommunications provider. Finally, I added the DLCI of 101, which indicates the PVC I want to use (again, given to me by my ISP) and assumes there's only one PVC on this physical interface.

That's all there is to it—if both sides are configured correctly, the circuit will come up.

Check out Hands-on Lab 7.3 in the *Sybex CCNA 640-802 Study Guide* for a complete example of this type of configuration, including instructions on creating your own Frame Relay switch from a router.

Subinterfaces

TABLE 10.10 Subinterface Commands

Command	Meaning
interface *interface*	Chooses the interface you are connecting Frame Relay to
encapsulation frame-relay	Sets the Frame Relay encapsulation to Cisco
encapsulation frame-relay ietf	Sets the Frame Relay encapsulation to IETF
interface *interface.subinterface_number* point-to-point	Creates a point-to-point subinterface
interface *interface.subinteface_number* multipoint	Creates a multipoint subinterface

TABLE 10.10 Subinterface Commands *(continued)*

Command	Meaning
frame-relay interface-dlci *dlci_number*	Assigns a DLCI to an interface; not required if you use a static mapping between IP addresses and DLCIs
frame-relay map *ip_address dlci*	Defines a static mapping between the destination IP address and the DLCI
no frame-relay inverse arp	Turns off inverse arp

You probably know by now that you can have multiple virtual circuits on a single serial interface and yet treat each as a separate interface—I mentioned this earlier. You can make this happen by creating *subinterfaces* (see Table 10.10). Think of a subinterface as a logical interface defined by the IOS software. Several subinterfaces will share a single hardware interface, yet for configuration purposes they operate as if they were separate physical interfaces, something known as *multiplexing*.

To configure a router in a Frame Relay network so it will avoid split horizon issues by not permitting routing updates, just configure a separate subinterface for each PVC with a unique DLCI and subnet assigned to the subinterface.

You define subinterfaces using a command like int s0.*subinterface number*. First, you have to set the encapsulation on the physical serial interface, and then you can define the subinterfaces—generally one subinterface per PVC. Here's an example:

```
RouterA(config)#int s0
RouterA(config-if)#encapsulation frame-relay
RouterA(config-if)#int s0.?
  <0-4294967295>  Serial interface number
RouterA(config-if)#int s0.16 ?
  multipoint       Treat as a multipoint link
  point-to-point  Treat as a point-to-point link
RouterA(config-if)#int s0.16 point-to-point
```

You can define a serious amount of subinterfaces on any given physical interface, but keep in mind that there are only about 1,000 available DLCIs. In the preceding example, I chose to use subinterface 16 because that represents the DLCI number assigned to that PVC by the carrier. There are two types of subinterfaces:

Point-to-point Used when a single virtual circuit connects one router to another. Each point-to-point subinterface requires its own subnet.

Multipoint This is when the router is the center of a star of virtual circuits that are using a single subnet for all routers' serial interfaces connected to the frame switch. You'll usually find this implemented with the hub router in this mode and the spoke routers in physical interface (always point-to-point) or point-to-point subinterface mode.

On multipoint interfaces you can either use inverse arp, which allows the ends of the connection to dynamically discover the DLCI of the remote end of the connection, or you use the frame-relay map command to create a static mapping of these values. On a point-to-point connection the frame-relay map command is not required because it is assumed that each end of the connection lies in the same subnet. Neither is the use of inverse arp since there is only a single remote destination on the PVC. To create a static mapping on a multipoint link, use the following command:

```
Router(subif)#frame-relay map ip 192.168.5.6 160
```

In the above example the remote IP address 192.168.5.6 is mapped to the DLCI 160.

Monitoring Frame Relay

Take a look at Table 10.11.

TABLE 10.11   Frame-Relay Verification Commands

Command	Meaning
show frame-relay ?	Displays all Frame Relay show commands.
show frame-relay lmi	Provides the LMI traffic statistics exchanged between the local router and the Frame Relay switch.
show frame-relay pvc	Provides you with a list of all configured PVCs and DLCI numbers. It provides the status of each PVC connection and traffic statistics too.
show interface interface	Displays interface information about the encapsulation, as well as layer-2 and layer-3 information. It also displays line, protocol, DLCI, and LMI information.
show frame-relay map	Displays the Network layer–to–DLCI mappings.
debug frame-relay lmi	Provides information to help you determine whether the router and switch are exchanging the correct LMI information.

Several commands are used frequently to check the status of your interfaces and PVCs once you have Frame Relay encapsulation set up and running. To list them, use the show frame ? command, as shown here:

```
RouterA>sho frame ?
end-to-end     Frame-relay end-to-end VC information
```

```
fragment        show frame relay fragmentation information
ip              show frame relay IP statistics
lapf            show frame relay lapf status/statistics
lmi             show frame relay lmi statistics
map             Frame-Relay map table
pvc             show frame relay pvc statistics
qos-autosense   show frame relay qos-autosense information
route           show frame relay route
svc             show frame relay SVC stuff
traffic         Frame-Relay protocol statistics
vofr            Show frame-relay VoFR statistics
```

The most common parameters that you view with the show frame-relay command are lmi, pvc, and map.

Now, let's take a look at the most frequently used commands and the information they provide.

The *show frame-relay lmi* Command

The show frame-relay lmi command will give you the LMI traffic statistics exchanged between the local router and the Frame Relay switch. Here's an example:

```
Router#sh frame lmi

LMI Statistics for interface Serial0 (Frame Relay DTE)
LMI TYPE = CISCO
    Invalid Unnumbered info 0      Invalid Prot Disc 0
    Invalid dummy Call Ref 0       Invalid Msg Type 0
    Invalid Status Message 0       Invalid Lock Shift 0
    Invalid Information ID 0        Invalid Report IE Len 0
    Invalid Report Request 0       Invalid Keep IE Len 0
    Num Status Enq. Sent 0         Num Status msgs Rcvd 0
    Num Update Status Rcvd 0       Num Status Timeouts 0
Router#
```

The router output from the show frame-relay lmi command shows you any LMI errors, plus the LMI type.

The *show frame pvc* Command

The show frame pvc command will present you with a list of all configured PVCs and DLCI numbers. It provides the status of each PVC connection and traffic statistics too. It will also give you the number of BECN and FECN packets received on the router per PVC.

Here is an example:

```
RouterA#sho frame pvc

PVC Statistics for interface Serial0 (Frame Relay DTE)

DLCI = 16,DLCI USAGE = LOCAL,PVC STATUS =ACTIVE,
INTERFACE = Serial0.1
 input pkts 50977876     output pkts 41822892
  in bytes 3137403144
 out bytes 3408047602    dropped pkts 5
  in FECN pkts 0
 in BECN pkts 0       out FECN pkts 0       out BECN pkts 0
 in DE pkts 9393      out DE pkts 0
 pvc create time 7w3d, last time pvc status changed 7w3d

DLCI = 18,DLCI USAGE =LOCAL,PVC STATUS =ACTIVE,
INTERFACE = Serial0.3
 input pkts 30572401     output pkts 31139837
  in bytes 1797291100
 out bytes 3227181474    dropped pkts 5
  in FECN pkts 0
 in BECN pkts 0       out FECN pkts 0       out BECN pkts 0
 in DE pkts 28        out DE pkts 0
 pvc create time 7w3d, last time pvc status changed 7w3d
```

If you want to see information only about PVC 16, you can type the command **show frame-relay pvc 16**.

The *show interface* Command

You can use the show interface command to check for LMI traffic. The show interface command displays information about the encapsulation, as well as layer-2 and layer-3 information. It also displays line, protocol, DLCI, and LMI information. Check it out:

```
RouterA#sho int s0
Serial0 is up, line protocol is up
 Hardware is HD64570
 MTU 1500 bytes, BW 1544 Kbit, DLY 20000 usec, rely
  255/255, load 2/255
 Encapsulation FRAME-RELAY, loopback not set, keepalive
  set (10 sec)
 LMI enq sent 451751,LMI stat recvd 451750,LMI upd recvd
```

```
164,DTE LMI up
LMI enq recvd 0, LMI stat sent 0, LMI upd sent 0
LMI DLCI 1023 LMI type is CISCO frame relay DTE
Broadcast queue 0/64, broadcasts sent/dropped 0/0,
 interface broadcasts 839294
```

The previous LMI DLCI is used to define the type of LMI being used. If it happens to be 1023, it's the default LMI type of Cisco. If LMI DLCI is zero, then it's the ANSI LMI type (Q.933A uses 0 as well). If LMI DLCI is anything other than 0 or 1023, it's a 911—call your provider; they've got major issues!

The *show frame map* Command

The show frame map command displays the Network layer–to–DLCI mappings. Here's how that looks:

```
RouterB#show frame map
Serial0 (up): ipx 20.0007.7842.3575 dlci 16(0x10,0x400),
              dynamic, broadcast,, status defined, active
Serial0 (up): ip 172.16.20.1 dlci 16(0x10,0x400),
              dynamic, broadcast,, status defined, active
Serial1 (up): ipx 40.0007.7842.153a dlci 17(0x11,0x410),
              dynamic, broadcast,, status defined, active
Serial1 (up): ip 172.16.40.2 dlci 17(0x11,0x410),
              dynamic, broadcast,, status defined, active
```

Notice that the serial interfaces have two mappings—one for IP and one for IPX. Also important is that the Network layer addresses were resolved with the dynamic protocol Inverse ARP (IARP). After the DLCI number is listed, you can see some numbers in parentheses. The first one is 0x10, which is the hex equivalent for the DLCI number 16, used on serial 0. And the 0x11 is the hex for DLCI 17 used on serial 1. The second numbers, 0x400 and 0x410, are the DLCI numbers configured in the Frame Relay frame. They're different because of the way the bits are spread out in the frame.

The *debug frame lmi* Command

The debug frame lmi command will show output on the router consoles by default (as with any debug command). The information this command gives you will enable you to verify and troubleshoot the Frame Relay connection by helping you determine whether the router and switch are exchanging the correct LMI information. Here's an example:

```
Router#debug frame-relay lmi
Serial3/1(in): Status, myseq 214
RT IE 1, length 1, type 0
KA IE 3, length 2, yourseq 214, myseq 214
PVC IE 0x7 , length 0x6 , dlci 130, status 0x2 , bw 0
```

```
Serial3/1(out): StEnq, myseq 215, yourseen 214, DTE up
datagramstart = 0x1959DF4, datagramsize = 13
FR encap = 0xFCF10309
00 75 01 01 01 03 02 D7 D6

Serial3/1(in): Status, myseq 215
RT IE 1, length 1, type 1
KA IE 3, length 2, yourseq 215, myseq 215
Serial3/1(out): StEnq, myseq 216, yourseen 215, DTE up
datagramstart = 0x1959DF4, datagramsize = 13
FR encap = 0xFCF10309
00 75 01 01 01 03 02 D8 D7
```

Troubleshooting Frame Relay Networks

Note the commands listed in Table 10.12.

TABLE 10.12   Verifying the Frame-Relay Encapsulation

Command	Meaning
configure terminal	Takes you to global configuration mode
encapsulation frame-relay	Sets your Frame Relay interface encapsulation to Cisco
encapsulation frame-relay ietf	Sets your Frame Relay interface encapsulation to IETF

Troubleshooting Frame Relay networks isn't any harder than troubleshooting any other type of network as long as you know what to look for, which is what I'm going to cover now. We'll go over some basic problems that commonly occur in Frame Relay configuration and how to solve them.

First on the list are serial encapsulation problems. As you learned recently, there are two Frame Relay encapsulations: Cisco and IETF. Cisco is the default, and it means you have a Cisco router on each end of the Frame Relay network. If you don't have a Cisco router on the remote end of your Frame Relay network, then you need to run the IETF encapsulation, as shown here:

```
RouterA(config)#int s0
RouterA(config-if)#encapsulation frame-relay ?
  ietf  Use RFC1490 encapsulation
```

```
<cr>
RouterA(config-if)#encapsulation frame-relay ietf
```

Once you verify that you're using the correct encapsulation, you then need to check out your Frame Relay mappings. For example, take a look at Figure 10.10.

FIGURE 10.10   Frame Relay mappings

```
RouterA#show running-config
interface s0/0
ip address 172.16.100.2 255.255.0.0
encapsulation frame-relay
frame-relay map ip 172.16.100.1 200 broadcast
```

So why can't RouterA talk to RouterB across the Frame Relay network? To find that out, take a close look at the `frame-relay map` statement. See the problem now? You cannot use a remote DLCI to communicate to the Frame Relay switch; you must use *your* DLCI number! The mapping should have included DLCI 100 instead of DLCI 200.

Now that you know how to ensure that you have the correct Frame Relay encapsulation and that DLCIs are only locally significant, let's look into some routing protocol problems typically associated with Frame Relay. See whether you can find a problem with the two configurations in Figure 10.11.

FIGURE 10.11   Frame Relay routing problems

```
RouterA#show running-config
interface s0/0
ip address 172.16.100.2 255.255.0.0
encapsulation frame-relay
frame-relay map ip 172.16.100.1 100
router rip
      network 172.16.0.0
```

```
RouterB#show running-config
interface s0/0
ip address 172.16.100.1 255.255.0.0
encapsulation frame-relay
frame-relay map ip 172.16.100.2 200
router rip
      network 172.16.0.0
```

Hmmmm, well, the configs look pretty good. Actually, they look great, so what's the problem? Well, remember that Frame Relay is a nonbroadcast multiaccess (NBMA) network by default, meaning that it doesn't send any broadcasts across the PVC. So, because the mapping statements do not have the broadcast argument at the end of the line, broadcasts, like RIP updates, won't be sent across the PVC.

GRE Tunnels

Generic Routing Encapsulation (GRE) is a tunneling protocol developed by Cisco. It is designed to manage the transportation of multiprotocol and IP multicast traffic between two or more site that only have IP connectivity. From a high level the steps to create a GRE tunnel are

1. Create the tunnel interface.
2. Specify the interface mode as tunnel (optional, this is the default).
3. Specify the tunnel source IP address.
4. Specify the tunnel destination IP address.
5. Configure an IP address for the tunnel interface.

The commands that are used are contained in Table 10.13.

TABLE 10.13 GRE Tunnel Commands

Command	Meaning
Tunnel source *ip_address*	Specifies the tunnel source IP address (in tunnel configuration mode)
Tunnel destination *ip_address*	Specifies the tunnel destination IP address (in tunnel configuration mode)
ip address *ip_address mask*	Specifies the IP address of the tunnel interface

Below is the configuration of two routers that lie on either end of a GRE tunnel. Notice that the IP addresses of the tunnel interface (192.168.5.4 and 192.168.5.5) must reside in the same network:

```
routerA(config)#interface tunnel0
routerA(config-if)# ip address 192.168.5.4 255.255.255.0
routerA(config-if)#tunnel source 209.16.5.5
routerA(config-if)#tunnel destination 209.16.6.7

routerB(config)#interface tunnel0
routerB(config-if)# ip address 192.168.5.5 255.255.255.0
routerB(config-if)#tunnel source 209.16.6.7
routerB(config-if)#tunnel destination 209.16.5.5
```

Verifying a GRE Tunnel

To verify the successful operation of the GRE tunnel you can use the three commands shown below with their output. The first two commands confirm the existence and proper operation of the tunnel and the third verifies the placement of the route in the routing table as a directly connected route.

```
RouterA#Show ip interface brief | include tunnel
Tunnel0        192.168.5.4   Yes manual          up         up


routerA#sh int Tunnel0
Tunnel0/0 is up, line protocol is up
  Hardware is Tunnel
  Internet address is 192.168.5.4
  MTU 17916 bytes, BW 100 Kbit, DLY 50000 usec,
      reliability 255/255, txload 1/255, rxload 1/255
  Encapsulation Tunnel   loopback not set
  Keepalive not set
  Tunnel source 209.16.5.5 destination 209.16.6.7
  Tunnel proticol/transport  GRE/IP
[output cut]


routerA#show ip route
[output cut]
C   192.168.2.0/24 is directly connected, Tunnel0
[output cut]
```

Chapter
11

IP Services

In addition to all of the features and services discussed thus far in this book, the Cisco IOS supports a collection of optional but helpful functions that Cisco refers to collectively as "IP services." These include two systems that can be used to monitor and manage the network, SNMP and Syslog and two first hop redundancy protocols, HSRP and GLBP that can be used to provide router redundancy and router load balancing respectively to hosts.

For up-to-the-minute updates for this chapter, check out www.lammle.com or www.sybex.com/go/iossurvivalgd

Network Monitoring and Management Services

Network device monitoring and management can be greatly simplified by the use of two IP services supported in the Cisco IOS. Simple Network Management Protocol (SNMP) is a standard application layer protocol that allows for extracting information remotely from devices that can be centralized, organized and viewed with graphing tools. Syslog is a protocol that allows system messages that are usually maintained locally on each device to be sent to a syslog server where it can be viewed and managed centrally. In this section the configuration of these IP servers is covered.

Simple Network Management Protocol (SNMP)

SNMP is an Application layer protocol that provides a message format for agents on a variety of devices to communicate with network management stations (NMSs)—for example, Cisco Prime or HP Openview. These agents send messages to the NMS station which then either reads or writes information in the database stored on the NMS that's called a Management Information Base (MIB).

The NMS periodically queries or polls the SNMP agent on a device to gather and analyze statistics via GET messages. End devices running SNMP agents would send an SNMP trap to the NMS if a problem occurs.

SNMP has three versions, with version 1 being rarely, if ever implemented today. Here's a summary of these three versions:

SNMPv1   Supports plaintext authentication with community strings and uses only UDP.

SNMPv2c   Supports plaintext authentication with MD5 or SHA with no encryption but provides GET BULK, which is a way to gather many types of information at once and minimize the number of GET requests. It offers a more detailed error message reporting method, but it's not more secure than v1. It uses UDP even though it can be configured to use TCP.

SNMPv3   Supports strong authentication with MD5 or SHA, providing confidentiality (encryption) and data integrity of messages via DES or DES-256 encryption between agents and managers. GET BULK is a supported feature of SNMPv3, and this version also uses TCP.

Configuring SNMP is a pretty straightforward process for which you only need a few commands. These four steps are all you need to run through to configure a Cisco device for SNMP access:

1. Enable SNMP read-write access to the router.

2. Configure SNMP contact information.

3. Configure SNMP location.

4. Configure an ACL to restrict SNMP access to the NMS hosts.

The only required configuration is the community string. The commands used to enable SNMP on a device are included in Table 11.1

TABLE 11.1   SNMP Command

Command	Meaning
snmp-server community *string* [ro|rw]	Defines the community access string with a read-only or read-write privilege
snmp-server contact *contact_name*	Sets the system contact name
Snmp-server location *location*	Sets the system location string

A sample configuration for a router named R2 is shown below. In this case a community string of Todd, a location of Dallas and a contact name of Lex Luther has been configured and both read and write access has been granted.

```
R2(config)#snmp-server community Todd RW
R2(config)#snmp-server location Dallas
R2(config)#snmp-server contact Lex Luther
```

Syslog

All Cisco devices generate system messages of various types and various levels of importance. These messages can be configured to be forwarded to various locations which can include

- Logging buffer
- Console line
- Terminal lines
- Syslog server

Reading system messages from a switch's or router's internal buffer is the most popular and efficient method of seeing what's going on with your network at a particular time. But the best way is to log messages to a *syslog* server, which stores messages from you and can even time-stamp and sequence them for you, and it's easy to set up and configure the IOS device!

Syslog allows you to display, sort, and even search messages, all of which makes it a really great troubleshooting tool. The search feature is especially powerful because you can use keywords and even severity levels. Plus, the server can email admins based on the severity level of the message.

When system messages are generated they are formatted into something like this:

```
Seq no:timestamp: %facility-severity-MNEMONIC:description
```

The system message format can be broken down in this way:

seq no   This stamp logs messages with a sequence number, but not by default. If you want this output, you've got to configure it.

Timestamp   Data and time of the message or event, which again will show up only if configured.

Facility   The facility to which the message refers.

Severity   A single-digit code from 0 to 7 that indicates the severity of the message.

MNEMONIC   Text string that uniquely describes the message.

Description   Text string containing detailed information about the event being reported.

The commands required to configure a device to send messages to a syslog server are contained in Table 11.2

TABLE 11.2   Syslog Command

Command	Meaning
logging {hostname| ip address}	Identifies the syslog server to receive login messages
logging-trap severity	Limits the syslog messages based on a severity level

The first command defines the syslog sever and the second defines the severity of messages to be sent. The seven possible levels are shown below.

Emergency	Level 0
Alert	Level 1
Critical	Level 2
Error	Level 3
Warning	Level 4
Notification	Level 5
Informational	Level 6
Debugging	Level 7

Understand that only emergency-level messages will be displayed if you've configured severity level 0. But if, for example, you opt for level 4 instead, level 0 through 4 will be displayed, giving you emergency, alert, critical, error, and warning messages too. Level 7 is the highest-level security option and displays everything, but be warned that going with it could have a serious impact on the performance of your device. So always use debugging commands carefully with an eye on the messages you really need to meet your specific business requirements!

In the example below the router R2 has been configured to send syslog messages to a server at 192.168.5.5 and to limit those messages to levels 3 and above (0-3).

```
R2(config)#logging 192.168.5.5
R2(config)#logging error
```

First Hop Redundancy and Load Balancing

First hop redundancy protocols (FHRP) are used to provide default gateway fault tolerance to hosts. While there is not a method available to configure a host with multiple default gateway addresses, by using first hop redundancy protocols, hosts can be provided with the IP address of a *virtual router* that represents two or more routers that are operating as a group to provide the same routing functions to the host as a single default gateway would do while also providing backup if a single router in the group fails. The configuration of Hot Standby Routing Protocol (HSRP), one such FHRP is covered in this section.

It is also a desirable to be able to load balance between multiple default gateways when they are available to achieve better throughput. While this can be achieved with HSRP, it can be done more easily by using Gateway Load Balancing Protocol (GLBP). Its configuration is also covered in this chapter as well.

Hot Standby Routing Protocol (HSRP)

Hot Standby Routing Protocol (HSRP) is a Cisco proprietary first hop redundancy protocol that can be run on most, but not all, of Cisco's router and multilayer switch models. It defines a standby group, and each standby group that you define includes the following routers:

- Active router
- Standby router
- Virtual router
- Any other routers that maybe attached to the subnet

The standby group will always have at least two routers participating in it. The primary players in the group are the one active router and one standby router that communicate to each other using multicast Hello messages. The Hello messages provide all of the required communication for the routers. The Hellos contain the information required to accomplish the election that determines the active and standby router positions. They also hold the key to the failover process. If the standby router stops receiving Hello packets from the active router, it then takes over the active router role.

When a host sends a packet to the gateway, the router that is performing the active role will actually route the packet. If that router is unavailable the standby router will take over the routing function for the group, but this failover process will be transparent to the hosts.

Virtual MAC Address

A virtual router in an HSRP group has a virtual IP address and a virtual MAC address. So where does that virtual MAC come from? The virtual IP address isn't that hard to figure out; it just has to be a unique IP address on the same subnet as the hosts defined in the configuration. But MAC addresses are a little different, right? Or are they? The answer is yes—sort of. With HSRP, you create a totally new, made-up MAC address in addition to the IP address.

The HSRP MAC address has only one variable piece in it. The first 24 bits still identify the vendor who manufactured the device (the organizationally unique identifier, or OUI). The next 16 bits in the address tell us that the MAC address is a well-known HSRP MAC address. Finally, the last 8 bits of the address are the hexadecimal representation of the HSRP group number.

Let me clarify all this with an example of what an HSRP MAC address would look like:

```
0000.0c07.ac0a
```

- The first 24 bits (0000.0c) are the vendor ID of the address; in the case of HSRP being a Cisco protocol, the ID is assigned to Cisco.

- The next 16 bits (07.ac) are the well-known HSRP ID. This part of the address was assigned by Cisco in the protocol, so it's always easy to recognize that this address is for use with HSRP.

- The last 8 bits (0a) are the only variable bits and represent the HSRP group number that you assign. In this case, the group number is 10 and converted to hexadecimal when placed in the MAC address, where it becomes the 0a that you see.

The commands used to configure basic HSRP are in Table 11.3.

TABLE 11.3 HSRP COMMANDS

Command	Meaning
standby *HSRP_group_number* ip *virtual_IP_address*	Activates HSRP on an interface for the specified group number using the specified virtual IP address
standby *HSRP_group_number* priority *priority _value*	Assigns a priority to the selected interface for the purpose of selecting the active router

In the example below the Fa0/1 interface of router R2 has been added as a member of HSRP group 2 and the interface has been assigned a priority of 125. The virtual IP address assigned is 192.168.5.6

```
R2(config)#int Fa0/1
R2(config-if)#standby 2 ip 192.168.5.6
R2(config-if)#standby 2 priority 125
```

Verification

To verify or troubleshoot an HSRP configuration there are several commands you can use to gather information about the current configuration. The show standby command (output shown below) gives you the quickest overview and includes the group number, state (status) the virtual IP address and additional information about the current configuration.

```
R2# show standby

FastEthernet0/1 - Group 2
  State is Active
   2 state changes, last state change 00:30:59
  Virtual IP address is 192.168.5.6
```

```
 Active virtual MAC address is 0000.0c07.ac02
 Local virtual MAC address is 0004.4d82.7981 (bia)
Hello time 4 sec, hold time 12 sec
 Next hello sent in 1.412 secs
Gratuitous ARP 14 sent, next in 7.412 secs
Preemption enabled, min delay 50 sec, sync delay 40 sec
Active router is local
Standby router is unknown
Priority 120 (configured 120)
 (output omitted)
```

Gateway Load Balancing Protocol (GLBP)

Gateway Load Balancing Protocol (GLBP) is a Cisco proprietary protocol that allows automatic selection and simultaneous use of multiple gateways. It provides the same fault tolerance features as HSRP but also allows for the use of multiple gateways at the same time for load balancing. It presents the hosts with a virtual IP address, but uses multiple virtual MAC addresses in its operation.

GLBP Functions

GLBP essentially provides clients with the following:

- An active virtual gateway (AVG)
- An active virtual forwarder (AVF)

It also allows members of the group to communicate with each other through Hello messages sent every 3 seconds to the multicast address 224.0.0.102, User Datagram Protocol (UDP) port 3222.

GLBP AVG

Members of a GLBP group elect one gateway to be the AVG for that group. Other group members provide backup for the AVG in the event that the AVG becomes unavailable. The AVG assigns a different virtual MAC address to each member of the GLBP group.

GLBP AVF

Each gateway assumes responsibility for forwarding packets that are sent to the virtual MAC address assigned to that gateway by the AVG. These gateways are known as AVFs for their virtual MAC address.

GLBP Per-host Traffic Balancing

These two steps will really help clarify how GLBP balances traffic using the round-robin algorithm:

1. When a client sends an ARP message for the gateway IP address, the AVG returns the virtual MAC address of one of the AVFs.

2. When a second client sends an ARP message, the AVG returns the next virtual MAC address from the list.

The commands used to configure basic GLBP are in Table 11.4

TABLE 11.4 GLBP COMMANDS

Command	Meaning
glbp *GLBP_group_number* ip *virtual_IP_address*	Activates GLBP on an interface for the specified group number using the specified virtual IP address
glbp *GLBP_group_number* priority *priority _value*	Assigns a priority to the selected interface for the purpose of selecting the active virtual gateway (AVG)
glbp *GLBP_group_number* preempt	Allows this interface to reassume the role of AVG if it loses that role as a result of a failure

In the example below the Fa0/ interface of router R2 has been configured as a member of GLBP group 3 using a virtual IP address of 192.168.6.3. It also has been assigned a priority value of 150 for the purpose of selecting the AVG and has been configured to reassume the role of AVG if it loses that role as a result of a failure.

```
R2(config)#int fa0/1
R2(config-if)#glbp 3 192.168.6.3
R2(config-if)#glbp 3 priority 150
R2(config-if)#glbp 3 preempt
```

Verification

To verify or troubleshoot a GLBP configuration there are several commands you can use to gather information about the current configuration. The show glbp command (output shown below) gives you the quickest overview and includes the group number, state (status) the virtual IP address and additional information about the current configuration.

```
R2 show glbp 3
```

```
FastEthernet0/1 - Group 3
  State is Active
    2 state changes, last state change 23:50:33
  Virtual IP address is 192.168.6.3
  Hello time 5 sec, hold time 18 sec
    Next hello sent in 4.300 secs
  Redirect time 1800 sec, forwarder time-out 28800 sec
  Preemption enabled, min delay 60 sec
  Active is local
  Standby is unknown
  Priority 150 (configured)
  Weighting 100 (default 100), thresholds: lower 95, upper 105
    Track object 2 state Down decrement 5
  Load balancing: round robin
  There is 1 forwarder (1 active)
  Forwarder 1
    State is Active
      1 state change, last state change 23:50:15
```

(output omitted)

Index

Note to the Reader: Throughout this index **boldfaced** page numbers indicate primary discussions of a topic. *Italicized* page numbers indicate illustrations.